Coastal Resource Management in the Wider Caribbean: Resilience, Adaptation, and Community Diversity

Coastal Resource Management in the Wider Caribbean: Resilience, Adaptation, and Community Diversity

edited by
Yvan Breton, David Brown, Brian Davy, Milton Haughton & Luis Ovares

Ian Randle Publishers
Kingston •Miami

IDRC CRDI
International Development Research Centre
Ottawa • Cairo • Dakar • Montevideo • Nairobi •
New Delhi • Singapore

First Published in Jamaica, 2006 by
Ian Randle Publishers
11 Cunningham Avenue
PO Box 686
Kingston 6, Jamaica W.I.
www.ianrandlepublishers.com

and the
International Development Research Centre
PO Box 8500, Ottawa, ON, K1G 3H9,
Canada
info@idrc.ca / www.idrc.ca
ISBN 1-55250-223-6 (ebook)

This book, and the completed IDRC catalogue, may be consulted at www.idrc.ca.

National Library of Jamaica Cataloguing in Publication Data

Coastal management in the wider Caribbean: resilience, adaptation and community diversity/edited by Yvan Breton

p ; cm

Includes index
ISBN 976-637-262-4(pbk)

1. Breton, Yvan

1. Coastal zone management – Caribbean Area. 2. Coastal zone management – Citizen participation. 3. Coastal zone management – Economic aspects.

333.91716 dc21

Book and Cover design by Ian Randle Publishers

Table of Contents

Foreword

Peruse almost any text on the Caribbean and one is struck by the critical importance of the region's coastal areas, whether as the main attraction for tourists who visit in the millions every year or for the many fisherfolk whose livelihoods depend upon its important natural resource base. Very few people, however, are aware of the escalating problems in coastal zone management and, even less so, the ineffectiveness of solutions developed to date. The more one begins probing into these issues, the more apparent the many problems become, whether related to biota loss such as declining stocks of fish and turtles, increased pollution of coastal bays, or destruction of critical ecosystems such as mangroves and seagrasses. Clearly, the Caribbean coasts are in a disturbing state, and all predictions suggest that this situation will only worsen.

In response to this crisis, Canada's International Development Research Centre (IDRC) and its Caribbean partners have been testing new and innovative approaches to the management of the region's coastal resources. One very promising approach is community-based management or "co-management." Co-management approaches, in a nutshell, involve the resource users themselves working in some form of shared or collaborative management with government authorities. In many parts of the world, such approaches have been shown to be effective in alleviating common problems of resource overuse and misuse. In the Caribbean, collaborative, community-based approaches are still at an early stage of testing, particularly in coastal zones. However, these techniques are beginning to show promising results in reversing some of the negative trends cited above, which have adversely affected the unique mix of culture and ecology in the Caribbean.

Although most Caribbean countries share the same ecosystem, there has been only very limited collaboration in managing the region's natural resources. This book presents a great opportunity for shared learning around this type of work as it explores, on a pan-Caribbean scale, the problems in coastal-zone management and offers possible solutions.

The authors seek to understand what role (and future roles) communities and individuals can play, at the local level, in the management of the resources upon which they are most dependent. The book focuses on the overall issue of heterogeneity — the need both to better understand its many shades and to probe how a better understanding of the complexity of Caribbean heterogeneity could lead to improved management and, ultimately, a reversal in the loss of precious natural resources. The book is the result of over five years of research on these issues and is part of a wider program to take these findings to various policy and decision-making fora at both national and pan-Caribbean levels.

Clearly, regional bodies such as the Caribbean Community (CARICOM) Secretariat and the Caribbean Regional Fisheries Mechanism (CRFM) Secretariat, will continue to play important roles in promoting more sustainable development policies. However, to do this effectively, there needs to be a better understanding of the root causes of current problems and, perhaps more importantly, the development of creative new solutions. This book offers a beginning to what I feel is an important option for our future.

EDWIN W. CARRINGTON
Secretary-General
CARICOM

Preface

This volume deals with community-based coastal resource management (CBCRM) in the insular and continental Caribbean. Supported by a small-grant programme from the International Development Research Centre (IDRC), and undertaken in collaboration with the International Ocean Institute (IOI) in Costa Rica and the Caribbean Regional Fisheries Mechanism (CRFM) in Belize, it summarises the results of a second phase that took place between January 2002 and February 2005. This programme was composed of 15 projects in 11 countries, with research teams coming from university research centres and various non-governmental organisations (NGOs). It was designed to better understand the heterogeneity of the Caribbean communities by taking a critical look at existing natural resource management (NRM) approaches in which, in our view, insufficient attention has been paid to the diversity of social institutions and ecosystems working at various scales in the management processes.

During Phase I, results of the project were summarised in individual case studies. In Phase II, more structured exchanges produced collective writing efforts, which gave the study a stronger comparative and analytical orientation. In addition to chapters dealing with analytical and methodological issues in coastal management, the essence of the volume lies in five comparative and synthesised case studies that focus on particular management problems in diverse social contexts.

Although this text is written primarily for a research audience, it should be of interest to coastal planners, decision makers, and funding agency representatives because this type of thinking needs to be shared far more widely among these groups in the Caribbean. For instance, we argue that particular attention should be given to reaching a better balance between natural and social sciences in the management of natural resources. We also need to deepen our understanding of local human contexts as part of the increasing tendency to decentralisation in many areas of the world. We hope that participants, individuals, and institutions have learned several lessons from this experience and that the programme will remain a valid, illustrative basis for further involvement in Caribbean coastal management issues.

The preparation of this book was funded by the IDRC. The editors and authors would like to thank Dr Alejandro Gutiérrez, Director del International Oceans Institute in Costa Rica, and Hugh Saul, Director of the Caribbean Regional Fisheries Mechanism in Belize, for their dedicated administrative support of this CBCRM programme in the Caribbean. We are also grateful to Manon Ruel and Sandra Baron, graduate students in anthropology at the Université Laval, Québec, Canada, for regularly submitting documentation to the projects and participating in finalising this publication.

The Scientific Committee of the CBCRM Programme in the Caribbean:

Yvan Breton	Université Laval, Canada
David Brown	Caribbean Regional Fisheries Mechanism, Belize
Brian Davy	International Development Research Centre, Canada
Milton Haughton	Caribbean Regional Fisheries Mechanism, Belize
Luis Ovares	International Ocean Institute, Costa Rica

List of Tables & Figures

TABLES

FIGURES

Abbreviations

ACS	Association of Caribbean States
AECS	Association of Eastern Caribbean States
APRM	managed resource protected areas
BAS	Belize Audubon Society
BFCA	Belize Fishermen's Cooperative Association
BJLI	Buyei Juan Lambey Institute (Panama)
BPTT	British Petroleum Company of Trinidad and Tobago
CARICOM	Caribbean Community and Common Market
CARSEA	Caribbean Sea Ecosystem Assessment
CBCRM	community-based coastal resource management
CBO	community-based organisation
CEN	Canadian Environmental Network
CFRAMP	CARICOM Fisheries Resource Assessment and Management Programme
CFTDI	Caribbean Fisheries Training and Development Institute
CFU	CARICOM Fisheries Unit
CIDA	Canadian International Development Agency
CINVESTAV	Centre for Research and Advanced Study, National Polytechnic Institute (Mexico)
CIRNAC	Research Center on Natural Resources (Mexico)
CITES	Convention on International Trade in Endangered Species
CITMA	Centro de Estudios Ambientales de Cienfuegos (Ministry of Science, Technology and Environment) (Cuba)
CNAP	National Centre for Protected Areas (Cuba)
CRFM	Caribbean Regional Fisheries Mechanism
CRIP	Regional Center for Fisheries Research
CZMAI	Coastal Zone Management Authority and Institute
EEC	European Economic Community
EEZ	exclusive economic zone
EIA	environmental impact assessment

EMA	environmental management authority
FAC	Fishery Advisory Committee
FAD	fish aggregation device
FAO	Food and Agricultural Organisation of the United Nations
FAS	fish aggregating sites
FENAPESCA	Federation of Artisanal Fishers (Panama)
FON	Friends of Nature
FTAA	Free Trade Agreement of the Americas
FUNDAECO	Foundation for Ecological Development (Guatemala)
GDP	gross domestic product
GEF	Global Environmental Facility
GESAMP	Joint Group of Experts on Scientific Aspects of Marine Environmental Protection
GPS	Global Positioning System
HABs	harmful algal blooms
IADB	Inter-American Development Bank
ICCAT	International Commission for the Conservation of Atlantic Tunas
ICM	integrated coastal management
ICZM	integrated coastal zone management
IDRC	International Development Research Centre (Canada)
IFREMER	French Research Institute on the Sea Resources (France)
IMA	Institute of Marine Affairs (Trinidad and Tobago)
IMSS	Mexican Institute of Social Security
INAPESCA	Instituto Nacional de Pesca y Acuicultura (National Institute of Fisheries and Aquaculture) (Venezuela)
INE	National Institute of Statistics (Mexico)
INP	Instituto Nacional de la Pesca (National Institute of Fisheries) (Mexico)
IOCARIBE	Caribbean Sub-commission of the United Nations Intergovernmental Oceanographic Commission of UNESCO
IOI	International Ocean Institute
IRD	Research Institute on Development (France)
IUCN	International Union for the Conservation of Nature
KSAC	Kingston and St Andrew Corporation (Jamaica)

LGEEPA	Ley General de Equilibrio Ecológico (Mexico)
MAC	Monitoring and Advisory Committee (Trinidad and Tobago)
MAFC	Ministry of Agriculture, Fisheries and Cooperatives (Belize)
MINGA	a Quechua word meaning communal work or cooperation; IDRC's Latin America programme
MIP	Ministry of Fisheries (Cuba)
MIZC	integrated management of coastal zones
MKGT	Kuna Model of Natural Resource Management (Panama)
MNRE	Ministry of Natural Resources and the Environment (Belize)
MPA	marine protected area
MPCC	multi-purpose community centre
NEPA	National Environment and Planning Agency (Jamaica)
NGO	non-governmental organisation
NRM	natural resource management
NSF-LTER	National Science Foundation's Long-term Ecological Research Programme
OECD	Organisation for Economic Cooperation and Development
OECS	Organisation of Eastern Caribbean States
PAN	National Action Party (Mexico)
PAR	participatory action–research
PESCACIEN	Empresa pesquera de Cienfuegos [fishing enterprise] (Cuba)
PNMPF	Punta Frances National Marine Park (Cuba)
PRI	Revolutionary Institutional Party (Mexico)
PROPESCAR	artisanal fishery (Dominican Republic)
RRA	rapid rural assessment
SAGARPA	Ministry of Agriculture, Livestock Farming, Rural Development, Fisheries and Feeding (Mexico)
SECOL	Secretariat of Ecology (Mexico)
SEMARNAP	Ministry of Environment, Agriculture and Fishing (Mexico)
SEMARNAT	Ministry of Environment and Natural Resources (Mexico)

SFA	Southeast Fishing Association (Trinidad)
SGA	small-grant approach
SNAP	National System of Protected Areas (Cuba)
SSA	Ministry of Health and Assistance (Mexico)
SWOT	strengths, weaknesses, opportunities, and threats analysis
T&T	Trinidad and Tobago
TEK	traditional ecological knowledge
TIDE	Toledo Institute for Development and the Environment (Belize)
TWOWS	Third World Organisation of Women in Science
UMA	Environment Unit (Cuba)
UNDP	United Nations Development Programme
USAID	United States Agency for International Development
UWI	University of the West Indies
UWISCS	University of the West Indies School of Sciences
WIFA	Women in Fishing Association (Trinidad and Tobago)
WWF	World Wildlife Fund

Introduction

Coastal Mangement in the Wider Caribbean: Resilience, Adaptation, and Community Diversity

Brian Davy and Yvan Breton

In recent years, concerns have been increasing over the deteriorating status of natural resources, or biodiversity depletion, particularly with respect to the impact of these changes on marginalised groups that are most dependent on the resources. These concerns have been summarised in a variety of international summits linked to sustainable development (Rio Conference 1992; Cairo Conference 1994; the Millennium Ecosystem Assessment 2001, Johannesburg Earth Summit 2002).

Coastal management efforts were initiated about 30 years ago. They represent one domain of natural resource management (NRM) that is underway in several countries and that has acquired high visibility, on both the academic and the public stages. Management efforts have generated numerous studies in which the notion of the scale of interventions is at the centre of discussions between researchers and practitioners. Studies have resulted in various management propositions and models designed to balance the local-global linkages in various ecological and socio-political contexts. The literature, however, indicates that the efficiency of many of these efforts remains to be demonstrated. In parallel with many other regions, the Caribbean has been the object of several interventions from international and regional agencies (Chakalall, Mahon, and McConney 1998; Garcia Montero 2002). To date, satisfactory results have been limited, and collaborative initiatives are still at an early stage of understanding.

Our work is guided by the development of new management theory and approaches in which users are more involved (Bradshaw 2003; Johannes 2002; Berkes et al. 2001; Charles 2001). This thrust has come about in response to increasingly rapid changes in these social-ecological systems, the need to examine the adequacy of current institutional mechanisms (Sick

2002; Berkes, Calding, and Folke 2003), and governance arrangements (Olsen 2001). Our work tries to marry theory with practice in community-based management, through a network of applied research across a mix of social and ecological systems throughout the wider coastal Caribbean. Our experiences suggest that to date, social-science approaches to research and management in the Caribbean have not been adequately considered. More importantly, the capacity to do so now and in the near future is extremely fragile. Therefore, we propose a follow-up research agenda based on improved understanding of the institutions and the heterogeneity factor in these systems, coupled with greater capacity building. We hope that this will lead to a new set of flexible institutions representing one approach to better management.

Problem setting and objectives

The Caribbean Sea is the second largest sea in the world, covering an area of approximately 2,648,000 km^2 (CARSEA 2003) comprising the territorial waters and coastal areas of 33 bordering countries and territories. In addition to representing a highly fragmented territory, the Caribbean is characterised by a mix of cultures derived from the former European and North American colonial powers. This heterogeneity is reinforced by strong external and internal migrations. The region's overall population is over 30 million, with a density higher than 300/km^2 in some small-island sections (Arias-Isaza 2003). Caribbean states are highly dependent on their ecosystem services to support human well-being. These services are under threat from many sources, including international marine shipping, waste from yachts and cruise liners, and large commercial fishing vessels from nations that are not indigenous to the region.

Over-harvesting of fish stocks and pollution from land-based sources negatively affect sustainable livelihoods (CARSEA 2003). Long economically dependent on agriculture and export, the Caribbean has now become an important tourist destination, with an expected 1,857,000 jobs in the tourism sector in 2003, representing 12 per cent of total employment and 13 per cent of GDP. With respect to fisheries, the number of people actively involved increased from 194,278 in the 1970s to 256,787 in the 1980s, and to 504,910 in the 1900s, which is of the same magnitude as the number of jobs produced by tourism. These numbers have generated additional pressure on marine ecosystems. Concurrent to this increase, there has been a steady increase in fish landings since the 1950s, with an average of about 1.1 million tons at the beginning of 2000. Peaking in the mid- to late 1990s, fish catches declined by about 33 per cent between 1990 and 2000 (CARSEA 2003). Such variations are influenced by the exploitation of new species or the depletion of others. It seems that in the Caribbean, as in many other areas of the world, the 'tragedy of the commons' is acquiring a growing visibility. Caribbean coastal ecosystems face a increasing challenges as a result of the decrease in quantity and quality of coastal resources.

Are existing approaches solving these problems? This question is difficult to answer because of the lack of data on clear trends. We feel that, given the deteriorating situation in many coastal communities, new or revised approaches to improved management of these critical resources must be examined. In the Caribbean, the Caribbean Sea Ecosystem Assessment (CARSEA) review is part of the UN Millennium Ecosystem Assessment, 2003. CARSEA provides a useful and up-to-date assessment, and has now taken this work further by producing a series of scenarios, trends, and responses. At both a general institutional level and a more specific programme level at IDRC, Sick reviews the rationale for the active involvement of user groups in management and suggests a valuable list of issues. Among these, we particularly note the necessity of 'better coordination of nested local, regional, and state co-management institutions, which draw on the strengths of various stakeholders at various institutional levels' (Sick 2002, iii).

More recently, Dietz, Ostrom, and Stern (2003) have reviewed this literature and suggest that locally evolved institutional arrangements have worked well when governed by stable communities. But others pinpoint the limits linked to the rhetoric of community-based resource management, especially when little attention is paid to the representations deployed in constituting those 'communities' and to their internal diversity (Brosius, Tsing, and Zerner 1998; Jones 2004; Varughese and Ostrom 2001).

Our work tests some of these evolving theories in an ongoing series of projects in the Wider Caribbean and, more specifically, examines new options for better understanding the causes of ecological degradation. We recommend possible solutions based on better understanding of the interactions between the social and ecological systems.

The Caribbean region has been the object of several interventions (Warner 1997; Chakalall, Mahon, and McConney 1998; Béné 2003; Linton and

Warner 2003; Ratter 2003; Haughton et al. 2004; Levitt 2004). These have led to new management approaches (the creation of several natural parks and reserves); promotion of new institutions (an increasing number of non-governmental organisations [NGOs] aiming at reinforcing the role of the civil society); capacity building (various graduate programmes in natural resources management in universities and research centres); and even new governance mechanisms (expanded regional collaborative mechanisms oriented toward the pursuit of a better equilibrium between environment and society). However, resource degradation and quality-of-life indicators suggest that most Caribbean ecosystems are increasingly threatened by natural and anthropogenic factors. This seems to occur at various scales, particularly at the local and regional levels.

First of all, we have tried to emphasise the increasing need to examine the importance of social capital, both among and by the users of such resources, as one option for improving present management approaches. Such issues are already discussed in an expanding body of literature (Bradshaw 2003; Brown 2003; Chevalier 2001; Warner 1997; Yanagi 2003); they are, however, too complex to permit much generalisation, and any tendency to oversimplify must be resisted.[1] Our intention is to focus on how a social and ecological analysis of coastal zones, and particularly a better understanding of the impressive array of sub-ecosystems (the interrelations and evolution of which are still inadequately understood), explain how various stakeholders cooperate or compete for access to resources. In the last 20 years or so, these zones, which often include terrestrial and marine components, have been the object of several interventions; they were not systematic, however, and are understood only at a superficial level.

Second, this publication will emphasise a scale of observation and intervention that targets primarily the local, or community, level. We believe this aspect has not been given the emphasis that it deserves in several management initiatives, compared with work at other, higher levels. Because they are basic social units encompassing various groups of stakeholders (in the domestic sphere or in larger social coalitions), communities represent the main administrative level in several political systems. Studying their social organisation should be the stepping stone for understanding the existing dyadic and polyadic relations as the basis of any management consensus.

These two basic concerns form what we have called CBCRM, although adaptive management might be a better term. We will examine them from the point of view of their diversity or heterogeneity, and from the perspective of the contribution they provide to Caribbean community resilience. We suggest that a better understanding of management options and governance mechanisms can provide guidance on how to reverse some ecosystem and quality-of-life trends.

Improved management of these resources is suggested as one solution to these problems. As well, a more people-centred approach to management should be promoted. To test some of these ideas, we have been operating a CBCRM network of research projects across a variety of Caribbean ecosystems. The projects address various issues relative to how communities deal with territorial delimitation, contamination, fishing conflicts, and marine reserves. The general objective of this network is to promote, through research, integrated multi-stakeholder and interdisciplinary community-based approaches along with CBCRM in the Caribbean, with a view to enhancing sustainable development.

The specific objectives are

- to encourage CBCRM projects that guarantee sustainability, improve standard of living for coastal populations, and address both biodiversity and gender issues;
- to demonstrate to policy makers and national institutions the benefits of multi-stakeholder and interdisciplinary CBCRM approaches that are conducted by a multidisciplinary team;
- to promote greater involvement of women and minority groups who depend upon the coastal resources for their livelihood, but who traditionally have operated at the margins of the planning and decision-making processes;
- to encourage, within the wider Caribbean, joint-venture projects between English and Spanish institutions as well as between groups of stakeholders, in order to enrich our vision of the interest in or potential participation with CBCRM; and
- to promote gradual collaboration at the regional level, by building upon the quality of the projects and the progressive involvement of the Caribbean Regional Fisheries Mechanism (CRFM) and the International Ocean Institute (IOI), which could result in the export of expertise and encourage promotion of CBCRM in the region.

The geopolitical and ecological characteristics, spatial dispersion, socioeconomic disparities, and cultural diversity of the Caribbean countries present unique challenges for sustainable development of the marine and coastal resources. There are striking differences among Caribbean countries in terms of their economic and political weight. There is also a great disparity in the number and quality of their research and natural resource management institutions, in availability of skilled human resources, and in the type and level of participation of local stakeholders in the development process. These countries are not equally part of or active in regional organisations such as the Caribbean Forum of Association of Partner States (CARIFORUM), WECAFC, ACS, CARICOM, or OECS. Several Caribbean countries are small-island developing states (SIDS), while others are continental countries. SIDS face special problems because of their small size, limited human and institutional capability, heavy reliance on coastal resources for economic development, and ecological and economic vulnerability to environmental and external economic shocks.

In addition, Caribbean countries are characterised by diverse cultures, languages (including Spanish, English, and, to a lesser extent, French and Dutch), and ethnicities. Ovares underlines this situation in chapter 1. Few cooperative programmes cross the linguistic and cultural barriers in the Caribbean, even in countries that share common borders, such as Belize and Honduras or Guyana and Venezuela. Our gradual, step-by-step approach will enable the CBCRM programme to maintain the high quality essential in both research and capacity-building objectives at acceptable operational costs.

Taking into account this diversity, the CBCRM programme is gradually developing a regional focus based on the cumulative experience of selected countries. The IDRC-CBCRM programme began in the Caribbean in 1999, following the La Havana international conference on the same topic in 1998 (Chircop and Rolson 1998). The programme received 125 applications for small-grant projects, among which 32 (17 in Phase I and 15 in Phase II) were given financial support. In this second phase, the programme was open to all countries in the region and strove to establish a balance between the region's geophysical, socioeconomic, linguistic, cultural, and ecological diversity. The IOI-Costa Rica and CRFM Secretariat, both based in Belize, were responsible for monitoring and providing technical support to the network of projects. They were assisted by consulting anthropologists from Laval University in Québec, Canada, and various staff members at IDRC in

Ottawa. Initial results of this CBCRM Caribbean network, or Costas, are summarised in an anthology entitled Balancing People and Resources: Interdisciplinary Research and Coastal Areas Management in the Wider Caribbean (IOI-CFU-LAVAL-IDRC 2002).

Now at the end of the second three-year phase, this programme generated a critical mass of work involving the role of male and female community stakeholders who are managing coastal areas. This publication aims to synthesize some of the results and to promote stronger pathways to decentralisation in the management of the area's natural resources. This orientation is important, because livelihood issues are becoming extremely complex owing to resource depletion in coastal areas and increasing conflicts between stakeholders (autochthonous and outsiders; see Chapin 2004). Because of the political uncertainty that prevails in several countries, it is challenging to establish long-term coordination in management decision-making between local and regional institutions.

We are increasingly concerned that existing management approaches do not give adequate recognition to or understanding of the importance of local diversity (what we call the heterogeneity factor). Almost by definition, centralised management forces a generalisation, or loss of heterogeneity, which leads to non-resilient management processes. We believe more research is needed so that some of the important heterogeneous factors that are being lost or inadequately recognised in present management plans can be more critically identified and understood.

Coastal zone management: a fragile coalition

Locally evolved institutions and governance arrangements have been suggested as critical elements in natural resource management (Dietz, Ostrom, and Stern 2003), and this orientation has been the object of many discussions for a few years. (Agrawal and Gibson 1999). Our review suggests that in the Caribbean, the institutional trajectory of coastal management has been focused mainly at regional and national levels without real mobilisation at the local level. Many institutions—namely the nation-state bureaucracies, environmental agencies, and NGOs—became the promoters of such initiatives. The institutions rely mostly on representatives of natural sciences, who are more numerous in the state apparatus than their social science counterparts. This orientation, coupled with the associated knowledge base, undoubtedly produced distorted analyses of many management approaches that neglected the rich cultural management practices which are being implemented elsewhere. Even though in the last decade some progress has been made to rectify the situation, interdisciplinary asymmetry remains a major characteristic of many research teams concerned with management issues. This is true whether they come from the government or the NGO sector.[2] The term 'integrated management' often corresponds more to a mix of natural sciences than to an adequate balance between natural and social sciences.

When transposed to marine and coastal areas, these overall features—which are easily detected at a general level—can have additional negative consequences. When marine and coastal zones became the object of management interventions after the UNCLOS conference in the 1980s (Nichols 1999), management models had already been used and consolidated in mainland areas for several decades. Agrarian or forest management approaches that encouraged conservation of natural resources in remote areas were uncritically transposed to coastal areas. The consequences were extremely negative in the Caribbean, because in many insular countries, especially SIDS, all the people live, de facto, in coastal zones. Unilateral decisions by the state authority to create protected areas (or similar processes) directly affected the people's lives and livelihood strategies. It has been mainly through the consolidation of biosphere reserves, including both land and marine zones, and buffer zones that are more sensitive to the presence of social factors, that these differences became better understood and the stakeholders' presence carried weight at the intervention level.

Another aspect to consider is that most state interventions for the conservation of coastal zones in the 1970s and 1980s took place simultaneously with a thrust to reinforce maritime nationalism, and the importance given to the actual conservation initiatives was exaggerated. Often, once an area was declared protected or included in a park or reserve, inadequate human resources were dedicated to management and enforcement efforts. Many of today's decision makers forget that the prevailing models of management of coastal areas were rooted in an orthodoxy prevalent two or three decades ago—an orthodoxy in which theoretical discourse and political visibility were more important than concrete interventions and practices. Finally, because of the open-access character of marine zones, their protected areas were often extended and delimited in an arbitrary way that did not take into account their human uses, so coastal communities located within or near these areas were not consulted. Even more important, communities' knowledge of these sub-ecosystems and the richness they included were rarely considered.

This publication seeks to demonstrate specific constraints that promoters of consolidated management initiatives in coastal zones have not sufficiently analysed.

The community level: conflicting interpretations

The CBCRM programme is primarily oriented towards validating the role of community stakeholders in the use and management of natural resources. This orientation is not fortuitous. Rather, it is at the heart of a strong conviction that communities (taken here in both a spatial and a sociological sense) must become key observation units and actors in management processes. This does not mean we believe that communities, especially small ones, are always conservers or even creators of biodiversity. Instead, we think that certain management practices start and keep developing at a local level. As well, there is increasing evidence that fishermen and other stakeholders contribute to the information and knowledge base that is so critical to improved resource management. In a given ecosystem, most small-scale producers expand the functional limits of the space they require for fulfilling their livelihood needs. This scale forms their basic perceptions and beliefs. It is also at this scale that the daily relations among themselves or with outsiders develop either a collaborative or a competitive nature.[3] Given the way that most management plans have been promoted—that is, with international guidelines influencing the initiatives of regional bureaucracies—insufficient space is left to local levels. From a 'logical' point of view, this top-down approach fits well with the rationalising orientation of government agencies, which aim to demonstrate good collaborative will with the international institutions, generally in conjunction with some financial incentives. However, agencies tend to associate the importance of their intervention with the dimensions of the territory they intend to manage. This is done without accounting for the context or heterogeneity of these spaces (various types of parks and reserves, for instance) which consist of distinct sub-ecosystems and co-evolved social systems of highly differentiated communities. Good management presupposes consensus, which can be obtained through considering the rationale and objectives that prevail at the upper levels, as well as the logic at the base. This means that the direct users of the ecosystems that are the object of the management interventions must be studied.

There are additional arguments for paying greater attention to the community level in coastal areas. In small island countries, as in the eastern part of the Caribbean, coastlines comprise the dominant ecosystem and are the main locus of interaction among the stakeholders. They become 'national' priorities, a situation that diminishes the weight of communities at the analytical and intervention levels, which then leads to a distorted interpretation of the term 'community.'

On the other hand, fishing is often associated with coastal areas and in many countries still represents the main economic activity. Management approaches here are critical because of their direct impact on the sustainability of the resource base. But this source of income is increasingly faced with internal and external pressures that jeopardise its potential contribution to the people's livelihood. When coastal fishermen and their family members must look for economic alternatives, tourism becomes an increasingly important solution. The differences that traditionally prevailed between communities in a given region are further compounded and enhanced by present-day economic trends, which are influenced by both the global market and transformations in the local ecosystems. Thus the divergences between various groups of stakeholders are accentuated.

Study of the trends in these growing differentiation processes, which is so essential to the understanding and promotion of good management devices, cannot be limited to the upper or middle decision-making levels. Instead, research must be rooted in the observation of people's daily lives and initiatives. Despite growing awareness of the need for changes in the current governance mechanisms and the call for greater decentralisation, many statements remain at a discussion level. This publication seeks to show the important role that communities can play in management initiatives.

Heterogeneity, resilience, and adaptation

The literature of natural resources management shows that many authors look for alternative governance devices in which the local level should gain importance. There are several debates around the 'tragedy of the commons' and the role that the state should play in common-pool resources. Embedded in such discussions is concern about access to and use of resources for which no formal authority exists. Unfortunately, the interest in communities does not generate homogeneous interpretations (Bardhan and Dayton-Johnson 2002). Instead, more and more studies underline the fact that communities must be perceived as including various groups of stakeholders with frequently opposing interests (Gillingham 2001). Although such diversity might pose problems for obtaining consensus, it can present certain advantages in a management perspective. These stakeholders, who are characterised by some forms of resilience, can possess a diversified (and, we believe, critically important) knowledge about certain resources. Brown emphasises this orientation in more detail in chapter 1.

At both the theoretical and empirical levels, this book underlines the diverse roles of Caribbean communities. Historically, this diversity has developed in a number of ways. We believe that with increasing globalisation and internationalisation trends in the Caribbean, we need to examine and understand these factors more carefully. In particular, we need to understand what parts of this diversity are important in the development of revised management approaches. Contrary to other regions, where CBCRM approaches are often rooted in a significant historical time span,[4] nothing equivalent exists in the Caribbean. For instance, during the colonial period the social organisation of native populations gave way to both assimilation and miscegenation, influenced by the presence of European, African, and Asian cultures, and to significant internal and external migrations. The establishment and development of communities resulted in very flexible social units, which now form the essence of the Caribbean cultures. Historically, this culture was driven, at least in part, by access to resources, such as fish. In spite of the absence of significant CBCRM applications in this region, in the present-day globalisation context this heterogeneity offers an opportunity for undertaking new management initiatives. Heterogeneity was at first considered a negative factor in the strengthening of collective action. Recent literature, however, presents new evidence that it is a challenge that can be overcome (Varughese and Ostrom 2001; Jones 2004).

The accent put on the heterogeneity of Caribbean communities as a key variable implies that management must be conceived through non-linear historical and spatial frameworks. This allows for resilience as well as adaptations by local actors who are closest to the resource both in time and space and who, therefore, are ideally suited to become stronger actors in the adaptive management that we foresee for the future. Rather than opposing these processes, we see them as mutually dependent. Resilience can be seen as a system's capacity to undergo change and disturbance, yet which persists with some form of control on its initial integrity.[5] All ecological and social systems are adaptive and characterised by complex dynamics, and are never in a state of perfect equilibrium. Indeed, a small perturbation can generate unexpected effects at the macro level; this becomes increasingly true as systems become more complex. Any system must possess some degree of resilience in order to survive, a resilience which derives from an ability to change adaptively and which is often rooted in flexibility. This is one of the main orientations we promote when referring to management issues. We intend to demonstrate that variations in the communities' social structure and organisation should be a cornerstone for understanding the essence of management problems and solutions.

Organisation of this book

This book includes three parts. The first contains an examination of the analytical and methodological issues linked to community studies in Caribbean systems; the second presents comparative, thematically oriented chapters detailing specific management issues at local levels; and the concluding section questions the gap between theory and practice in coastal zone management.

There are eight chapters. The first provides an overview of Caribbean social science paradigms in the last decades, showing how the extremely variable nature of Caribbean communities made it difficult to obtain a robust epistemological basis for the study. It discusses issues linked to the blurred notion of community in the Caribbean social sciences, the slow emergence of a maritime socio-anthropology, and the numerous analytical challenges linked to the communities' ethnicity and spatial morphology. The second chapter underlines the usefulness of interdisciplinary approaches for grasping the web of relations between people and ecosystems in different small-community contexts.

The next five chapters are devoted to a comparative examination of various management issues. They illustrate how similar management problems can be solved differently, according to the specifics of various communities. The first example looks at the importance of territoriality, technical revitalisation, and symbolism in three Garifuna and Kuna communities on the Atlantic Caribbean coast, and illustrates how management can be promoted through different cultural logics. The second deals with the presence of communities in three protected marine areas of Mexico, Dominican Republic, and Cuba. It explores the different governance mechanisms that offer management solutions based on the communities' distinct features, while considering their relations with their respective state agencies. The third chapter examines how communities in Cuba and Venezuela can be mobilised for and involved in solving problems of coastal bay and lagoon contamination. The fourth chapter examines how seaweeds and mangroves in Mexico and Jamaica represent additional coastal natural resources that can provide various livelihood initiatives for fishing communities. The fifth contribution looks at the socioeconomic and political organisation in three fishing communities in Grenada, Trinidad, and Belize. This chapter demonstrates the role of local knowledge and institutions that could reinforce more functional management systems.

The final chapter raises questions about the gaps between theory and practice in coastal resource management, with specific reference to the Caribbean context. It examines the analytical and methodological issues linked to resilience, meso-levels of governance, and paradigmatic shifts in management approaches. It then seeks to pinpoint and discuss some lessons that stem from this CBCRM Caribbean experience, and concludes with a list of recommendations to researchers and decision makers who are involved in the development of the region.

Notes

1. See Belfore (2003) for an overview of initiatives undertaken in integrated coastal management at the world level. The author mentions that in 2002, 145 countries, semi-sovereign states, and international organisations had initiated 698 ICM initiatives at that level. For a synthesis of issues in fisheries governance in the Caribbean, see Chakalall, Mahon, and McConney (1998).
2. The publication of the first phase of the CBCRM programme, Balancing People and Resources: Interdisciplinary Research and Coastal Areas Management in the Wider Caribbean (2002), directly addresses issues linked to interdisciplinary asymmetry.
3. In agreement with many critics of the stereotypical view of the community as a homogeneous and bounded social unit that is often promoted by those emphasising the usefulness of PRA (Cooke and Kothari 2001; Agrawal and Gibson 1999), we see the community as a flexible entity whose frontiers and

internal features are subject to constant change and evolution. Brown strongly emphasises this point.

4. We do not mean to imply that the CBCRM models in other parts of the world, like Asia or Oceania (see Johannes 2002), are perfectly adequate and need not be transformed. On the contrary, many examples now show that they have to be modified to some extent to accommodate new management realities. Nevertheless, they have been in use longer and their content is more established, and they can be reinforced with decentralisation trends.
5. For a good discussion of links between resilience and adaptation, see Levin et al. 1997; Walker et al. 2002.

References

Agrawal, A., and C.C. Gibson. 1999. Enchantment and disenchantment: The role of community in natural resource conservation. *World Development* 27: 629–49.

Arias-Isaza, F. 2003. Advances on GIWA region 3 'Caribbean Sea.' Manuscript. Trinidad: CARSEA.

Bardhan, P., and J. Dayton-Johnson. 2002. Unequal irrigators: Heterogeneity and commons management in large-scale multivariate research. In *The drama of the commons*, ed. Elinor Ostrom, 87–112. Committee on the Human Dimensions of Global Change. Washington, D.C.: National Research Council, National Academy Press.

Belfore, S. 2003. The growth of integrated coastal management and the role of indicators in integrated coastal management: Introduction to the special issue. *Ocean and Coastal Management* 46: 225–34.

Béné, C. 2003. When fisheries rhymes with poverty: A first step beyond the old paradigm of poverty in small-scale fisheries. *World Development* 31(6): 949–75.

Berkes F., J. Calding, and C. Folke, eds. 2003. *Navigating social-ecological systems: Building resilience for complexity and change.* Cambridge, UK: Cambridge University.

Berkes, F., R. Mahon, P. McConney, R. Pollnac, and R. Pomeroy. 2001. *Managing small-scale fisheries. Alternative directions and methods.* Ottawa: IDRC.

Bradshaw, B. 2003. Questioning the credibility and capacity of community-based resource management. *Canadian Geographer* 47(2): 137–50.

Brosius, J.P., A. Tsing, and C. Zerner. 1998. Representing communities: Histories and politics of community-based resources management. *Society and Natural Resource* 11: 157–68.

Brown, N.D. 2003. The global environmental change and Caribbean food. Conference in the IHDP open meeting on the Human Dimension of Global Environmental Change, Montréal, 16–18 October, 2003.

CARSEA. 2003. Caribbean sea ecosystems assessment, summary report. Port of Spain, Trinidad.

Chakalall, B., R. Mahon, and P. McConney. 1998. Current issues in fisheries governance in the Caribbean Community (CARICOM). *Marine Policy* 22(1): 29–44.

Chapin, M. 2004. A challenge to conservationists. *World Watch Magazine*, Dec. 17–31.

Charles, A. 2001. *Sustainable fishery systems.* Fish and Aquatic Resources Series 5. London: Blackwell Science Ltd.

Chevalier, J. 2001. Stakeholder analysis and natural resource management. Ottawa: Carleton University, June. www.carleton.ca/~jchevali/STAKEH2.html.

Chircop, A., and S. Rolson, eds. 1998. *Taller internacional sobre formación de capacidades para el manejo de las costas y los océanos en el Gran Caribe.* Palacio de Convenciones de la Habana, Cuba: Comisión Oceanográfica Intergubernamental. Informe de Reuniones de Trabajo no. 16.

Cooke, B. and U. Kothari, eds. 'The case for Participation as Tyranny.' In *Participation: the new Tyranny.* London: Zed Books.

Dietz, T., E. Ostrom, and P.C. Stern. 2003. The struggle to govern the commons. *Science* 302: 1907–12.

Garcia Montero, G. 2002. The Caribbean: Main experiences and regularities in capacity building for the management of coastal areas. *Ocean and Coastal Management* 45: 677–93.

Gillingham, S. 2001. Social organization and participatory resources management in Brazilian ribeirinho communities. A case study on the Mamiraua Development reserve, Amazonas. *Society and Natural Resource* 14: 803–14.

Haughton, M., R. Mahon, P. McConney, A. Kong, and A. Mills. 2004. Establishment of the Caribbean Regional Fisheries Mechanism. *Marine Policy* 28: 351–59.

IOI-CFU-LAVAL-IDRC. 2002. *Balancing people and resources: Interdisciplinary research and coastal areas management in the wider Caribbean.* Heredia, Costa Rica: Editorial Fundación, UNA.

Johannes, R.E. 2002. The renaissance of community-based marine resources management in Oceania. *Annual Review of Ecology and Systemics* 33: 317–402.

Jones, E.C. 2004. Wealth-based trust and the development of collective action. *World Development* 32(4): 691–711.

Levin, S., S. Barrett, S. Aniyar, W. Baumol, C. Bliss, B. Bolin, P. Dasgupta, C. Ehrlich, C. Folke, M. Gren, C.S. Holling, and A.M. Jansson. 1997. Resilience in natural and socioeconomic systems. *Beijer Discussion Papers* 100: 2–11.

Levitt, K.P. 2004. Independent thought and Caribbean community. *Canadian Journal for Development Studies* 30(2): 225–37.

Linton, D.M., and G.F. Warner. 2003. Biological indicators in the Caribbean coastal zone and their role in integrated management. *Ocean and Coastal Management* 46: 261–76.

Nichols, K. 1999. Coming to terms with 'integrated coastal management.' Problems of meaning and method in a new arena of resource regulation. *Professional Geographer* 51(3): 388–99.

Oslen, S. 2001. Future directions in coastal governance: The consensus from Block Island. Draft paper. Rhode Island: Coastal Resource Center.

Ratter, M.W. 2003. *Resource management changes in the Caribbean: The eco-eco approach.* Hamburg: University of Hamburg.

Sick, D. 2002. *Managing environmental processes across boundaries: A review of the literature on institutions and resource management.* Ottawa, Ontario: IDRC.

Varughese, G., and E. Ostrom. 2001. The contested role of heterogeneity in collective action: Some evidence from community forestry in Nepal. *World Development* 29(5): 747–65.

Walker, B., S. Carpenter, J. Andries, N. Abel, G.S. Cumming, M. Jassen, L. Level, J. Norberg, G.D. Peterson and R. Pritchard 2002. Resilience management in social-ecological systems: A working hypothesis for a participatory approach. *Conservation Ecology* 6(1):art.14.

Warner, G. 1997. Participatory management, popular knowledge, and community empowerment: The case of sea urchin harvesting in the Vieux-Fort area of St Lucia. *Human Ecology* (25): 29–46.

Yanagi, T. 2003. Toward coastal zone management that ensures coexistence in small-scale fisheries: Is ecotourism an empty promise? *Marine Pollution Bulletin* 47: 1–4.

1

Social Sciences and the Diversity of Caribbean Communities

Yvan Breton, David N. Brown, Milton Haughton
Luis Ovares

1: THE HISTORICAL AND SOCIOLOGICAL BASIS OF THE CONCEPT OF COMMUNITY IN THE CARIBBEAN CONTEXT (DAVID BROWN)

Many social scientists, particularly anthropologists and sociologists, become frustrated when they attempt to precisely define the concept of community. For some, the exercise is simply illusory. George Hilley, an American sociologist, identified 94 different definitions of community (Farrar 2001). For other social scientists, the term consistently defies scientific definition (Barrow and Murphee 1997). Still others think that the reason is the absence of any theory of community. When ideologies step in, the problem becomes even murkier. Bell and Newby (1971) are quoted in Farrar (2001) as differentiating between realists, who define the concept in terms of area, commonalities, and social interaction, versus idealists. They follow the Symbolic Interactionists of Weberian interpretive sociology and the functionalist school of thought, and stick to the elements of shared patterns of thought, norms, values, and meanings. It is these interpretations that constitute a source of 'epistemological' confusion to students and researchers (Farrar 2001). The meaning seems to change according to the theoretical and ideological perspectives of the author. Today's scholars, who face these challenges while they attempt to precisely define the concept, have their roots in the nineteenth century's founding fathers of sociology and anthropology.

Theoretical underpinnings

The evolutionary and neo-evolutionary theorists of society, who take their cue from social Darwinists, considered social change as the evolution of society through broad categories of stages from the traditional to the modern, as depicted in the works of Herbert Spencer, L.H. Morgan, and Auguste Comte. To them, specific historical events such as colonialism and slavery, which are so critical for understanding the makeup of today's Caribbean society, are not necessary. Following in their footsteps, others of similar persuasion developed what is termed the 'ideal typical, bi-polarised systems of social organisation' to represent the extremes of traditional and modern societies (Brown 1981, 11). Ferdinand Tonnies differentiates between community (*gemeischaft*) and society (*gesselschaft*). Following his approach, Charles Cooley differentiates between primary and secondary attachment; Howard Becker writes about sacred and secular societies; and Henry Maine differentiates between status and contract relations. Emile Durkheim characterises communities as homogeneous societies based on mechanical solidarity and urban settings as heterogeneous societies based on organic solidarity.

In these formulations, community is equated with the rural as opposed to the urban, or the village as opposed to the town or city. The former is small, homogeneous, less differentiated, and traditional. According to this school of thought, such societies tend to keep to tradition and the status quo and stick to particularistic religious, ethnic, and kinship affiliations as well as relatively harmonious social relationships. Hence, they are not progressive and are anti-market in orientation. The latter, in contrast, is large, heterogeneous, and more differentiated; integrated and secularised; and characterised by market orientation, progress, modernity, and rationality. From this basis, one could hypothesise that the more urban a society becomes, the greater the loss of community.

Critique of the notion of community

The interpretation of community confronts the student of community-based coastal resource management (CBCRM) with severe challenges. Community is erroneously equated with many confusing characteristics. Depending on interpretation, the term signifies rural and small, fixed territories; relative isolation that is not overly influenced by external forces and which sticks with the status quo; the quality of being less socially differentiated, while simultaneously having shared values, norms, and social relationships that are largely harmonious.

Researchers may start by assuming the existence of all these characteristics in the community being studied. Subsequently, while in the field, they realise that the community in question does not exhibit these characteristics, and that the research has commenced based on fundamentally flawed conceptual and methodological premises. The dilemma lies in how to deal with unanticipated socially fractured rural communities as well as multiple stakeholder groups with particularistic and potentially conflicting and incompatible interests. This challenge is complicated by the need to figure out how to engender participatory and collaborative efforts under such conditions and circumstances, knowing that these are basic requirements of CBCRM.

The assumption that communities are rural, small and characterised by structural homogeneity and social harmony is a premise that simply cannot be sustained in the face of empirical evidence in the Caribbean. There are examples all over the region of contentious community-based fisher organisations in coastal areas that disintegrate almost as fast as they are formed, due to incompatible interests and conflicts. Sandersen attributes this to divisive forces creating dissension and disunity, and argues that many rural communities and organisations in the region are 'less communitarian and more individualistic' (Sandersen, 1998, 26). There is also empirical evidence of fishers in coastal communities who strenuously compete for access to, and use of, scarce resources. Sometimes they use rough tactics against each another, particularly when inshore fisheries with depleting stocks are in question. Wilson called this tendency to try to pull down one's competitors as 'crab antics', analogous to crabs confined in a barrel attempting to climb out to freedom, with those gaining the upper hand being dragged down by those still at the bottom. (Wilson 1973, 58). Nowadays, political affiliations and patronage produce shifting political alliances that cut across ethnic and religious lines and frequently produce social conflict in rural communities. Whether inspired by political patronage or by industry, differential access to resources leads to differential channels of influence and widens social cleavages in coastal communities.

The issue is more complex than Durkheim's characterisation of rural communities as being homogeneous and urban settings as heterogeneous societies. As we will be contending in the next section, in the Caribbean, social structures and relationships can be as varied in rural communities as they are in urban settings. This section presents some of the weaknesses in the argument for homogeneity and social harmony based on 'shared meanings and ... shared norms' as contended by Etzioni and others who are concerned with the loss of community accompanying increased modernization (Etzioni 1995, 24). It is these variations in social structures and relationships that the researcher in CBCRM should pursue, not the overly romanticised harmony of rural communities.

Finally, one must address the claim that communities are anti-progress and anti-market-oriented and could, therefore, be obstacles to efficient and rational organisation of resource use and sustainable development. The underlying assumption leads some researchers and managers away from consulting and negotiating with stakeholders in the communities, even if they are supposed to be the intended beneficiaries of the projects to be implemented. They assume that the target groups lack the understanding and capacity to participate in the decision-making processes or do not possess the right attitudes towards progress and development. The managers would therefore rather impose decisions on the stakeholders than build their capacity to participate as partners in the research and implementation processes. This is a negative and unsustainable approach to CBCRM research and development efforts.

The Caribbean region's history illustrates how citizens took over the plantations which were previously owned and run by European settlers and diverted their energy into planting other exportable crops in the post-colonial era. According to Mintz (1996), labour was imported primarily to work on plantations which, over time, produced sugar, molasses, rum, tobacco, cotton, indigo, coffee, and other staples for European markets. After the slave trade and then slavery ended, these enterprises were partly adapted to produce bananas, coconuts, pineapples, nutmeg, and, these days (though not quite on a plantation scale), marijuana.

Societies possessing such entrepreneurial qualities hardly deserve the labels of anti-progressive and anti-market-oriented. It is our contention that CBCRM practitioners must strive harder to meaningfully involve their community-based stakeholder groups in the decision-making process, and ensure that consultation and negotiation become inextricable elements of the research and decision-making processes.

History, modernity, and heterogeneity

The arrival of European powers in what is now known as the Caribbean ignited a near elimination of indigenous peoples in the area. The Maya, Caribs, and Arawaks were initially targeted; next the Garinagu (Garifuna people) were dislodged from their original settlements in St Vincent and the Grenadines and scattered through Belize, Honduras, Guatemala, Nicaragua, and other areas. The remaining indigenous populations, reduced to insignificant numbers, were pushed to the back burner of history. This posed a real challenge to early social scientists, especially anthropologists, who were looking for their favourite subjects—natives and primitives—to study.

In their place, Africans were forcibly uprooted from Africa and transplanted as slaves to the Caribbean to provide cheap labour for profit-based, European-owned plantations. These enterprises were plantation-cum-agro-industrial complexes, run along modern factory lines. As Mintz puts it:

> As the first part of the non-Western world to endure an era of intensive westernizing activity, the Caribbean oikoumene became "modern" in some ways even before Europe itself while the history of the region has left it a coherence, not so much cultural, as sociological. (Mintz 1996, 305)

The word *oikoumene* means the historical production of a distinctive synthesis, with outcomes that are also unique, such as a unique history that produces unique outcomes. The Caribbean development of 'precocious modernity' predated the Industrial Revolution in England (Mintz 1996, 289). As Sandersen states, these Caribbean societies were 'the oldest modern societies in the world', considering how labour was organised on the plantation-industrial complexes (Sandersen 1998, 9). This economic system was outward-looking, specifically designed to produce and export commodities to feed European consumer markets. Hence, as Mintz notes, the system depicted the merger of production and processing, field work and factory labour, and producer colonies feeding the metropolitan centres with consumer commodities. Enslaved Africans became an instant proletariat, and class structures of capitalist and working classes began to emerge. The commodities exported from the Caribbean to urban centres included sugar, coffee, bananas, rum, and raw rubber. It was the beginning of the integration of the Caribbean economies into the world's capitalist-dominated economy. This instant process of working-class formation was a unique historical development, never replicated elsewhere in the world.

Workers of African origin were later joined on the plantations by East Indian indentured labour. In the English-speaking Caribbean, East Indians were settled particularly in Guyana and in Trinidad and Tobago. Wolf and Hansen wrote about 'closed communities' of East Indians and 'open communities' of Creoles in Spanish-speaking Caribbean countries (Wolf and Hansen 1972, 73-4). The former were inward-looking and oriented towards the community, whereas the latter were outward-looking, oriented towards the city, the region, the nation, and the world. This phenomenon was observed among Indians who adhered strictly to the Hindu religion and way of life in Guyana and Trinidad until midway through the twentieth century. Organisation of production—the control over the factors of production, including both technology and labour force—on the haciendas in the Spanish-speaking Caribbean was derived mainly from a patron-client relationship – a more personal relationship between individuals, rather than the means of production being in the hands of external companies as in the plantation system. Each racial or ethnic group experienced the Caribbean in different ways (Cudjoe 2001).

The peopling of the colonies increased with the arrival of other ethnic and racial groups including the Chinese in Cuba, Jamaica, and Guyana; the Javanese in Suriname; and the rebellious ex-slaves called Maroons in Hispaniola (now Dominican Republic and Haiti), Cuba, Puerto Rico, Jamaica, and some of the Eastern Caribbean islands. Europeans of Caucasian descent settled mainly in those colonies ruled by their countries of origin, namely the English, French, Dutch, and Spanish. As the process of miscegenation set in, hybrid populations began to appear—for example, the Mulattoes, Mestizos, Dougla and Creole.

Because rural communities were the loci of the agro-industrial complexes, the social structures of these communities became heterogeneous, incorporating people of different races and ethnicities, different religious persuasions and creeds, and with different roles to play in the process of production. This is very different from what the founding fathers postulated about rural communities. For them, structural heterogeneity was a phenomenon of urban, industrial settings. The Caribbean example had demonstrated a number of features hardly ever replicated anywhere else. A distinctive history resulted from the way the region was populated—first by African slaves and Indian indentured labour, followed by waves of other ethnic and racial groups—and the emergence of 'hybrid populations'. Modern agro-industrial economies evolved in rural communities through processes that bypassed the usual mechanisms leading to industrialisation.

Another unusual feature of the Caribbean communities was cultural. African slaves were 'deculturalised' through forced dislodgement from their original homelands and because the colonial powers attempted to 'reculturate' them in the European way of life (Henry 1989, 9). This is what Mintz called 'cultural stripping and rebuilding' (Mintz 1996, 289). The process of 'cultural assimilation' on the plantations produced a sizeable number of Christians, predominantly Roman Catholic in the Spanish-speaking Caribbean and Protestant in the English-speaking Caribbean (Carew 2001, 5). Many, however, adhered to remnants of traditional African religions, which they tried to piece together on the margins of colonial society. Other imported religions such as Hinduism and Islam further complicated the picture.

Left with only remnants of their traditional cultures and religions, African slaves and their descendants cobbled together a juxtaposition of those remnants. Sandersen describes this process as the creation of 'dynamic kaleidoscopic cultures', contending that the Caribbean is not culturally homogeneous but a conglomeration of bits and pieces retrieved from past cultures (Sandersen 1995, 9). Therefore, the concept of a 'culture area' as postulated by classical social evolutionary theorists, based on social order, bereft of contradictions and conflicts, cannot be applied to the Caribbean. It is the 'common historical experience of slavery, indentured labour, colonial rule, plus bonds of race and culture, that continue to link the peoples of [this] region together' (Carew 2001, 4). According to Carew, 'the past has left the Caribbean with a legacy of class, race, caste, colour, religious and ethnic contradictions'.

Class structures in the Caribbean emanate from different relationships associated with means of production, status, competition, and conflict, all of which emanate from the assemblage of race, ethnicity, and religion. Considering this, we can see that Caribbean communities are highly diversified social units. Education is another factor that heightens differences in both class and status, as well as power relations, political patronage, and alliances; the result is differential access to resources. To this mix must be added the drive toward economic diversification (in fisheries, tourism, construction, and industrial openings), which has created competition and conflict over access to and use of resources in the coastal communities, and the problems of deforestation, sedimentation, pollution, and overfishing. Mention could also be made of the illusory urban-rural boundaries, with their spillover rural populations living in squalid slums; these 'bridges' sometimes make it difficult to identify the dividing line between rural communities and townships. The reality is one of coastal communities with heterogeneous social structures, which possess contradictory class, status, and power relations along with a complex assemblage of competing and sometimes seemingly irreconcilable interests. The potential for social conflict is great and ever-present.

In the absence of the cementing effect of a unifying culture, the work of the researcher and manager interested in CBCRM becomes a Herculean task. How can they achieve the objectives of their research and projects under these conditions and circumstances? In response, we advance the following propositions.

- Assume a complex assemblage of stakeholders who are not easily discernible at first glance.
- Assume heterogeneity and potentially contradictory interests, and the potential for conflict.
- Develop a strategy for a thorough identification of all stakeholders, bearing in mind that some hitherto-unknown stakeholder groups may emerge.
- Conduct a full stakeholder analysis.
- Develop an implementing strategy that takes into account all the major differing and competing interests of stakeholders.
- Adopt a participatory approach to decision-making, research, and project implementation. Negotiation and consultation should always be guiding principles to keeping all stakeholders on board.

The implementation of a CBCRM approach in the Caribbean presupposes a substantial methodological carefulness that can be enriched only through time. However, taking the communities' heterogeneity into account does not imply an endless series of community studies or management monographs. Instead, it emphasizes the need for researchers to engage in various middle-range comparative efforts that will help them grasp the communities' elasticity in given regional or sub-regional contexts.

2: MARITIME SOCIOANTHROPOLOGY AND CARIBBEAN FISHING COMMUNITIES: AN EMERGENT FIELD (YVAN BRETON)

Given the historical and present-day importance of coastal fishing communities, it would be a truism to assume that they represent key observation units in this CBCRM programme. Indeed, most of the projects selected for inclusion in this book have something to do with fisheries management and governance problems, because fishing represents the main livelihood for the communities studied. However, in comparison with other regions of the world, social studies of coastal communities have not given rise to a great number of scientific publications in the Caribbean. Several exist in master's or doctoral theses and various types of technical reports, but these have not had a significant influence on the academic and intervention scenes. Only recently have we seen more structured efforts that are beginning to counterbalance the numerous contributions stemming from the natural sciences. In other words, as is the case in several countries where fisheries represent an important economic sector, we know more about the reproductive mechanisms of fish species in the Caribbean than about the socioeconomic and political organisation of the fishermen and their families.

We believe a stronger concern for the internal features of fishing communities, including their heterogeneity, will enhance our understanding of the shortcomings linked to the promotion of CBCRM approaches.

Fish have always been an important natural resource in the Caribbean, fulfilling the dietary needs of natives as well as those immigrants who gradually became established in the area. Long before the advent of industrial capitalism, the presence of salt deposits along the coasts allowed producers to develop an exchange economy with a regional basis. Recent archaeological work, for instance, shows that some pre-colonial Maya communities relied heavily on marine resources for their subsistence and engaged in export of salted fish to mainland markets (Quezada 1980, 1999). Pearl fishing was the basis of a mercantile capitalism by Spaniards in the early days of colonisation—for instance, in Margarita Island in Venezuela (Mendez-Arocha

1963). During the colonial period, prebendal domains—concessions of a given exploitation zone made to an individual by the official authorities for a given period of time with exclusive rights— served as a mobilisation device for many fishermen in lagoons of the Gulf of Mexico, and there existed a significant internal market in the Valley of Mexico (Breton and Lopez-Estrada 1988, 1989). As time evolved, the economic importance of fishing has greatly increased (with some variations between countries). In 2000, the number of fishermen in the overall Caribbean region reached 500,000, with the main insular fishing countries being Jamaica, Haiti, the Bahamas, Dominican Republic, and Trinidad and Tobago (CARSEA 2003). In addition to this numerical increase, the activity has been characterised by an important internal differentiation at the capture level and a significant expansion in its recreational and sport sectors. The end result is that fishing communities in the Caribbean form a wide array of social units in which a growing diversity prevails.

In addition to the usual distinction between industrial and artisanal fishing, within each category significant modifications are now taking place that are linked to the depletion of existing species or the introduction of new ones. Particularly striking is the fact that artisanal fishing communities, because of their location in and exploitation of coastal areas, are very sensitive to drivers that are external to the fisheries themselves. Such driver mechanisms include the expansion of tourism, increase in international marine shipping, and the offshore petroleum industry. While the majority of artisanal fishermen remain in rural areas, an increasing number are now located in semi-urban centres. Examples include Cuba, with its state control of the industry, and seaport areas of large cities, as in Jamaica. In these instances, management issues are largely influenced by the predominant presence of stakeholders who are not directly linked to fishing. On the other hand, several coastal states have now established marine parks and reserves—and in these situations, most fishermen were not directly consulted. This changing procedural context generates and accentuates differential perceptions between various groups of fishermen and enhances the element of uncertainty that has always been a part of their livelihood strategies.

Neglect of maritime cultures

In spite of their historical depth and current economic importance, Caribbean fishing communities have not been the object of systematic social studies. The result is that our understanding of these communities remains relatively weak in terms of capital accumulation, governance issues, and market-oriented linkages.

Several factors explain this. The first is the historically low political visibility of fishermen in various parts of the world over the centuries. Generally distant from administrative centres and dealing with natural 'free-access' resources, this group does not draw much attention from the state authorities and does not engage in significant political movements, as is the case in the agrarian sector. In general, this apparent lack of social pathology was not very appealing to social researchers. Another factor pertains to the rapid agro-export orientation that occurred the Caribbean during and after the colonisation period. This process was greatly enhanced by the forced migration of enslaved African and indentured Asian labourers. This gave rise to a cultural mix that was not 'Western enough' to fit the concerns of sociologists and not 'native enough' to fit fully into the 'savage slot,' where anthropologists found their preferred subjects (Trouillot 1992, 20).

Needless to say, the importance of the plantation economy relegated fishing to a very secondary if not minimal role. A third factor is linked to the relatively late consolidation of a maritime socioanthropology as a specific discipline on the Western academic scene. It became a more structured field in the 1970s and 1980s, as the conflicts between artisanal and industrial fishing gained importance and as maritime nationalism emerged. The fisheries sector then began to acquire a stronger political dimension with increasing social pathologies. A fourth factor is the advent of integrated coastal management and CBCRM programmes in the Caribbean. Models of integrated coastal management were first implemented outside the Caribbean area but they quickly influenced the situation that prevailed in the Caribbean with the same basic shortcomings. In many parts of the world, interest in 'integrated approaches' and 'communities' was promoted mostly by scientists and non-governmental organisation (NGO) representatives, from the perspective of natural-science disciplines. Despite good intentions, and sometimes strong conviction that the social dimension was inescapable, researchers often came up with simplified or generic visions of what should have emanated from social analysis. Finally, since socioanthropological studies have so far been more common in English-speaking countries, an institutional asymmetry emerged with their Spanish counterparts. Language barriers prevented significant exchanges between researchers.

The foregoing points are intended to show that the relative weakness, or lack, of social studies on fishing communities is, within a programme that seeks to consolidate a CBCRM approach, a very real constraint that hides the communities' diversity and internal differentiation. Additional efforts must be made in the Caribbean to enrich both the knowledge of and our vision of the stakeholders who live in these communities, and of the specific institutional and governance linkages upon which they depend.

Institutionalisation of maritime socioanthropology

In order to expand on these issues, we briefly review some socioanthropological studies of fishing communities in the Caribbean over the previous decades. While providing the reader with some factual observations on these communities, this examination should reinforce the arguments put forward above. We claim neither exhaustiveness nor statistical representativeness in dealing with the literature, even though we had the opportunity to closely follow its evolution in the last 30 years. At the beginning of the 1990s, two studies summarised publications on artisanal fishing in the Caribbean; however, these limited themselves to insular countries (Pizzini 1990a; Freon, Gobert, and Mahon 1991).

A first period can be identified, with the work of Cohen (1954), Davenport (1956, 1960), Comitas (1962), Edel (1967), and Epple (1973, 1977). In accordance with the pattern that prevailed at the larger social-science level, all these studies concerned English-speaking countries, namely Jamaica and Grenada; only one study was conducted in Venezuela (Orona 1969). Most stemmed from the authors' doctoral research, at a time when maritime socioanthropology was still in an incipient phase of consolidation. Rather than entering into the social reproduction processes that characterised these communities and seeking to grasp their specificity, the researchers used ethnography as an illustrative basis for larger debates within the disciplines. These debates were related to culturalist paradigms centred on the fishermen's individualism or technological acculturation, or to the substantivist or formalist oppositions in economic anthropology. The main observation units consisted of the fishermen's cooperatives and extended families, not the community as whole. This orientation confirms the difficulty of dealing with the notion of 'community' from the social-science perspective. In a smaller way, a group of anthropologists from Montréal University, under the direction of Benoist

(1959), undertook studies in Martinique in the 1960s in which research interests evolved more around cultural than organisational features of the communities, despite their monographic orientation.

A second period corresponds to the emerging debates in many countries around the extension of the exclusive economic zones and the growth of maritime nationalism in the 1970s and 1980s. Within the social sciences, this coincided with the gradual transformation of culturalist paradigms and the advent of historical materialism. Sociomaritime anthropology also became better recognised on the academic scene. A series of studies, initially conducted through doctoral fieldwork, mostly in the Gulf of Mexico and Eastern Venezuela (Breton 1973, 1979; Dumas 1982; Lopez-Estrada 1989; Quezada 1993; De La Cruz Rock 1993; Lebail 1983; Fraga Berdugo 1993; Arnaiz Burne 1996), paid attention to the economic organisation of fishing communities and their relations to the state. Especially in Mexico, fisheries governance mechanisms underwent drastic changes that caught the attention of the researchers. While many concerns still existed concerning the role of the fishing cooperatives in these studies (Pizinni 1990b), several of the researchers relied on a class-analysis approach that represented an attempt to differentiate the stakeholders according to their relationship to the means of production (Breton and Lopez-Estrada 1989). The orientation towards historical materialism led researchers to consider the numerous conflicts that existed between industrial and artisanal fishermen. In some cases, reference was made to the growing importance of tourism, namely in the Yucatan Peninsula, after the collapse of the hennequen (sisal) industry. This second period, therefore, corresponded to an improved understanding of what concerns the socioanthropological studies of fishing communities in the Caribbean. However, it remained principally confined to Spanish-speaking countries, particularly Mexico, and gave more importance to the notion of social class than to community. As in the first period, however, most studies took place within graduate programs. Therefore, results were disseminated slowly, and language barriers continued to prevent significant exchanges with researchers from other countries.

The third and most recent period is characterised by an opening to interdisciplinarity and political-ecology approaches. These orientations were undoubtedly influenced by the emergence of various paradigms linked to such coastal resource management programmes as integrated coastal zone management (ICZM), natural resource management (NRM), and the

Community-based Coastal Resource Management (CBCRM). Socioanthropological studies of fishermen's management problems are now more widespread and include English, Spanish, and French countries. For instance, CARICOM researchers have undertaken numerous research activities in the small-island states (Brown 1998; Brown and Pomeroy 1999), and Mexican anthropologists at both University of Yucatan (Quezada and Breton 1996) and Cinvestav in Mérida (Fraga Berdugo 1999; Chuenpagdee, Fraga Berdugo, and Eúan-Ávila 2002) have set up research programmes involving several undergraduate and graduate students. Similar initiatives are underway in Cuba (Doyon 2003), with the recent establishment of an interdisciplinary master's degree programme in integrated coastal management in that country's national universities, as well as in Belize (Palacio 1999, 2001) and in the French Caribbean (Andre-Bigot 1998; Blanchet, Gobert, and Guérédrat 2002). But as was the case in the previous phases, despite more precise concerns for coastal management problems, most of these studies resulted from individual efforts. With a few exceptions, unequal attention is paid to the social reproduction of the communities themselves and to the collaboration/opposition mechanisms between their stakeholders. Because the linguistic barriers remain, there is a lack of institutional visibility and scaling-up efforts.

This attempt at categorising the development of socioanthropological studies of fishing communities in the Caribbean reveals several constraints and shortcomings that should be reduced if a real CBCRM approach is to be implemented. These can be summarised as follows.

1. Most research efforts were conducted by individual researchers without sufficient institutional support that could have ensured stronger continuity at the research and result-dissemination levels. Several of the studies were MA or PhD theses, and many represented a single output that was not followed by additional research. There was a clear lack of comparative efforts to develop a cumulative data bank that could have allowed researchers to improve their regional vision of management problems within the fisheries.[1]
2. In addition to the difficulty of relying on a Western social-science epistemology for the study of Caribbean communities in general, researchers who were interested in fishing communities did not have a set of well-defined concepts and methods at their disposal. It took

a few decades before a maritime socioanthropology became consolidated on the academic scene. The Caribbean fishing ethnography presents some particular features that cannot be easily synthesised without a clear but flexible analytical framework.

3. In matters related to marine affairs or maritime communities, natural scientists were and are far more involved than the social scientists. Natural scientists can rely on a long research tradition that gives them more weight in the decision-making processes linked to research programmes and policies on coastal management. Their growing openness to social science and stronger community studies is positive, but also requires some caution because it can lead to diluted or distorted orientations when not conducted appropriately.
4. Linguistic barriers are a scholarly handicap that amplifies intellectual parochialism within the disciplines. It restricts the range of comparisons and the number of territories studied, and promotes superficial similarities (Trouillot 1992, 35). The discussion above shows that there is still little connection between English, Spanish, and French studies of fishing communities in the Caribbean.

In spite of these constraints, we believe that some progress has been made in recent years. Social scientists are now acquiring more visibility in some institutions, and social sciences are represented more adequately in emerging interdisciplinary programmes. However, since fishing communities are and will remain important social units and because they are inescapable elements in many CBCRM efforts in the Caribbean, their systematic study should be the object of stronger promotional efforts in the future. In addition, special attention should be given to the fairly recent introduction of massive shrimp aquaculture as an industrial activity that has a tremendous impact on both land and adjoining communities. To accomplish this goal, more sophisticated statistical data must be obtained, which would permit a better establishment of the profile of fishermen and of their communities in various countries. In addition, a series of socioanthropological community studies on a cross-comparative scale need to be undertaken. These studies should not be strictly project- and deadline-driven, and subsequently evaluated according to outside standards. Instead, they should be developed within a regional, institutional framework that considers the specificity of both local and regional fisheries (at the ecological, economic, and social levels). As well, studies should promote a cumulative-knowledge orientation. In this regard, it would be useful to synthesise the already existing studies through temporal and sub-regional categories that would better highlight the development of maritime communities' studies in the Caribbean in recent decades. There must also be considerable reflection on how to encourage younger researchers to become more involved in the 'social mapping' of these communities. While consolidating a better social-sciences approach in CBCRM projects in the Caribbean, this orientation could certainly help to persuade the natural scientists working there to have a greater appreciation of the complexity of stakeholder analysis from a management perspective.

3: ETHNICITY AND CULTURAL IDENTITY (LUIS OVARES)

Whatever criteria are used to define it, the Caribbean region is a cultural mosaic. It has become multiracial, multilingual, and multicultural over several centuries. The Wider Caribbean, the Antilles, Mesoamerica, the West Indies, the insular Caribbean, the Caribbean basin, and simply 'the Caribbean' are labels used by different authors to describe the region. Some daring individuals separate this magnificent region according to the origins of its inhabitants, giving rise to Spanish, French, English, Dutch, and American Caribbean designations. These peoples have their own ways of life, their idiosyncrasies and cultural values rooted in a continuous re-identification process that is based on individual identities, ethnic group, and other self-identities which have been gradually integrated as a result of various distinct ethnic traditions and social forms (Polo 2001). This flexibility has led to a certain degree of semantic and conceptual confusion. What is indeed real is that the Caribbean has given form to very diverse and complex cultures that are a mix of elements from various parts of the world. This is one of the reasons its inhabitants have tried to maintain significant links with their ancestral countries, even as they are contributing to the formation of new and different cultures. The ancestral influences include European, African, Asian, and Middle Eastern. New trans-Caribbean characteristics have also been incorporated. In addition, since the beginning of the twentieth century, this cultural mix has been enriched by elements stemming from the Caribbean diaspora. Migration and interactions between Caribbean peoples and North America and Europe have also had a significant impact (Khan 1998).

Ethnicity is undoubtedly a dynamic phenomenon if viewed from a humanistic perspective, in contrast with the traditional Western conception. Within that framework, there is a tendency to deny the existence of minority ethnics (especially indigenous populations) because it challenges the nation-state model which assumes the homogeneity of the national population (Urioste 2001). Ethnicity remains a useful variable to help understand the changes occurring in many societies. Ethnicity is one of the historical factors that has generated conflicts between countries and between communities within the same country. It has also helped to consolidate relations between scattered groups sharing common ethnic roots. On the one hand, ethnicity has been the basis for formulating collective social objectives and strategies of action. On the other hand, the globalisation of economic processes has promoted standardisation and homogenisation in very diverse societies (such as those in the Caribbean), in which new 're-ethnification' processes have begun to emerge (PRMDR 2001).

In the case of the Caribbean, ethnicity has been shaped through and influenced by religion, language, and region of origin. Even though racial conflicts are infrequently spoken of in the Caribbean, well-documented political conflicts rooted in racial differences exist. In countries that are the most pluralistic and socially fragmented, such as Trinidad and Tobago, tensions and fights continue between African and Asian groups. Similar problems have occurred in Suriname between Hindus and Afro-Caribbean groups of Creoles and Maroons. Additional conflicts have arisen on the island of Hispaniola, where the Dominicans of Haitian origin are discriminated against by the majority Mestizo population, in spite of the fact that they speak Spanish. These cases illustrate the tortuous road involved in bringing together the different ethnic groups, even within the internal boundaries of individual countries in the Caribbean.

Language and culture

The language of the Great Caribbean has been designated in some scientific studies as the *lengua única* (sole language). It is the product and heritage of slavery and the forced migration of Africans brought by Europeans to work on their Caribbean plantations. At the same time, this *lengua única* is the product of the coexistence of peoples with different religions, races, languages, and cultures, including aboriginal groups, such as the Caribs, Mayans,

Arawaks, Garifuna, Chibchas, Tainos, and Ciboneys, who mixed with the immigrants. There is no doubt that in a globalised world, a multilingual culture composed of multiple intertwined elements allows many forms of expression and has advantages compared to a monolingual culture.

Although English and Spanish are two dominant languages in the Caribbean, historical and cultural dynamism has generated creole and patois languages—Papiamento Kreyol (Dutch Antilles) and Sranan Tongo, Ndjuka, Saramaccan, Kromanti, Hindustani, Bhojpuri, and Urdu (Suriname and Trinidad). The combination of African linguistic structures with European words gave rise to the French creole in Haiti, Martinique, Guadeloupe, St Lucia, Dominica, and French Guiana. In the islands under Dutch influence, the merging of Dutch, Portuguese, English, and African languages generated Papiamento. In Jamaica, English Creoles, patwa, and Kromanti developed alongside English (Premdas 1996). Creoles as well as patois have been spoken for the last two centuries. They have usually been the languages of the poor, who historically have lacked work and educational opportunities. In some countries, their use has been discouraged in favor of the use of European languages. Fortunately, this has changed recently with the resurgence of nationalistic movements that defend the cultural importance of Creoles (Cariforum 2004).

It is not easy to establish a linguistic typology for the Caribbean region. Nevertheless, four major groups exist.

- 'Castellano' (Castilian) is the dominant language in Cuba, Dominican Republic, and Puerto Rico. Of the 33 million Caribbean people, 60 per cent speak Spanish.
- The English Caribbean is represented by Jamaica, Trinidad and Tobago, Barbados, Guyana, Belize, the Bahamas, Antigua, St Kitts and Nevis, St Lucia, Grenada, Dominica, St Vincent and the Grenadines, Montserrat, Anguilla, Barbuda, the Cayman Islands, Turks and Caicos, and the Virgin Islands (both British and US).
- The French Caribbean includes Haiti, Martinique, Guadeloupe, and French Guiana. A French Creole is spoken in Dominica and St Lucia.
- The Dutch Caribbean is composed of Suriname, Aruba, Curaçao, Bonaire, Saba, St Maarten, and St Eustatius.

Is there a Caribbean identity?

The anthropologist Trouillot (1992) assumes that it is very difficult to define the concept of 'Caribbean' and Caribbean cultural identity, because of a series of contradictions present in the region. One of the best ways to understand its ethnic or communal identity is through the use of imagination. For instance, the terms used by most Caribbean people when they interact with each other—'brother' or 'sister'—are automatically rejected because, unlike other places—other cultural areas—people do not know or mix very much with their compatriots (Said 1995). This has motivated some 'pan-Caribbeanists' to promote the idea of a regional nationalism. This strategy avoids ethnocentrism and nationalism, which are so common in other areas, causing racial and ethnic tensions and prejudices that can lead to internal armed conflicts.

This apparently fragile and fleeting regional nationalism seems to strengthen when the region is subjected to external intervention. For example, in response to the Monroe Doctrine, the Cuban José Martí said 'America for the Americans but the Antilles for the Antillians' (Ferrer 1986). Similarly, in recent years, increasing economic, social, and cultural globalisation has influenced the Caribbean countries to strengthen pan-Caribbean integration efforts. Back in the 1970s, Serbin (1977) called this movement the 'epistemic regional community'. The idea was to develop a common regional front that could eventually negotiate commercial agreements with the United States and the European Community. One example of these efforts is the Free Trade Area of the Americas (FTAA) agreement, still under negotiation.

Today's Caribbean is developing under a dualistic conceptual framework. On the one hand, we find a heterogeneous geographical region with a heritage of slavery embedded in a plantation system. On the other hand, the Caribbean is a self-defined, internally-oriented region with its own characteristics. It is oriented towards local development with an internal dynamism. It acknowledges its differences and simultaneously embraces them so as to address common interests (Mori Gonzalez 2002).

From a Caribbean focus to a transnational community

According to Ralph Premdas (1996), to conceive of the Caribbean as a unified area that integrates the concepts of citizenship and community would not only be an exercise of imagination but would also represent an attempt to arbitrarily integrate what has existed for centuries. Various authors assume that national identity is a cultural creation resulting from social and historical processes. Ferdinand De Saussure thought that language was the key to understanding the culture of a given group. However, it is difficult to assume that a pluralistic region such as the Caribbean could be so easily homogenised and integrated. This is why some anthropologists do not hesitate to call it the 'open frontier' (Trouillot 1992).

Normally, anglophones use the term *Caribbean people* to describe the inhabitants of the English-speaking countries of the Caribbean or those belonging to CARICOM, while they use 'Wider Caribbean' for other countries in the region. However, the Spanish-speaking Caribbean people have the perception that they are *caribeños* as well as Latin Americans. Puerto Ricans, who live in a US protectorate, consider themselves to be Latin Americans. Their nationalistic roots are linked to the culture, language, and history of Latin America. They reject the term *Caribbean* because it refers to an anglophone, socioanthropological definition. Similarly, inhabitants of Central America (part of the greater Caribbean), identify themselves more with the people of Latin American and the isthmus of Central America. They prefer to designate their coastal zone along the Caribbean coast as the 'Atlantic region'. The terminology evokes sympathy for Central Americans of African heritage, as suggested by the Haitian anthropologist Casimir and the Puerto Rican historian Gaztamabide-Geigel, both of whom argue that this is the product of an ethnohistorical conceptualisation of the region (Girvain 2000).

The overall population of the Caribbean includes individuals of various ethnic origins (European, African, Indian, Indonesian, Chinese, and Native American, and the Mestizo descendants of all of these groups). However, there is a tendency in English-speaking countries to use a racial typology categorising people as white, black, brown, red, and mixed-blood. Among the Spanish-speaking people of the Caribbean, the categories are reduced to white, black, Chinese, and indigenous.

Pan-African and pan-Indian elements are present in some of the English-speaking countries. This phenomenon, which might be called 'Iberoamericanism', is almost non-existent in Spanish-speaking countries (Girvain 2000). Affinities with Europe are minimised, and autonomy from Spain maintained. In a systematic way, the English-speaking people have minimised the Spanish cultural identity. It has been associated with the expansionism and 'annexionism' of the United States in the past (Mori 2002). More recently, it has been associated with geopolitical and hegemonic initiatives, such as the commercial strategy of the Caribbean Basin Initiative (Cuenca del Caribe) or the most recent US intervention in Haiti.

Throughout the Caribbean's history, there has always been a central question among its inhabitants. Do you belong to a biracial or multiracial culture? In the Spanish Caribbean, the Afro-Caribbean people are frequently called 'Blacks', implying an ethnic group. The term does not, however, signify an erosion of their Latin-American identity. In contrast, in the English Caribbean, the term 'Negro' has long been viewed as denigrating because of its resonance of the colonial period and American plantation slavery. This could be a significant cultural difference between the English and the Spanish Caribbean. Another important difference has been noted in studies conducted among Caribbean migrants to the United States. These studies show that the English-speaking people frequently use the term 'America' to refer to the United States, whereas Spanish migrants use the term 'United States' but not 'America'. It is important to remember that in Latin American geography classes, America is a continent that goes from Alaska to Cape Horn. It is not a country.

The degree of integration, assimilation, and acculturation of Caribbean peoples in the United States has been determined by their ethnicity, language, country of origin, and cultural identity. Black immigrants from Spanish-speaking countries have succeeded in integrating themselves as part of the Latin-American minority living in the United States, in the same way white immigrants have. Their Latin-American background, more than their Caribbean culture, explains this situation. Many young Puerto Ricans and Dominicans have identified with the African diaspora. This reinforces their identification and solidarity with African Americans, especially in New York City. In contrast, for the majority of Black and English-speaking CARICOM immigrants, integration into US society is somewhat different. Their ethnicity and language have facilitated their integration into the Black minority in the United States; however, they try to maintain their Caribbean identity, since they perceive a loss of status when they are identified as Black US citizens. These variations also presuppose that there are differences between Blacks of Latin American backgrounds and those with English-speaking cultural backgrounds (Ostine 2003).

Such realities show that ethnicity is an inescapable variable when dealing with the Caribbean's heterogeneity from a management perspective. All the countries include various ethnic groups whose social organisation and systems of beliefs influence their relations with other groups as well as with the state bureaucracy. In this context, management initiatives must pay attention to the differentiated governance mechanisms that link the communities with decisions emanating from upper levels.

4: ECOSYSTEMS AND SPATIAL MORPHOLOGY AS DIFFERENTIATION FACTORS (YVAN BRETON AND MILTON HAUGHTON)

Like many other coastal areas around the world, the Caribbean region is characterised by the presence of highly diversified ecosystems that give rise to numerous productive activities around which human settlements and communities have developed. Without entering into a discussion of geographical determinism that negatively affected various social-science paradigms, we now explore the extent to which some functional relations exist between various types of ecosystems and communities' spatial arrangements. Convinced that space is intimately linked to social relations (in its use and appropriation mechanisms), we think that our quest for deepening our understanding of the Caribbean communities' heterogeneity can be enriched by referring to the basic features of their geographical settings and ecological characteristics.

Insular and continental dichotomy

The first striking element in this regard is the existence in the Caribbean of areas that are insular and areas that are continental. National territories vary greatly in size, a situation that generates discrepancies at the demographic and economic levels. The Caribbean is also highly fractionalised, comprising over 30 countries. For instance, among the 35 million people living in the insular zone, nearly 28 million belong to the two largest islands, Cuba and Hispaniola. The same contrast can be found between the coastal areas of the Gulf of Mexico, home to cities like Mérida, Campeche, and Veracruz, and the low population density found on the Atlantic side of Central American states. A direct correlation can be easily established between the number and size of the countries and their linguistic and cultural diversities, especially in the insular states.

When history is coupled with a fractionalised space, it is easier to explain the diversity of national contexts that emerged from the interaction between various groups of people, be they natives, colonisers, slaves, or other types of migrants. The present-day heterogeneity of the Caribbean communities can be first understood by referring to this relationship between general geographical features of the area and their progressive occupation and utilisation by individuals characterised by various cultural and technical traditions. Quoting Turner, Davidson-Hunt, and O'Flaherty (2003, 439):

> A well known facet of ecosystems is that the edges (the boundaries or transitions from one ecosystem to the other) often exhibit high levels of species richness or biodiversity. These transitional areas often show features of species composition, structure, and function representative of the ecosystems they transcend, as well as having their own unique array of species and characteristics. Cultural transitional areas (zones where two or more cultures converge and interact) are similarly rich and diverse in cultural traits, exhibiting cultural and linguistic features of each of the contributing people. This results in an increase in cultural capital, and resilience, by providing a wider range of traditional ecological knowledge and wisdom on which to draw, especially in times of stress and change.

In other words, this insular and continental dichotomy remains valid at a general level but is also the object of gradual transformations. Since the 1980s, the Central American coastline from Belize to Panama has been an area of large-scale in-migration from the highlands. The result has been the settlement of thousands of people who traditionally are not coastal and who are quickly adjusting to the economic opportunities they see available.

The diversity of marine ecosystems

The Caribbean region has an area of approximately 15 million km^2 of which about 1.9 million km^2 is shelf area. Within the Caribbean area, there are three large marine ecosystems: the Gulf of Mexico, the Caribbean Sea, and the Guiana-Brazil shelf. The oceanography of the Caribbean is highly complex and both spatially and temporally variable, with the west-to-northwestward-flowing Caribbean Current being the dominant surface current system in the region. The Caribbean's oceanographic characteristics are also greatly influenced by freshwater runoff from several large river systems, including two of the largest rivers in the world, the Amazon and the Orinoco. Average annual surface water temperature of the ocean is 27°C with seasonal changes of ±3°C.

The shallow shelves of the coastal waters are ideal locations for coral reefs, seagrass beds, mangrove swamps, and white sand beaches. Approximately 14 per cent of the world's coral reefs are found in the Wider Caribbean. The Meso-American Barrier Reef system lying off the Caribbean coast of Mexico, Belize, Guatemala, and Honduras is the second largest barrier reef in the world (Haughton and Brown 2002). There are variations in the width of the continental shelf, which is relatively narrow in most of the small-island states and parts of the Atlantic coast of Central America. This results in high diversity of Caribbean marine resources, warm climate, crystalline water, and numerous white sand beaches. It is obvious why the Caribbean is particularly attractive to various groups of marine users, be they industrial, artisanal, or recreational fishermen or scuba divers and other tourists.

Tourism is now the principal economic activity in many Caribbean states, particularly the small-island developing ones, and is also a major driver of social transformation and economic revitalisation in coastal communities. Over the past 30 years, tourism has gradually replaced traditional agriculture, fishing, and forestry as the main engine of economic growth and development, in several contexts (Haughton and Brown 2002). Tourism is based primarily on the highly diverse ecosystem resources, including the combination of sea, sand, sun, and the associated coral reefs and fish stocks. Major destinations such as Cancún in Mexico, Ocho Rios and Negril in Jamaica, San Pedro in Belize, and Puerto Plata in the Dominican Republic are all valued primarily for their diverse natural coastal and marine ecosystems.

Tourism is not everything, however. In all the communities involved in this programme, the fishery is one of the main livelihoods, and fish species vary greatly from one community to another. This implies reliance on diverse marine sub-ecosystems, among which coral reefs and estuarine areas are predominant, and reliance on different techniques for exploitation of the natural resources. This techno-ecological diversity is mirrored by the presence of differentiated labour mobilisation mechanisms, capital assets, and social coalitions. All contribute to Caribbean communities' specificity as well as the differential nature of their management problems.

Variations in settlement patterns

A comparative look at the spatial morphology of coastal regions and communities is also very instructive and indicates significant variations. Small-island states such as St Vincent and the Grenadines, St Lucia, and Barbados are de facto coastal areas in themselves. They thus present specific environmental challenges in which the communities, as units of observation, are intimately linked to or sometimes merged with 'national' priorities. This contrasts with larger countries in which coastal communities are scattered over a wider area, embedded in different administrative units. In these cases, communities have developed stronger regional identities that influence their governance mechanisms with the presence of a significant urban/rural dichotomy. In Cuba, for instance, major cities are all located around bays that serve as protected areas for navigation. Over the passage of time in these areas, a high concentration of population and developed industries has generated specific contamination problems that are now at the core of several national management issues. This issue is directly addressed in chapter 5.

If we contrast the central part of the Atlantic coast with the Pacific side, the reduced importance of the continental shelf explains why there are fewer people involved in the fisheries. Settlement patterns are generally based on a series of relatively small, scattered communities who are engaged in artisanal fishing. Most indigenous groups of the area are among these. In addition, given the significant presence of estuarine areas and coral reefs, many communities, such as those of northeastern Costa Rica, face management problems linked to the increasing presence of sport fishermen and scuba divers. In several coastal communities across the Caribbean, traditional fishers and others who are dependent on the fisheries are faced with numerous problems arising from the expansion of tourism and tourist-related activities, which create direct competition for access to and use of the same coastal resources.

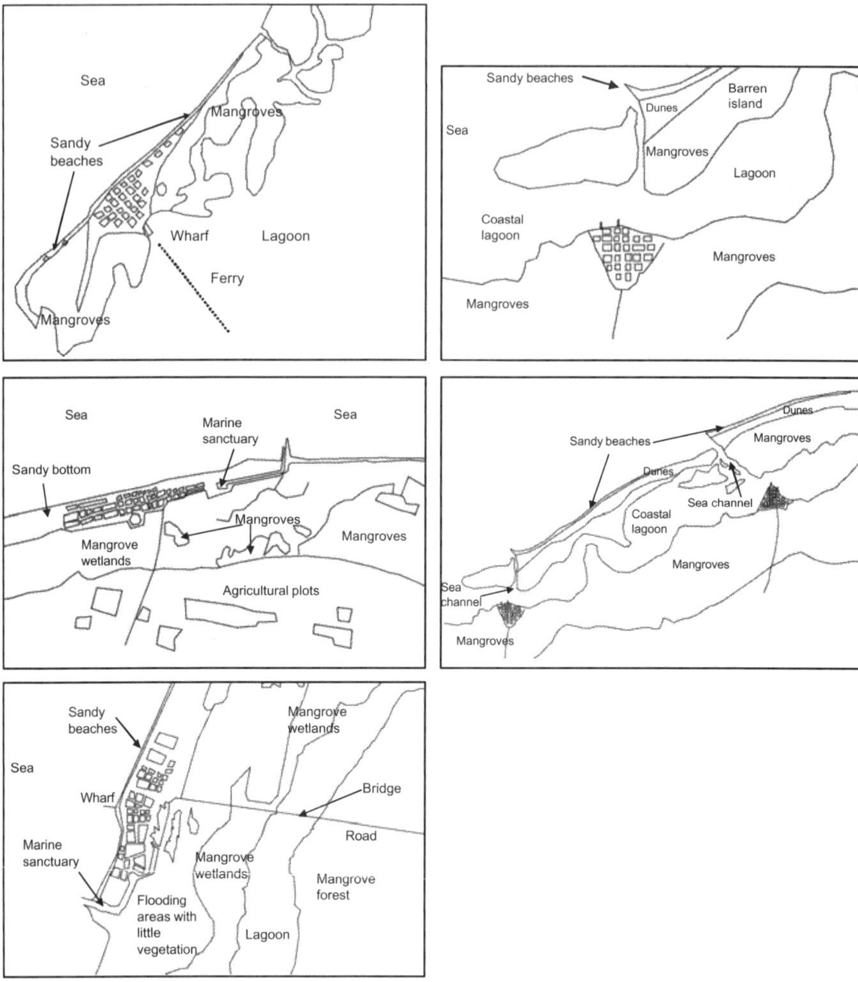

Figure 1
Ecosystems and variations in the settlement patterns of various communities

On the other hand, in some countries—for instance, Trinidad and Tobago—the presence of offshore petroleum wells along the coast, along with prohibited-access areas, has affected local fishing communities. Depending on the season, fishermen rely on a strong spatial mobility that, in spite of their variable locations, does not prevent them from developing a strong sense of sociological belonging. Here is a different type of community dependent upon specific ecological and economic drivers. For similar reasons, mainly to do with the location of fishing grounds, fishermen from communities like Sarteneja in Northern Belize have to undertake weekly migrations that greatly influence the social life of their community. Additional examples could be used here—while avoiding any form of geographical determinism—to explain how environmental features can influence the spatial morphology and the social organisation of communities. This situation is certainly not unique to the Caribbean region. However, at both macro and micro levels, this reality includes some details that must be taken into account if we are to better understand these communities' differences and the nature of their management problems.

Another important point is that people living in coastal areas are at the junction of mainland, marine, and mixed ecological niches. These areas possess high natural diversity, which potentially increases the internal diversity of the communities and the nature of their responses to environmental challenges. Finally, in spite of the establishment of exclusive economic zones under the 1982 UN Convention on the Law of the Sea, the exploitation of fisheries resources is overwhelmingly done by artisanal fishermen. The fisheries have evolved and continue to operate in a more or less 'open access' context that allows crowding and intensive harvesting within the narrow limits of the available island or continental shelf areas. This situation reinforces the communities' and the peoples' specialisation, yet fractionalises their management problems.

Space and people's places

Up to now, our inquiry into the relations between the environment and spatial morphology of the communities in the Caribbean has been based mostly on its physical features. Undoubtedly, management problems imply references to the ways people have access to, use, and share their environmental resources. Many management plans or initiatives rely at the beginning on mapping of given areas, focusing first on the boundaries of given zones and progressively detailing their various elements.

However, it is important to remember that ecosystems are not static and can undergo important transformations. They are subject to uncertainty and variable forms of resilience. At the same time, these ecosystems and their use are embedded in and influenced by various human perceptions. In recent articles, Ingold (2002) and Cheng, Kruger, and Daniels (2003) pose interesting statements regarding the relationship between people-place connections and strategic behaviour in the politics of natural resources. Not only do they suggest a strong connection between self-identity, place, and how individuals perceive their environment, but they also assume that the politics of natural resources is as much a contest over place meanings as it is a competition among interest groups over scarce resources. The Kuna example presented in chapter 3 is instructive in this regard. In other words, the emergence and persistence of community-based collaborative partnerships since the early 1990s implies that they are generally composed of individuals who, despite diverse backgrounds and frequently opposing perspectives on natural resources management, work together to define and address common-resource management issues bounded by a geographic place.

The authors clearly pinpoint the differences between real community-based management efforts involving various stakeholders, and the interactions in formal political processes. The latter include those that occur in legislative arenas or agency planning processes, and in which single-issue policy positions favoured by a coalition of interest groups are approved or opposed. In light of our previous remarks, this suggested orientation seems valid and supports forthcoming observations in the following chapters.

A stratified sample of selected communities

We end this section by presenting an overview of the communities selected in this Phase II of the CBCRM programme. They are located in 11 countries and include three in Cuba, two in Mexico, and two in Belize. The rest generally consist of one community per country. A strong emphasis has been put at the beginning of this phase on the selection of one community per project, in order to accentuate the CBCRM approach of the programme. It has not been possible in all cases, however, to identify a specific one.

This situation underlines some specific features of the Caribbean communities. In some places such as eastern Trinidad, Grenada, and Dominican Republic, the 'community' selected consists of a series of human aggregates characterised by the strong mobility of fisher people. Because they usually live close to their extended families and are embedded into larger kinship ties, over the years fishers have developed some technical specialisations that require back-and-forth migrations to various fishing sites with a frequency that varies according to their fishing seasons. The result is that, although at given moments of the year the fishers might be scattered in various fishing 'communities' with specific names, within the annual cycle a partial re-composition of these settlements occurs. From a sociological point of view, the overall community is more significant than its various sub-components and constitutes the ultimate reference in terms of belonging and identity in the group.

The information included in the chapter 2 shows that the demographic size of the communities ranges from 300 people in Cocodrilo, Cuba, to 12,000 in Liwingston, Belize. In addition to their locations in various ecosystems (estuarine, bay, mangrove, and beach) and administrative units (inside and outside various types of protected areas), there is a wide array of populations. These include Afro-Caribbean, Mestizo, and indigenous representatives such as the Garifuna in Belize and Guatemala and the Kuna in Panama. Such diversity represents an important challenge at the analytical level. Nevertheless, it enriches the comparative basis that underlines the need to take into account the local context in promoting a CBCRM approach.

Communities' heterogeneity is present in several parts of the world; it does not represent a unique Caribbean feature. But the essence and the elasticity of the Caribbean's heterogeneity vary according to several factors that have been shaped and influenced by history, environment, and culture. Before questioning and assessing the usefulness of a CBCRM approach in the Caribbean, we believe the strong specificity of this region's communities must be thoroughly understood.

Note

1. In a review of *Caribbean Studies* for the period 1988–95, we found only one article dealing with fisheries (Adams 1992).

References

Adams, J.E. 'Fish lovers of the Caribbean' In *Caribbean Studies*, Vol.25 No.1-2:1-10, 1992.

Andre-Bigot, H. 1998. 'D'eau et de rêve.' Une identité en transformation: Trois générations de pêcheurs de Sainte-Lucie (West Indies). PhD diss., EHESS.

Arnaiz Burne, S.M. 1996. De la pesca al turismo: Los cambios socio-económicos en San Pedro, Ambergris, Belize. PhD diss., Université Laval.

Barrow, E., and M. Murphee. 1997. *Community conservation from concept to practice. A practical approach.* Manchester, UK: Institute for Development Policy and Management.

Bell, C., and H. Newby. 1971. *Community studies.* London: George Allen and Unwin.

Benoist, J. 1959. Individualisme et traditions techniques chez les pêcheurs martiniquais. *Les Cahiers d'Outre Mer* 12(47): 265–85.

Blanchet, G., B. Gobert, and J.A. Guérédrat. 2002. *La pêche aux Antilles: Martinique et Guadeloupe.* Paris: Editions IRD.

Breton, Y. 1973. A comparative study of rural fishing communities in Eastern Venezuela: An anthropological explanation of economic specialization. PhD diss., Michigan State University.

———. 1979. The introduction of capitalism in Yucatan coastal fishing. In *New Directions in Political Economy,* ed. M. Leons and F. Rothstein, 144–51. Westport, CT: Greenwood Press.

Breton, Y., and E. Alcala. 1972. Chabihau: Una comunidad campesina de pescadores. Anales del Instituto Nacional de Antropología y historia. *México* 7(IV): 263–301.

Breton, Y., and E. Lopez-Estrada. 1988. Oyster and shrimp producers in estuarine areas of the Gulf of Mexico: Ecological constraints, economic incentives, and conflictual management. *Journal of Shellfish Research* 7(2): 319–27.

———. 1989. *Ciencias sociales y desarrollo de las pesquerías. Modelos y métodos aplicados al caso mexicano.* México: INAH.

Brown, D. 1981. The political economy of dependence and underdevelopment in Ghana (1844–1966). MA thesis, McMaster University.

Brown, D.N. 1998. Creating social institutions for fisheries management in the CARICOM region. Paper presented at the 7th Conference on Common Property, Vancouver, 1998.

Brown, D.N., and R.S. Pomeroy. 1999. Co-management of Caribbean community (CARICOM) fisheries. *Marine Policy* 23(1): 549–70.

Carew, J. 1999. *Afro-Latin America and Afro-Caribbean identity: An interpretation of Caribbean identity.* Issues in Caribbean Amerindian Studies. Caribbean Amerindian Center Link, Maximillia C, Forde (2001, 1-7); *http://www.africana.com/Articles/tt_910.htm.*

Cariforum. 2004. Cultural Review of the Caribbean. www.cariforo.org.

CARSEA. 2003. Caribbean sea ecosystems assessment. Summary report. Port of Spain, Trinidad.

Cheng, S.A., L.E. Kruger, and S.E Daniels. 2003. 'Place' as an integrating concept in natural resource politics: Propositions for a social science research agenda. *Society and Natural Resources* 16: 87–104.

Chuenpagdee, J. R. Fraga Berdugo, and J. I. Euán-Ávila. 2002. Community perspectives toward a marine reserve: A case study of San Felipe, Yucatán, México. *Coastal Management* 30(2): 183–91.

Cohen, Y.A. 1954. The social organization of a selected community in Jamaica. *Social and Economic Studies* 2(4): 104–33.

Comitas, L. 1962. Fishermen and cooperation in rural Jamaica. PhD diss., Columbia University.

Cudjoe, S. 2001. Identity and Caribbean literature. Lecture delivered to the Japanese Black Studies Association, Nara Women's College, Nara, Japan.

Davenport, W. 1956. A comparative study of two Jamaican fishing communities. PhD diss., Yale University).

———. 1960. Jamaican fishing: A game theory analysis. In Yale University Publications in Anthropology, 57–64, ed. S. Mintz. New Haven: Yale University.

De La Cruz Rock, J.L. 1993. La dinámica conflictual de las cooperativas pesqueras en México: al caso de la Laguna de Tamiahua. PhD diss., Université Laval.

Doyon, S. 2003. L'environnement 'révolutionnaire': Pratiques, discours et dynamique socio-environnementale de la gestion des ressources côtières à Cuba. PhD diss., McGill University.

Dumas, M. 1982. Pequeña producción mercantil y capitalismo en Chabihau. In *La organización de la producción de los Mayas de Yucatán,* ed. Y. Breton and M.F. Labrecque, 305–61. México: INI.

Edel, M. 1967. Jamaican fishermen: Two approaches in economic anthropology. *Social and Economic Studies* 16: 432–39.

Epple, G.M. 1973. Group dynamics and the development of fish-marketing co-operative: The La Baye fishermen-townsmen of Grenada, West Indies. Ph.D. diss., Brandeis University.

———. 1977. Technological change in a Grenada W.I. fishery. In *Those who live from the sea,* ed. E. Smith, 173–94. St. Paul: West Publishing Company.

Etzioni, A. 1995. *Old chestnuts and new spurs. New communitarian thinking. Persons, values, institutions, and communities.* Charlottesville: University Press of Virginia.

Farrar, M. 2001. Re-thinking 'community' as a utopian social imagery. Paper presented to Class, Space and Community—A Workshop Conference, Department of Sociology, University of Durham, 2001.

Ferrer, J. 1986. *Antillanísimo y anticolonialismo en Betances, Hostos y Máximo Gomez.* Mayagüez: Universidad de Puerto Rico.

Fraga Berdugo, J. 1993. La migración y sus principales efectos en la costa yucateca: Estudio de caso en Célestun and Sisal. Master's thesis, Universidad Autónoma de Yucatán.

———. 1999. Política ambiental y relaciones de género en una área natural protegida: La relación global-local en Rio Lagartos, Mexico. PhD diss., Université Laval.

Freon, B., B. Gobert, and R. Mahon. 1991. La recherche halieutique et les pêcheries artisanales dans la Caraïbe insulaire. In *La recherche face à la pêche artisanale,* ed. J.R. Durand, J. Lemoalle, and J. Weber, 1:195–222. Symposium international ORSTOM-IFREMER, Montpelier, France.

Girvain, N. 2000. Reinterpretar al Caribe. México. *Revista Mexicana del Caribe* 7:1–18.

Haughton, M., and D.N. Brown. 2002. An overview of present-day ecological and social issues. In *Balancing people and resources: Interdisciplinary research and coastal areas management in the Wider Caribbean*, ed. IDRC-CFU-IOI-LAVAL, 27–60. Heredia, Costa Rica: Editorial Fundación UNA.

Henry, P. 1983. Decolonization and cultural underdevelopment in the commonwealth Caribbean. In *The newer Caribbean—decolonization, democracy, and development*, ed. P. Henry and C. Stone. Institute for the Study of Human Issues.

Ingold, T. 2002. *The perception of the environment: Essays in livelihood, dwelling, and skill*. New York: Routledge.

Khan, A. 1998. Identity, personhood, and religion in the Caribbean context. Latin America in the 21st Century, Working Paper no. 97–98, New York: David Rockefeller Center.

Lebail, J. 1983. Le rôle des activités halieutiques dans le développement régional de la péninsule du Yucatan. Ph.D. diss., Université de Bretagnes.

Lopez-Estrada, E. 1989. Industria camaronera y cooperativas pesqueras: El capitalismo halieútico en Ciudad del Carmen, México. PhD diss., Université Laval.

Mendez-Arocha, A. 1963. *La pesca en la Isla Margarita*. Caracas: Fundación LaSalle de Ciencias naturales.

Mintz, S. 1996. Enduring substances, trying theories: The Caribbean region as Oikoumene. *Journal of the Royal Anthropological Institute* 2(2): 289–311.

Mori Gonzalez, R. 2002. La construcción de la identidad caribeña: La utopía inconclusa. Catédra Eugenio de Hostos. Mayagüen: Universidad de Puerto Rico.

Orona, A. 1969. The social organization of the Margariteño fishermen. Ph.D. diss., UCLA.

Ostine, R. 2003. *Caribbean immigrants and the sociology of race and ethnicity: Limits of the assimilation perspective*. Ann Arbor: University of Michigan.

Palacio, J. 1999. Reconstructing Garifuna oral history—techniques and methods in the story of a Caribbean people. *Journal of Eastern Caribbean Studies* 24(1): 1–24.

———. 2001. Past and current methods of CBCRM in the southern coast of Belize. IDRC-CBCRM Project Report.

Pizinni, Valdés M. 1990a. Fishermen associations in Puerto Rico: Praxis and discourse in the politics of fishing. *Human Organization* 49(2): 164–73.

———. 1990b. Etnología crítica del trabajo en las pesquerías de Puerto Rico y el caribe insular. *Caribbean Studies* 23(1–2): 61–82.

Polo, J. 2001. *Identidad étnica y cultural en una frontera del caribe: La guajira colombiana y venezolana*. Beca de Investigación Cultural. Colombia: Universidad de Cartagena.

Premdas, R. 1996. Ethnicity and identity in the Caribbean: Decentering a myth. Working paper no. 234, St Augustine:University of the West Indies.

Programa Regional de Maestria en Desarrollo Rural (PRMDR). 2001. Texto del curso derechos comunitarios, ethnias, y desarrollo rural. Heredia, Costa Rica: Universidad Nacional.

Quezada, R.D. 1980. La pesca entre los Mayas prehispánicos: Una relación sociedad naturaleza. Tesis de Licienciadura. México: ENAH.

———. 1993. Papel y transformación de las unidades de producción pesquera ejidales en el sector halieútico de Yucatan, Mexico. Ph.D. diss., Université Laval.

———. 1999. Los recursos marinos: Una alternativa alimenticia para los mayas prehispánicos. *Perspectivas Rurales* 3(2): 48–68.

Quezada, R.D., and Y. Breton. 1996. *Antropología marítima: Pesca y actores sociales.* Mérida: Universidad Autonoma de Yucatan, Fomes.

Said, E. 1995. East isn't east. *Times Literary Supplement* (February).

Sandersen, H. 1995. Co management in Caribbean fisheries? The case of St. Lucia. Paper presented at the 5th Common Property Conference, International Association for the Study of Common Property, Bodo, May 24–28.

———. 1998. The quest for community—culture, institutions, and organized collective action in the Eastern Caribbean. Paper presented at the 23rd Caribbean Studies Association conference, Antigua and Barbuda, May 26–30.

Serbin, A. 1977. *El ocaso de las islas: El gran caribe frente a los desafíos globales y regionales.* Caracas: Nueva Sociedad.

Trouillot, M. 1992. The Caribbean region: An open frontier in anthropological theory. *Annual Review of Anthropology* (21): 19–42.

Turner, N.J., I.J. Davidson-Hunt, and M. O'Flaherty. 2003. Living on the edge: Ecological and cultural edges as sources of diversity for social-ecological resilience. *Human Ecology* 31(3): 439–61.

Urioste, B. 2001. *La era post-nacional en Amerindia: La diversidad se oficializa.* Barcelona: Instituto Internacional de Governabilidad de Catalunya.

Wilson, P. 1973. *Crab antics—the social anthropology of English-speaking Negro societies in the Caribbean.* New Haven: Yale University Press.

Wolf, E., and C. Hansen. 1972. *The human condition in Latin America.* London: Oxford University Press.

2

Interdisciplinary Research and Collaborative Management in Small Coastal Communities

Jorge I. Euán-Ávila, Julia Fraga Berdugo, Silvia Salas Márquez, Daniel Robledo Ramirez, Ratana Chuenpagdee

This chapter summarises an experiment using an interdisciplinary approach to understand coastal issues that relate to social and ecological diversity in the context of community-based management of coastal resources. We present a conceptual and methodological framework of reference for interdisciplinary research developed during a project, conducted from March 2000 to June 2004, that focused on management of a protected natural area. This project is part of the community-based coastal resources management programme (CBCRM) in the Caribbean, financed by the International Development Research Centre of Canada (IDRC).

The content is methodological, and its geographic dimension is restricted to two communities in the northeastern portion of the Yucatan Peninsula in Mexico. We discuss the capacity and degree of incursion in a collaboration between sciences, where special emphasis is on the local level of the study. This is where we believe the heterogeneity of the communities, researchers, and collaborators is best reflected, as are the problems it poses for the project development.

An interdisciplinary approach is frequently recommended for studying resource use and management. Such advice is found in Agenda 21 and in documents produced by the Joint Group of Experts on Scientific Aspects of Marine Environmental Protection (GESAMP),[1] the National Science Foundation's Long-term Ecological Research Programme (NSF-LTER) and the Organisation for Economic Cooperation and Development (Agenda 21 1992, OECD 1993a, 1993b), among others. The intention is to promote collaboration between the social and natural sciences in applied research projects, especially in situations where environmental uses and impacts are mutually incompatible. Yet this recommendation has seldom been accompanied by any guidelines, experience, or discussion to facilitate its implementation, and this lack has perhaps slowed its adoption and effective use. Turner and Carpenter (1999) point out that there is no ready recipe for an interdisciplinary approach to ecosystem science, and Heemskerk, Wilson, and Pavao-Zuckerman (2003) note that the mechanisms currently employed are seldom discussed.

It is clear that in order to facilitate interdisciplinary work, experiments must be publicised so that they can be evaluated, adapted, and explored in each situation. The experience of these and other authors such as Ander-Egg (1999) suggests that the move to interdisciplinarity implies that the teams share certain values, recognise the complexity of these systems, and adopt a systems focus. To the foregoing, we may add that there are other obstacles, as reflected in institutional approaches, that project an image of openness to collective research but continue to promote evaluation based strictly on individual disciplines. This situation does little to encourage the formation of interdisciplinary teams. Fortunately, several international organisations support development projects, such as IDRC, UNDP, the FAO, and the Third World Organisation of Women in Science (TWOWS). These particular organisations are giving greater encouragement to this practice through financial and technical support for projects experimenting with interdisciplinary work. This chapter shares some of the local experiences in a geographically small area of study, and demonstrates that the results would not have been possible in an exclusively unidisciplinary approach.

This chapter is divided into four sections. The first establishes the conceptual and methodological framework for what we understand interdisciplinarity to mean (along with its related concepts of pluri-, multi-, and transdisciplinarity). The second sets the frame of reference for an interdisciplinary orientation within the CBCRM focus, at two levels of analysis: the Wider Caribbean, through the IDRC programme, and the specific case of the Yucatan Peninsula. The third section reviews our case study, examining two phases of a project; and the fourth points to some lessons learned regarding both the conceptual and methodological framework and the case study.

Conceptual and Methodological Frame of Reference

Collective work presupposes collaboration by two or more individuals towards a common goal. There are many ways of understanding the goal, many forms of collaboration, and differing degrees of commitment and participation in such a collective undertaking. In addition, there are various ways of organising the work. In this collaboration, each of the disciplinary inputs can be delimited from the outset and will make a particular contribution, depending on the research needs. Alternatively, the collective work may transcend disciplines.

In the past three decades, the concepts of interdisciplinary, multidisciplinary, and transdisciplinary work have been evident in major scientific forums, conferences, and research proposals. According to Rosaura Ruiz (2000), the interdisciplinary concept was used in 1937 by Louis Writz but did not come into general use until the 1960s. Ruiz offers a comparative table of the different concepts, recognising that for interdisciplinarity to occur, there must be interaction as well as reciprocal transformation of some disciplines to others in relation to a complex study. As well, these disciplines must unite around a common problem. The multidisciplinary approach combines various disciplines, but the individual viewpoints of each discipline prevail. Transdisciplinarity is a new concept that transcends the disciplinary approaches that gave it origin. There is, then, an appreciable difference in methodological and epistemological terms between these research processes. In the multidisciplinary and pluridisciplinary approaches, there are sectoral and methodological contributions from various disciplines to the study of a topic. However, in the interdisciplinary approach, the problem is posed in such terms that it cannot be resolved by one single discipline.

Resolving problems from the disciplinary perspective is part of the tradition of scientific research. But despite its great utility, highly specialised and discipline-bound research generally offers only partial explanations of environmental problems, and tends to overlook other areas of the same discipline (Daly and Cobb 1994). On the other hand, the multidisciplinary, hybridised, interdisciplinary, and transdisciplinary approaches open the possibility of more comprehensive or holistic explanations by filling the gaps left by specialisation and the limited involvement of professionals from some disciplines. It is important to note that these approaches do not replace nor do they conflict with the disciplinary approach. On the contrary, rigorous disciplinary perspectives, and even highly specialised ones, are required. In seeking holistic solutions to problems, interdisciplinarity must be seen as a form of cooperation between disciplines that allows researchers to address the complexity of environmental problems and to discern better solutions.

The task of developing a programme for managing natural resources and spaces with long-term strategies is complex and requires a great deal of information gathering, analysis, and decision making. As well, it usually involves ecologists, engineers, administrators, anthropologists, economists, lawyers, and other professionals of various disciplines who work with administrators and users. These so-called multidisciplinary groups have been winning acceptance for resolving environmental and planning problems. Parker (2003) notes that the approaches dominated by individualism, a monodisciplinary focus, and specialisation are losing ground to ways of working where rigid organisation is replaced by fluid collaboration; where centralised power is replaced by the empowerment of participants; and where hierarchy yields to reticular or horizontal structures.

According to Ander-Egg (1999), the interdisciplinary notion is relatively easy to formulate if we stick with the 'what' (what we want to do), which is generally understood as trying to move beyond fragmented analysis and gain a better overall comprehension of phenomena. The problem is greater when we come to the 'how'—how to work in an interdisciplinary manner. He proposes four structural principles to serve as a guide. These are the use of mathematics, general systems theory, the notion of structure in Piaget's thesis, and the logic of complexity in the Morin thesis. Yet, as Ander-Egg (1999) also mentions, an intellectual propensity to interdisciplinarity (a determined 'mentality') is also needed. Organisation by programmes, mechanisms for horizontal integration between laboratories, departments, or institutions, and the development of collective working strategies can constitute forms of academic organisation that promote structures favourable to such a mentality. A schematic formulation of the elements involved in interdisciplinary work is shown in Table 1.

TABLE 1
AN INTERDISCIPLINARY SCHEME FOR ADDRESSING PROBLEMS OF NATURAL RESOURCE USE AND MANAGEMENT

<table>
<tr><td>What do we want to do?
Move beyond fragmented analysis for a comprehensive understanding of phenomena</td><td>How to achieve interdisciplinarity?
An intellectual attitude conducive to interdisciplinarity and development of collective working strategies</td></tr>
<tr><td colspan="2">Interdisciplinarity</td></tr>
<tr><td>Foster a holistic vision in seeking solutions to development problems</td><td>Encourage the sharing of diverse perspectives on common research subjects</td></tr>
</table>

The design and effective implementation of coastal management policies require a sound understanding of the condition of the resources and of the impact of human activities on the environment. We learn from multiple sources (Euán-Ávila 1997) that this requires, among other things,

1. the detection, distribution, and quantification of physical changes;
2. an evaluation of the conditions of the natural system;
3. analysis of the local specifics of soil uses and ground cover;
4. quantification of current and future rates of resource use; and
5. quantification of current and future wastes generated in the region and in other areas that are discharged along the coast.

Most of the data come from various sources in multiple ecosystems that, in the case of tropical coastal zones, include mangrove swamps, lagoons, barrier islands, urban areas, agricultural developments, reefs, submerged vegetation, and open water. Data gathering is currently facilitated with highly synoptic and dependable technologies, such as remote sensing and geostatistics, and tools for compiling and integrating data, such as geographic information systems. These technologies have been recommended and used in the development of integrated coastal management (ICM) programmes (Kay and Alder 1999; Cicin-Sain and Knecht 1998; Euán-Ávila and Witter 2002). These technologies facilitate the multidisciplinary and interdisciplinary focus that is required for solving these research questions.

Natural resource management used to be dominated by the biophysical aspects, but more recently the human behavioural aspects have been expanded, and the human dimension integrated into the biological, as a way of presenting sound solutions in management programmes (Decker et al. 1992). Today, it is much more widely accepted that effective decision making requires familiarity with human responses, over both the short and long terms, to the effects of current and planned actions. In particular, precautionary or anticipatory decisions must anticipate the human reactions that management proposals produce in order to evaluate and prepare strategies for their adoption. Several authors emphasise that an understanding of social, cultural, and economic aspects can improve the selection of policies and strategies for resource management (Payton 1984, 1990; Decker et al. 1992; Liu 2001; Weisbuch 2000). The following points are mentioned by Kellert (1980), Senger (1990), and Guirdham (1999) as being among relevant data for any social component applied for management purposes:

1. traditional uses;
2. preferences by project type;
3. preferences for short-term versus long-term economic returns;
4. preferences for the location of projects;
5. level of knowledge about resources and the environment;
6. levels of organisation;
7. aspirations;
8. potential response to programmes;
9. knowledge of competing groups;
10. attitudes;
11. cultural values (naturalist, ecological, utilitarian, etc.); and
12. economic values such as those of use, option, existence, and legacy.

A fuller description of the last two aspects can be found in Barbier (1994) and Kellert (1980). An evaluation that considers the knowledge of individuals and their attitudes and perceptions, whether they are fishers, industrialists, students, tourists, or homemakers, will provide information about the likelihood of success in the design, implementation, and future outcomes of management programmes (Chuenpagdee, Fraga, and Euán-Ávila 2004). The demonstrated complexity of socioecological systems has led the scientific community and administrators to insist on the need for an interdisciplinary analysis of major coastal issues. These information needs were summarised in the paper 'The contributions of science to integrated coastal management'

(GESAMP 1999). It presents the various stages of ICM as well as factors that have facilitated or impeded the incorporation of science into management. It has also established guidelines for the approaches used in many scientific projects currently underway.

The CBCRM Focus in the Wider Caribbean

The CBCRM programme of IDRC has two major features: it is an interdisciplinary method whose focus is on the community. This programme was approved in January 1999 to contribute to sustainable development in coastal areas of island and continental Caribbean countries. The programme seeks to promote concrete local action, as well as to foster collaboration, networking, and dissemination of information on coastal management issues among various users and agents. Another goal is to strike a balance between the natural and social sciences as they relate to natural resources, while developing further understanding of local human aspects (Savard and Breton 1999; Savard 2001; Breton, Davy, and Buckles 2002).

From experience with the first phase of the programme, Palacio (2002) emphasised that one characteristic of many case studies was a limited knowledge of social-science methods and an inability to apply them to advantage in the field. Instead, typically there was too much reliance on traditional ethnographic approaches, even though there were applied approaches available through participatory action–research (PAR) and rapid rural assessment (RRA), as well as in co-management. According to the programme's scientific committee, many of the projects submitted under CBCRM called for using social-science researchers merely to be considered eligible. Subsequently, these researchers were given only a limited role in the actual work, which was conducted primarily by researchers from the natural sciences.

One of the programme's strengths was to encourage researchers who were accustomed to working alone to establish multidisciplinary and interdisciplinary links and to pool their efforts in the field in a concrete common study of the Wider Caribbean. Therefore, the programme was a test of both local and sponsors' capacity to take a participatory focus, in spite of the short time and limited financing available for this type of research. In total there were 32 projects in 22 Caribbean countries that exhibit linguistic and ethnic barriers, while sharing some common problems such as pollution, overfishing, and conflicts between the oil industry and fishing or between fishing and tourism. The specific interest in the programme was how the CBCRM focus and the interdisciplinary approach could be combined to move forward on these broad socioenvironmental problems. When IDRC sponsored a second phase of the programme, it selected projects in which the notion of 'community' played a more visible role than it had in the first phase, and it sought to achieve closer linkages among the projects. One of the approaches has involved joint work among members of different groups and the exchange of ideas at meetings sponsored by the CBCRM programme. Finally, IDRC has supported preparation of this joint publication, in which the different case studies are compared, experiences are shared, and methodological approaches are discussed.

Implementing the Approach in the Yucatan Context

The inhabitants of coastal communities in the Yucatan Peninsula, like many others around the world, are facing pressures that are growing with the new global relationships. These are reflected in moves by governments and the international market to reduce subsidies, prices, and international interest rates, to handle great volumes, and to comply with international standards. These factors, combined with the continuing deterioration of ecosystems and their resources, pose a threat to the sustainability of traditional livelihoods. As well, they point to an uncertain future for these communities. According to Lebel, the health of human communities depends on the state of their ecosystems and their resources (Lebel 2001). To maintain the health of ecosystems we must contend with new environmental policies and global relationships that are forcing changes in traditional forms of exploitation, organisation, and marketing. Concerned by these problems, the international community has put special stress on improving or developing local capacities in the communities of developing countries. The goal is to alleviate, at least, or, in the best case, to improve living conditions within a healthy environment. Mexico is no exception.

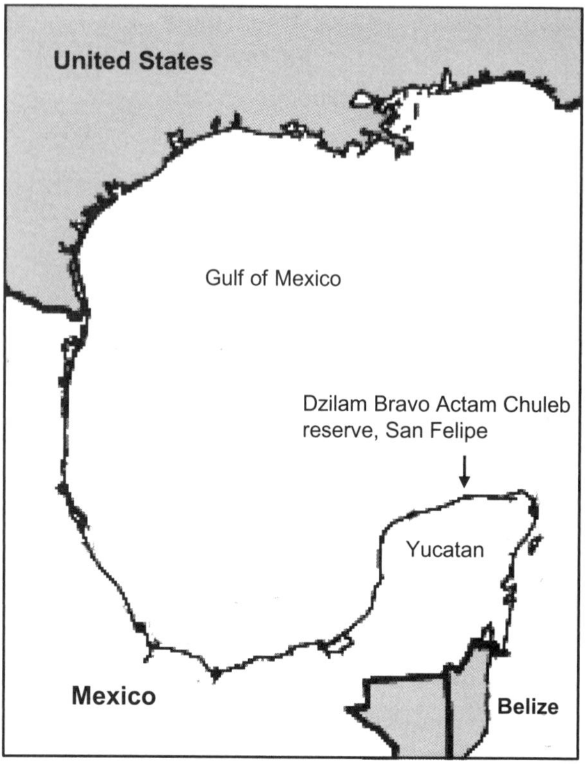

Figure 2
San Felipe, Santa Clara, and Dzilam Bravo, Yucatán

Frequently, the ideal approach to these problems exceeds the human and material resources available to traditional research groups, not to mention the capacity of individual efforts. Forging links with other groups and researchers is one way to expand the availability of resources and open a range of real possibilities for developing a better understanding of the processes associated with the identified problems. This is why international agencies tend to encourage partnerships.

The actions taken and problems faced during the project in two coastal communities of Yucatan are outlined in Table 1 (see p. 54). These communities, which share a protected area and common interests, serve to describe some of the relevant factors for guiding future strategies, improving work both within the research groups and among members of the community, and indicating future challenges. The description is given in three stages:

1. gestation of the Phase I research proposals that come together in the process of multidisciplinary integration;
2. a description of community activities; and
3. a summary of personal and professional experience in fostering collaborative work among professionals of different disciplines.

These points are expanded upon below.

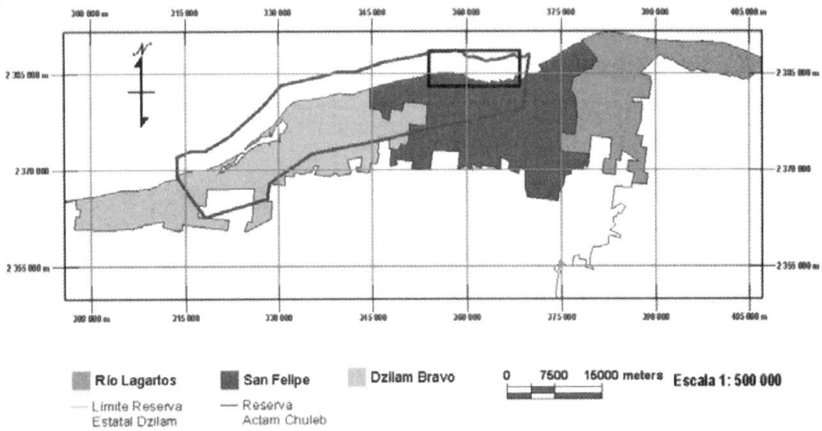

Figure 3
Location of the marine reserve and the coastal communities of Dzilam Bravo and San Felipe, Yucatan, Mexico

Gestation of the Phase I research proposal

The establishment of this working group was motivated by our thinking about multidisciplinary and interdisciplinary work and our view that one of the strengths of the CBCRM-IDRC programme was that bringing together researchers from the social and natural sciences was an eligibility criterion for research projects, along with participatory focus.

Our multidisciplinary collaboration was launched on the basis of the enthusiasm and interest of four researchers who had previously been in communication on coastal studies and their dimensions. The working group consisted of two natural scientists (biologists), a systems engineer, and a social anthropologist. The project for 'community-based management of a protected marine reserve' (Phase I) involved four research departments in Mexico and Canada.[2]

In addition to the core group of four researchers, a number of community members were hired to help administer questionnaires. This group was joined by an administrator, a communications specialist, and a fisher. Initial contact among the core group members took place in Mexico during three days of intensive work. Initially proposed programme objectives were reviewed, and two days of fieldwork validated our observations and our initial statement of the problem, which involved answering four questions.

1. On the economic front: What are the resources and habitats that people use in their activities?
2. On the social front: What are the perceptions of and attitudes to the marine reserve?
3. On the administrative and legal front: How is the protected area being managed?
4. On the ecological front: Why is the habitat being protected?

At the meeting we also discussed tools that would help answer these questions. During this exercise, we came to understand each other's working styles, including the methodological procedures of the various disciplines. We recognised the need to use qualitative and quantitative techniques in our research. These included a questionnaire to prioritise damage to resources and activities, community workshops, open-ended interviews, life histories, and remote sensing for studying submerged aquatic vegetation.

Community activities under Phase I

The tools were designed to be used with groups of respondents from the community and beyond. Remote sensing technologies were used to study the seabed within the reserve, with participation by community members. The questions posed in the project implicitly contained the four broad dimensions of the study of the society-nature relationship, or the relationship between people and the environment.

Based on selection between pairs of possible responses that were analysed using the method proposed by Dunn-Rankin (1983), one of the instruments used in the programme study was discussed and adopted for gathering data on preferences and knowledge. This was a keystone of the research process. It provided information on legal and social aspects, as well as on the perceptions and attitudes of users and administrators of natural resources, as they related to a protected marine area. To get feedback from the questionnaire results, we held a community workshop in which we had face-to-face contact with groups of respondents and with the authorities.

That workshop was attended by 38 members of the fishing cooperative, ranchers, and independent fishers, among others. The group dynamics generated results consistent with those of the fieldwork, including the perception of the impact of human activities on marine ecosystems, and aspects relating to management of the reserve. In addition, participants indicated the need for training courses dealing with natural resource conservation, as well as further research and a cleanup campaign in the area. They also recognised the need for financial support for these activities, and the need to secure community and government commitment. When local informants were consulted, they said there was wide recognition that 'what is being done in the reserve is really producing results', since 'we can see that species are recovering, and the people working there can testify to this'. Participants also recognised the value of having a legal framework to give continuity to the reserve, although some pointed out that 'we are not protected, we need to have regulations. That's what we are missing—the danger we face is the lack of laws to protect us.'

Summary of experience during Phase I

This phase opened the way for an informal exchange of knowledge and experience, and allowed for initial recognition of the various specialities included in the group. Each member took responsibility for a section in order to support the work of other members, and each of us worked with the community. The anthropologist's role was crucial to maintaining contact with the community. These dynamics were strengthened when it came to preparing the final project report, some joint publications, and presentations to various forums. To achieve this, we invited two community members to participate, who served as wardens patrolling the marine reserve.

In designing and applying the techniques, and particularly in analysing the results for feedback to the community, we encountered barriers to the use of clear and comprehensible academic language. It was challenging to put concepts and viewpoints into a common context, not as a set of definitively achievable goals but rather as a gradual process of understanding each other's professional perspective. It became clear that different members of the team did not understand one another's specialities or professional jargon. Nonetheless, we recognised that the various professional profiles must be linked in order to better understand community processes and needs. There were also some language barriers due to the participation of Canadian colleagues; these became apparent during the training in field techniques and in communication with the community. Understanding of the project's methods and techniques improved with practice, and after holding a community workshop.

The goals in Phase I were to contribute to discussions among the various community groups which were involved in using and managing the reserve in order to identify activities consistent with their management goals. While this did not crystallise at that time, an initial contact was established for dialogue with the various community groups, as well as between them and the government. The community workshop was the platform that permitted this initial dialogue. The results of the project laid the foundations for future exploration of cooperative management, community management, and other types of arrangements appropriate to administering coastal resources in San Felipe, and which could serve as a model for other communities (Chuenpagdee, Fraga, and Euán-Ávila. 2002, 2004; Fraga et al. 2002).

The results of the first phase were encouraging both for the researchers and for various members of the community, who asked that the project continue, particularly given their interest in developing the organisational structure for the marine reserve and the idea of developing a multi-purpose community centre (MPCC) in San Felipe.

Gestation of Phase II

From the demands mentioned above and after considering the results of Phase I, we developed some initial ideas regarding how to strengthen the process of multidisciplinary integration. These were applied in the planning process for Phase II. In the programme submissions for the period from June 2002 to November 2003, a project which would tackle the community management of a protected natural area in Yucatan was proposed. This proposal reflected the need for continuity on the basis of the results of Phase I, and called for incorporating a second locality (Dzilam Bravo). This location was selected as a site where an exploratory process could be initiated to study the perceptions of the local populace and the socioeconomic context. This type of information was relevant because of the identified need for the two communities to cooperate while they proposed strategies for collaborative community management.

The core group for Phase II retained the previous project's disciplinary balance, but the gender balance shifted from two men and two women to three women and one man. The director of the algae-growing project was later added to this group.

For Phase II of the project we posed the following questions:

1. How can we move ahead with the organisational structure of the Actam Chuleb protected marine area?
2. Can we propose a model for collaboration between San Felipe and Dzilam Bravo so as to manage the reserve?
3. What does the community of Dzilam Bravo know and think about the marine reserve?
4. Does the community still entertain the idea of developing a multipurpose community centre in San Felipe, and does it still have the desire to improve the capacities of that community?

Coincidentally, another research project was suggested for this programme from the same institute, which also happened to be working in the community of Dzilam Bravo. IDRC proposed pooling efforts to ensure efficient use of economic and human resources, and to increase the prospects of success through synergy. An additional interest of IDRC was to convert both projects into an example of multidisciplinary work.

The project known as Commercial Cultivation of Marine Algae in Yucatan had its origins in 1994, when research first began into the algae resources of the Yucatan Peninsula. Five years later, experience with the pilot project was used to evaluate the technical and biological feasibility of the systems for raising algae in the sea. The project sought to lay the basis for sustainable development of algae culture as an alternative economic pursuit that would be more than a curiosity. It was hoped it would become an activity of genuine interest, one that would help the shift from fishing to aquaculture, with attendant economic benefits in additional incomes. The objectives were

1. to improve seeding techniques through the use of various substrata and depths;
2. to compare different production systems for establishing the economic potential of the activity;
3. to evaluate the possibilities of disseminating this activity among other interested groups in the community; and
4. to conduct a socioeconomic diagnosis of the community.

This working group consisted primarily of natural-science professionals: two marine biologists, four chemists (industrial chemistry and nutritional chemistry), and an oceanologist.

Preparation and composition of the Phase II working groups

Although we had some experience with fieldwork and community workshops, it was proposed that an expert in PAR should work with us at the beginning of Phase II. For this purpose, we established terms of reference that would allow us to select an individual from among three candidates: two agricultural engineers and a social anthropologist with many years of experience in PAR. The anthropologist was selected because his proposal best fit the bill.

Based on the final report from Phase I of the project and the proposal for Phase II, the expert designed a training workshop to help integrate the group into the communities, using the theoretical and methodological tools of PAR. Essentially, the objective was to promote personal interaction, to standardise fieldwork strategies, and to prepare a working guide for the workshops in San Felipe and Dzilam Bravo. While initial plans did not include a workshop in Dzilam Bravo for the algae-growing project, it was felt that it was best to pool efforts in this activity.

The training workshop for promoters, as we called the three working sessions at the beginning of this phase, fostered a multidisciplinary and interdisciplinary approach to experimentation. With 25 hours of intensive work during this workshop, for the first time the group was subjected to the phenomenon of group dynamics while considering and analysing problems. We created an atmosphere of trust and sparked greater interest among the participants in becoming more actively involved in both projects. Participants declared that the lectures and discussions, along with interaction through a 'social drama', heightened their interest in multi- and interdisciplinary work and in community work. It became clear that the dynamics inherent in a participatory and a multidisciplinary perspective are much more demanding than the traditional research approach, as Leff (1998) has indicated.

Phase II community activities

Several meetings were needed to define the joint activities for the two projects, to establish points of intersection and interests in light of the characteristics of the two communities. Because both projects called for a socioeconomic evaluation in Dzilam Bravo, different members of the teams provided input for the overall information collected, and we avoided saturating community members with similar questionnaires.

As part of the activities, we conducted a community workshop in San Felipe in November 2002 for the purposes of

1. presenting the results of Phase I;
2. evaluating the community's continuing interest in establishing an MPCC;
3. determining the feasibility of the project;
4. defining training needs; and
5. confirming the needs of an organisational structure for managing and administering the Actam Chuleb marine reserve.

After two sessions of one day each, the workshop's objectives were covered, and a total of 60 participants readily joined in the group dynamics. The field results were confirmed by the workshop in terms of users' perceptions of resource use and management. We confirmed interest in moving ahead with the organisational structure of the marine reserve and in establishing a multipurpose community centre. The plan was for it to serve as an interpretive museum and computer centre. Authorities from the state government and other centres attended the workshop but played a rather passive role. In fact, the workshop failed to stimulate interaction between community members and the authorities because there was no basis for defining the points of reference of each side, particularly the latter.

Meanwhile, we added new members to the group, including three more biologists, another anthropologist, an oceanologist, and a fisheries expert. The structure was not static but shifted steadily: the group included a floating population, as members voluntarily joined and departed. Moreover, in addition to the permanent and semi-permanent members, we could count on the voluntary support of several students and friends, including administrators, biologists, and anthropologists.

The second activity undertaken in the communities was the workshop held in April 2003 in Dzilam Bravo. It was held after the application of several of the instruments for socioeconomic diagnosis and after a questionnaire was completed that gathered perceptions of resource use and management in the state reserve. Antonio Cupul, a fisherman coordinating the algae group in Dzilam Bravo, was an important interlocutor for the group working with the community. We also received support from teachers in the Dzilam Bravo technical high school. They helped in the field, facilitating interviews with students, and made their facilities available for holding the community workshop.

The workshop was held over a period of two days and involved 45 people, including members of the community and some representatives of government agencies and non-governmental organisations (NGOs). Its objectives were

1. to explain the results of the fieldwork conducted through questionnaires and socioeconomic surveys;
2. to evaluate community members' knowledge with respect to the location and composition of the Dzilam Bravo and Actam Chuleb reserves;
3. to report on aspects of the reserve's legal framework and to identify users' preferences with respect to management;
4. to generate information on the structure and social interactions of the community and on the level of people's confidence that the expected functions would be fulfilled, as a measure of social capital;
5. to determine the levels of perception of the use of resources and activities that impact the coastal zone, and to appreciate expectations and options for productive activities as potential alternatives to fishing, including algae growing; and

6. to measure the degree of interest among stakeholders (local users and administrators) in managing coastal resources and their potential for collaborative management with the community of San Felipe.

Members of government agencies and non-governmental organisations presented some projects underway in the area, and members of the promotional team presented the results of the surveys, before we began the group dynamics.

Most of the 38 members of the group who were interested in algae attended the workshop during the first day and took an active role in it. On the second day, although attendance declined because of adverse weather, there was a good audience; in particular, many women turned out despite the weather. The results of the group dynamics confirmed and enriched the fieldwork results. It is important to note that the government representatives were surprised by the response of the community participants and their active involvement in the group dynamics. People asked for more workshops of this kind; this was particularly true of the women who, although they attended the workshop in fewer numbers, were more enthusiastic. The workshop and the fieldwork served to open new channels of communication and opportunities for thinking about interdisciplinary work among the participants. In addition, the implications of PAR processes in the context of an expanded group emerged from the two projects.

Back in San Felipe, a third activity involved holding a second workshop in June 2003, for the purposes of

1. providing information on legal aspects of the Dzilam Bravo reserve and its relationship with the Actam Chuleb preserve;
2. moving ahead with the organisational structure of the marine reserve;
3. exploring the prospects for the multipurpose community centre;
4. allowing members from San Felipe and Dzilam Bravo to exchange experiences; and
5. promoting the exchange of experiences between visitors from various Caribbean countries and members of the San Felipe community.

At this workshop, efforts were directed at getting members of the two communities to share experiences about their productive activities, such as algae growing in Dzilam Bravo and the process of creating the marine reserve in San Felipe. As well, representatives of the Dzilam Bravo state reserve were invited to provide information on its management. The results of the previous workshop were presented, and the MPCC idea was again discussed. Information gathered at the previous workshop was described to the community in the form of a social drama, in which both community members and visiting foreign guests (project leaders) participated. We took advantage of the presence of these individuals (who included two fishermen) so they could share their knowledge and experiences from their home countries relating to community work and problems encountered, as well as ways of seeking options to resolve those problems (Leaders Workshop Synthesis 2003).

The response of community members and programme visitors was very positive. One of the ideas that received the greatest support was the MPCC. Several community members proposed initiatives for making this project a reality. Among the actions taken were the donation of land for the centre by the municipal government and the development of a construction plan and concrete proposals for the modules that the centre would include. The availability of computer equipment donated by the project to the community was mentioned in connection with the MPCC and the training courses. The community proposed courses in English, administration, and psychology, among other things. It was suggested that 'seed groups' be set up to take the courses first, and then to pass on what they had learned to other members of the community. In this context, it is clear that the community is beginning to take its own initiatives, with the hope that the group will support them, but with very clear ideas about the direction they should take that are quite independent of the promoter group. This is a clear indication of the need for interdisciplinary collaboration to meet increasingly complex demands (Echeverria et al. 2003).

Analysis and reflection

Working in an interdisciplinary way has not proved easy. This effort is not as highly appreciated as is claimed: it is the specialists who are most highly valued, and those who venture across frontiers are regarded with suspicion as 'Jacks of all trades'. In reality, such people represent bridges for building linkages, because they can understand language and outlooks from different angles. This does not mean that everyone must venture into inter-

or multidisciplinarity. Specialists are essential, just as both basic science and applied science are essential. But the process is complex: the conceptual question, which appears so simple, can turn out to be a laborious exercise in exchanging ideas.

This experiment revealed pronounced differences in the ways the natural sciences and the social sciences perceive things. Such differences produced divergences at various stages in the process, showing up in three principal areas: conceptual-disciplinary, the specific interests of researchers, and community expectations.

Conceptual-disciplinary area

Given participants' limited knowledge of other disciplines, we seized on the idea of holding seminars for sharing knowledge and standardising criteria. The seminars' scope was limited to putting forward the primary objectives of the project within strict time constraints. For various reasons, seminars were frequently postponed; nonetheless, they were an important and ongoing activity for broadening outlooks, facilitating work, and promoting interaction within the group. While the differences might have seemed a threat at some point, once they were recognised and clearly stated we understood that, however intimidating they might appear, they actually represented the seeds of curiosity and an opportunity to generate new ideas to modify or adapt existing ones.

This perception was facilitated within the group because most of the participants had been exposed, to some degree, to ideas and materials from more than one discipline and had confronted social issues that had sensitised their thinking. Despite this, a major and still pending task is to test and systematise working techniques and compare them for understanding the scope of the concepts involved in interdisciplinary practice. The strategies for overcoming these difficulties focused on standardising the meaning given to a word when it generates confusion or conflicting interpretations, analysing from concrete and commonly understood situations instead of starting from theoretical abstractions, and focusing on possible routes to resolution of the problems.

Individual aspects

There were important differences in peoples' levels of participation. This was because, quite apart from the particular interest that each member had in the two working groups, everyone was working within an intensely academic setting. All had other research projects underway; they had to devote time to preparing and conducting teaching assignments; they were under pressure to maintain such activities as publishing articles in international journals. Being published is considered an important yardstick of evaluation in research centres, where performance is judged by the quality and quantity of scientific publications produced. The institutional mandate makes no allowance for outreach activities. Thus, institutional demands in terms of teaching and other academic commitments limit the time available for building bridges to the productive sector—in this case, to the coastal communities. On the other hand, once work in the community begins, its members demand greater attention, greater involvement, and greater time on site. All of this requires time, personnel, and resources.

Therefore, care must be given to sorting out the differences among and expectations of team members and defining a common view of what we are seeking as a group and as individuals. This is crucial so that future strategies will take into account personal and institutional interests as well as those of community members, who have their own obligations to maintain.

Other individual attributes that were essential in interpersonal interaction within the group and that generated benefits for our work included sustaining interest and respect for each other's knowledge and contributions. This is also a point of departure for recognising the limitations of what we may not know but can find, fortunately, in the baggage of other persons within the team. Thus, despite personal differences and differences in ways of thinking and in academic or technical training, we were able to wrap up these phases smoothly. This does not mean that there was always agreement. On the contrary, working days were long precisely because of the need to discuss differences and strike compromises. A source of strength for the project was the commitment that each person showed to the work, in terms of supporting individuals or groups involved in community development. Far from being a paternalistic approach, this meant recognising the potential value of scientific work, and the personal and collective effort toward community improvement.

Problems with the community

Interaction with the communities generated expectations and demands for work that at times were difficult to meet, either because the work was beyond our abilities or scope or because of lack of time or personnel. We enjoyed the support of many people, but few were able to devote themselves full-time to the projects. People were constantly coming and going because of their personal commitments. The lack of any economic incentive for keeping people permanently involved was a constraint. Despite this, it was clear to us that the communities' demands will be met over time, with or without outside help. However, if we are to provide ongoing coaching and support for this community development, we will need to procure the support of a defined allotment of personnel and time. A planning exercise requires taking account of the personal agendas of the team members involved, as well as those of the community members. We must be careful not to create expectations beyond those that can realistically be achieved, even with an interdisciplinary team approach.

The complexity and particular contexts of the communities involved in the projects, the processes of community development, and the empowerment of their members that will allow them to devote themselves to community management of their natural resources require different routes. This is particularly true given the contexts, timing, and sequencing of the various processes, which are distinct. These conditions, however, do not preclude the possibility of building links between the two communities. Despite their differences, they share many common interests, in terms of both culture and natural resources. There is a long road ahead, but it is full of possibilities as long as we recognise the differences and can turn them to advantages.

On the other hand, the interests of the members of each community and of the organisations involved in managing the reserves are varied and sometimes contradictory, and involve a political context that goes well beyond the group's capacities. This implies understanding the community's social context, and requires many hours of hands-on work in the communities, compiling and analysing information. To some extent this defines the scope that the group may have over the short, medium, and long term, in addition to the strategies to be adopted for achieving a specific goal. Under these conditions we can take several approaches.

1. We can use a participatory focus, with the personal and institutional implications that this approach involves in terms of time, human resources, and financing.
2. We can work in a conventional way with unidisciplinary bases, occasionally combining experiences and, if possible, using some PAR tools, and accept the limited degree of involvement with the community and the constricted scope of activities.
3. We can achieve the objectives set forth in the projects by the financial donors through conventional research, and recognise, in combination with the community, the factors preventing a greater scope.

At this stage, the team is somewhere between the limits of 2 and 3, as described above. To reach level 1 will take more time and a high level of commitment, as well as the human and economic resources needed to achieve results over the short term, and perhaps even over the medium and longer terms. But that is not a reason to discard this approach, even if the process is relatively longer. In fact, the seeds have been sown in the community of San Felipe, and a series of processes has been launched that could succeed in making a reality of the plans that the community and the promotion team are promoting. Success may well be achieved with the proper advice and training. In Dzilam Bravo, more work and time are needed to produce concrete results. But the potential is there, and a number of its members have taken initiatives to maintain contact with our group.

To the foregoing we must add that the stance of IDRC, through its representatives, has encouraged and facilitated the work of the project coordinators. Strict respect has been maintained for the purposes of the project and facilitating local initiatives. For example, IDRC has supported familiarisation sessions during the projects, even though they were not initially planned. Such sessions fostered a better understanding of management practices in each region. As well, IDRC has taken an active role in the programmes through periodic visits to the work sites.

To conclude, we must admit that some activities take a lot of time: getting involved in community work through linkages with other disciplines is one example. The communities are pursuing their processes and continue to involve us in them, in the hope of responses, which must be timely and concrete. This is clear in the context of the MPCC being promoted in San Felipe. To date, land has been donated, construction plans have been prepared, and the community has submitted a project for funding the materials; labour will be provided by the community itself. The training courses planned for the centre have been started and are continuing. In addition, discussions have begun with the state authorities for implementing the management plan for the Actam Chuleb marine reserve, as part of the management plan for the Dzilam Bravo state reserve. A new committee of community representatives has been legally established and is in contact with the administrators, monitoring their administrative and technical processes. In the case of the algae-growing project, a group of women in San Felipe has shown an interest in the activity. They have been seeking advice from the researchers on this project, while also looking at strategies for geographic expansion and methodological and technical upgrading.

Future actions

The future activities of the group involve further 'community coaching'. This might occur within a limited framework, particularly given the time and personnel constraints on the communities. It is also important to look for strategies that will optimise the efforts of participants and to search for alternatives that will satisfy the community's interests as well as the personal, academic, and general interests of the researchers and promoters (see Fraga et al. 2003).

There is a continuing interest in promoting multidisciplinary seminars that will involve other colleagues from our centre, so that, over time, they will become interested in these dynamics and will also support initiatives of this kind. This requires high-level action to evaluate the scientific work and its impact on society. Often the expected linkages are not as strong as they appear, and the costs seem to outweigh the benefits for those who devote themselves to interdisciplinary research and linkages. New forms of academic evaluation at different levels seem to favour individualism over collaborative work. We must seek effective ways of operation that allow for high-level academic work while at the same time encouraging coordination involving social linkages—and not only industrial ones, which, generally speaking, seem to be better appreciated.

It is clear that actions are needed at various levels. Included in this are the personal contexts in which individual work and the routes to be followed are defined, work within the community, the time constraints within academic work and institutional work. Another important consideration is the external component, which also influences the specific activities of our research. This is a long and intricate road down which few venture.

Acknowledgements

We wish to thank our collaborators for the support they provided at different stages throughout the projects: Nidia Echeverría, Miguel A. Cabrera, Karin Alvarez, Martha Uc, Ana Cristina Gavaldón, Hector Rodríguez, Laura Vidal, Ma. José Espinosa, Josefina Morales, Rodolfo Olguín, Carlos Vásquez, and Eliseo Ortiz. We are also grateful to Juan Carlos Mijangos, who worked with us for part of the process and shared with us his experience with PAR, and to Tiburcio Castro, who helped with the launch of Phase II of the project. No less valuable were the cooperation and support offered by the people and authorities of San Felipe and Dzilam de Bravo, who patiently answered our questions and graciously welcomed us into their homes, and who attended and participated enthusiastically in the workshops in both communities. Our thanks also to IDRC, which sponsored this chapter and provided funding for the project's successive phases, and to Dr Alejandro Flores who, as Director of the Unidad Mérida, offered standing support for activities under the projects and encouraged the collective effort.

Notes

1. Sponsoring organisations are the International Maritime Organization (IMO), the Food and Agriculture Organization of the United Nations (FAO), the Intergovernmental Oceanographic Commission (IOC)/United Nations Educational, Scientific and Cultural Organization (UNESCO), the World Meteorological Organization (WMO), the World Health Organization (WHO), the United Nations (UN), and the United Nations Environment Programme (UNEP).
2. Those institutions are the Departments of Human Ecology and Maritime Resources of the Centre for Research and Advanced Studies of the National Polytechnic Institute, Mérida Unit, in Mexico, and the Department of Natural Resources and the Fisheries Centre of the University of British Columbia, Vancouver, Canada.

References

Agenda 21. 1992. Earth Summit: The United Nations Programme of Action from Rio. United Nations Conference on Environment and Development (UNCED), Rio de Janeiro, June 3–14.

Ander-Egg, E. 1999. *Interdisciplinariedad en educación*. Buenos Aires: Magisterio del Río de la Plata.

Barbier, E.B. 1994. Valuing environmental functions: Tropical wetlands. *Land Economics* 70(2): 155–73.

Breton, Y., B. Davy, and D. Buckles. 2002. Balancing people and resources: Interdisciplinary research and management of coastal areas in the Caribbean. In *Balancing people and resources: Interdisciplinary research and coastal area management in the Wider Caribbean*, ed. IDRC-CFU-IOI-LAVAL, 15–24. Heredia, Costa Rica: Hefuna.

Chuenpagdee, R., J. Fraga Berdugo, and J. I. Euán-Ávila. 2002. Community perspectives toward a marine reserve: A case study of San Felipe, Yucatan, Mexico. *Coastal Management* 30(2): 183–91.

———. 2004. Progressing toward co-management through participatory research. *Society and Natural Resources* (17): 147–61.

Cicin-Sain, B., and R.W. Knecht. 1998. *Integrated coastal and ocean management: Concepts and practices*. Washington. DC: Island Press.

Daly, H.E., and J.B. Cobb Jr. 1994. *For the common good*. Boston: Beacon Press.

Decker, D.J., T.L. Brown, N.A. Connelly, J.W. Enc, G.A. Pomerantz, K.G. Purdy, and W.F. Siemer. 1992. Toward a comprehensive paradigm of contemporary wildlife management: Integrating the human and biological dimensions of management. In *American Fish and Wildlife Policy: The Human Dimension*, ed.. W. R. Mangun,. Carbondale, IL: University Press.

Dunn-Rankin, P. 1983. *Scaling methods*. Hillsdale, NJ: Lawrence Earlbaum Associates.

Echeverria, N., J. Euán-Ávila, J. Fraga Berdugo, and L. Uc. 2003. Construyendo capacidades: El reto de la vinculación comunitaria y los múltiples interesados. In *Manejo comunitario de un área natural protegida en Yucatán, México*. Final report for Phase II. Mexico: CINVESTAV-Unidad Mérida.

Euán-Ávila J. 1997. Physical and human dimensions for integrated coastal management: Assessment of coastal changes and resident knowledge base in coastal areas of the Yucatan Peninsula. PhD diss., Michigan State University.

Euán-Ávila, J., and S.G. Witter. 2002. Promoting integrated coastal management in the Yucatan Peninsula, Mexico. *Journal of Policy Studies* 12: 1–16.

Fraga Berdugo, J, J. Euán-Ávila, R. Chuenpagdee, and R. Torres. 2002. Manejo Comunitario de una reserva marina en San Felipe, México. In *Balancing people and resources: Interdisciplinary research and coastal area management in the Wider Caribbean*, ed. IDRC-CFU-IOI-LAVAL, 278–311. Heredia, Costa Rica: Hefuna.

Fraga Berdugo, J., J. Euán-Ávila, S. Salas and R. Chuenpagdee. 2003. Construyendo futuras colaboraciones: ¿Es posible el manejo colaborativo en la Reserva Estatal de Dzilam? In *Manejo comunitario de un área natural protegida en Yucatán, México*. Final report for Phase II. Mexico: Cinvestav-Unidad Mérida.

GESAMP (Mixed Group of Experts on Scientific Aspects of Marine Environmental Protection). 1999. The contributions of science to integrated coastal management. *Rep. Stud. GESAMP* 61: 65.

Guirdham M. 1999. *Communication across cultures*. Ichor Business Books. West Lafayette, IN: Purdue University Press.

Heemskerk, M., K. Wilson, and M. Pavao-Zuckerman. 2003. Conceptual models as tools for communication across disciplines. *Conservation Ecology* 7(3): 8.

Kay, R., and J. Alder. 1999. *Coastal planning and management*. London and New York: Spon Press.

Kellert, S.R., and J.K. Berry. 1980. *Knowledge, affection, and basic attitudes toward animals in American society: Phase III*. Washington, DC: US Department of the Interior, Fish and Wildlife Service.

Leaders Workshop Synthesis. 2003. CBCRM/IDRC Programme/Cinvestav. Unidad Mérida/Yucatán. México, 2–6 June.

Lebel, J. 2001. *Health: An ecosystem approach*. Ottawa: IDRC.

Leff, E. 1998. *Saber ambiental. Sustentabilidad, racionalidad, complejidad, y poder*. México: Siglo Veintiuno editores.

Liu, J. 2001. Integrating ecology with human demography, behavior, and socioeconomics: Needs and approaches. *Ecological Modelling* 140: 1–8.

OECD. 1993a. *Coastal zone management: Integrated policies*. Paris: Organization for Economic Co-operation and Development.

———. 1993b. *Coastal zone management: Selected case studies*. Paris: Organization for Economic Co-operation and Development.

Palacio, J. 2002. Ecosystems and social actors: Comparative results. In *Balancing people and resources: Interdisciplinary research and coastal areas management in the Wider Caribbean*, ed. IDRC-CFU-IOI-LAVAL, 483–500. Heredia, Costa Rica: Hefuna.

Parker, G.M. 2003. *Cross-functional teams*. New York: Jossey-Bass.

Payton, R. B. 1984. A typology of natural resource issues with implications for resource management and education. *Michigan Academician* 17(1): 49–58.

———. 1990. Institutional and public constraints on dynamic management of fish and wildlife resources. In *Management of Dynamic Ecosystems*, ed. J. M. Sweeney, 155–69. West Lafayette, IN: Wildlife Society.

Ruiz, R. 2000. Multidisciplina e interdisciplina en el postgrado de la UNAM, Mexico City.

Savard, K. 2001. Context, statement. In *Participatory research and CBCRM: In context*, ed. V. Brzeski, J. Graham, and G. Newkirk, 8–11. Ottawa: IDRC.

Savard, K., and Y. Breton. 1999. Social sciences and coastal management. In *Social sciences and community-based resource management*, ed., 1–12. Ottawa: IDRC.

Senger, P.M. 1990. *The fifth discipline. The art and practice of the learning organization*. New York: Doubleday Currency.

Turner, M.G., and S.R. Carpenter. 1999. Tips and traps in interdisciplinary research. *Ecosystems* 2: 275–76.

Weisbuch, G. 2000. Environment and institutions: A complex dynamical systems approach. *Ecological Economics* 34: 381–91.

3

Territoriality, Technical Revitalisation, and Symbolism in Indigenous Communities

Joseph Palacio, Camilo Coral, and Hugo Hidalgo

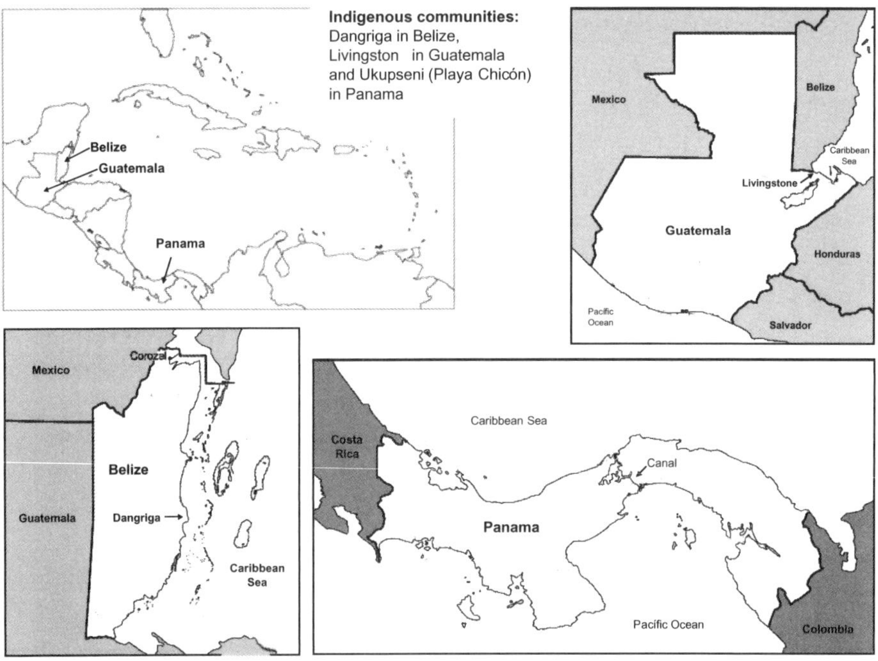

Figure 4
Location of selected communities

We can no longer be content with writing only the history of victorious elites, or with detailing the subjugation of dominated ethnic groups. Social historians and historical sociologists have shown that the common people were as much agents in the historical process as they were its victims and silent witnesses. We thus need to uncover the history of "the people without history"—the active histories of "primitives", peasants, laborers, immigrants and besieged minorities. (Wolf 1982)

In this chapter, we focus on technical revitalisation, territoriality, and symbolism among indigenous communities as indicators of the heterogeneity of Caribbean communities, together with their resilience and adaptive responses in coastal management. We start by outlining where our perspectives on these three factors contribute to the literature in terms of the management of coastal resources. We do likewise for the concept of indigenous peoples within the circum-Caribbean.

Having defined the scope of our contribution to this anthology, we spend considerable time on the three main parts of this chapter—the setting of the studies, the community groups, and research methods. Together, they ground our research within its empirical parameters. For us the setting is not only the location where the research takes place. It is also the larger geographical context, the socioeconomy, and the circumstances that predisposed the community for the study. This led to a spotlight on the community groups who became our field counterparts. We attempted to show that the groups were the core who, to a large extent, determined what would take place in the field as well as the outcome. There was a logical link to the next phase, which was our field methods, many of which were relatively new in the field of coastal resource management.

We conclude this chapter with a review of the contributions that we are making to an appreciation of community-based coastal resource management (CBCRM)[1] within the Caribbean. The technical-revitalisation component of our study introduced a new dimension, where community members found they could exercise more control over their coastal resources by breeding fish. In turn, this resulted in their needing to actively manage their coastal resources. In the case of territoriality, our focus was on the overlapping of ethnicity with marine tenure, along with the social forces that two groups can muster for the benefit of their overall community. Finally, our analysis of symbolism considered the epistemology of our informants, who had to rationalise a management system for their natural resources, demonstrating a capability that is not normally associated with indigenous peoples. Our studies, however, transcend boundaries separating the West from the rest of the world in the management of coastal resources.

Conceptual Orientation

There are two main orientations underlying this study. The first is the core content of this chapter—technical revitalisation, territoriality, and symbolism. The second relates to the community we researched: the indigenous peoples of the circum-Caribbean.

In the study of fisheries management, technical revitalisation remains confined within the field of traditional ecological knowledge at the anecdotal level, where rural people are praised for maintaining their traditional ways. In Mexico and the Caribbean, there has been little depth applied to this, in contrast to what is found in language retrieval (England 2003, 733–43) and agroforestry management (Bray 2000). In Southeast Asia there are many references to detailed studies of traditional fishery methods (Ferrer, Poloton-de la Cruz, and Domingo 1996, 2001). But the emphasis is still on techniques and their biological effectiveness. There is little appreciation of where they fit within the history and socioculture of the community or of their viability for economic development. These are topics we highlight in our description and analysis of the revitalisation of two Garifuna fishing methods in Dangriga, Belize.

Probably because territoriality can generate a lot of animosity, it is a subject that has received considerable analysis in coastal studies. Some main topics include comparison with systems of land tenure (Bavinck 2001), degrees of competition between artisanal and industrial fisheries (ibid.), and reciprocal exchanges among indigenous peoples in Oceana (Johannes 2000, 317–40). Our study adds to the methods of appropriating marine territory by indigenous people within a historical context. It also includes group mobilisation as a form of mitigating inter-ethnic conflict around marine resources. Our information extends from the causes of social conflict to making efforts to find solutions.

A basic premise of ours is that territoriality is a right for a group, even when they have been denied their physical territory. The Garifuna in Livingston are a prime example. At various times in their past, government authorities have denied them territory, both as house lots and as farmland. Our study shows that, notwithstanding this history, for over 200 years they have established indisputable territoriality over their fishing grounds.

Attributing meanings to little-understood phenomena, symbolism has attracted much attention from scholars in the disciplines of psychology, architecture, cultural geography, and anthropology. This perspective is dominated by Western scholars who create explanations that are culture-bound (Dakin 2000, 185–200; Demerrit 2000, 761–90; Laviolette 2000, 215–240). Our contribution comes from broadening the analogy from the West to the world of an indigenous nation, namely the Kuna. We explore a system of managing the universe and its parts that the Kuna have maintained for generations. While Western natural resource management is based upon the centrality of humankind, the Kuna model starts with the centrality of the spirit world, in which humankind is one of several species. Environmental stewardship among the Kuna, therefore, has a higher point of reference than the welfare of humankind. In other words, the Kuna believe in a mystical balancing force that keeps the entire universe in check.

Our study's focus on indigenous peoples effectively neutralises the debate about whether such people still exist in the circum-Caribbean. Our two protagonists, the Garifuna in Belize and Guatemala and the Kuna in Panama, are indigenous peoples with biological and cultural roots within the Caribbean Basin that pre-date Columbus. Because of their extensive intermixture with non-indigenous peoples, they have been called 'colonial tribes' by Helms (Wolf 1982, 155). This is merely a handle that anthropologists use which unintentionally hides the integrity of peoplehood that these two nations have steadfastly preserved.

If anthropologists have difficulty placing the Garifuna and Kuna, it is even more difficult for others whose training and expertise lies in identifying fish species. In his study of traditional fishing habits in Belize, cultural geographer Craig (1966) was able to distinguish traits specific to various ethnic groups. But that was the end of his interest in socioculture. Marine biologists Heyman and Graham (2000) recently conducted baseline studies on fishing in the three countries in the Gulf of Honduras—Belize, Guatemala, and Honduras. However, just like Craig, they displayed little interest in ethnic differentiation and its association with the behaviour of fishers.

While indigenous peoples have little doubt about their cultural identity, others certainly have difficulties with their identification. It may not be the case in homogeneous communities like Ukupseni in Panama, where Coral did his study. On the other hand, many indigenous peoples are now living in heterogeneous localities, where they could be identified as Latinos or other black people. Within the hierarchical social stratification underlying the Caribbean, they are the objects of racial discrimination. The Garifuna are the victims of racial discrimination in Livingston, not because they are indigenous people but because they are black. To avoid this stigma, thousands have emigrated from Guatemala and Belize into the United States, where they are able to find jobs and escape the downward spiral of poverty in their homeland.

The Setting

TABLE 2
THE SELECTED COMMUNITIES

	Dangriga	Livingston	Ukupseni
Country	Belize	Guatemala	Panama
Location	30 miles south of Belize City	Amatique Bay, east coast	Eastern coast, San Blas region
Population	8,000	12,000	1,600
Economy	Little fishing, public services, migrant labour	Artisanal fishing, construction, tourism	Artisanal fishing, agriculture, artisan work
Other	66% are Garifuna with matriarchal kinship system	35% are Garifuna with matriarchal kinship system	Administrative autonomy of San Blas area

Dangriga within southern Belize

Belize lies in the southernmost portion of the Yucatan Peninsula. The northern part of the country, which extends from the border with Mexico as far south as Belize City, consists of flat limestone terrain. It also includes the predominantly Yucatec Maya culture found in the rest of the peninsula (see Figure 5). There are marked differences from Belize City south to the border with Guatemala. The extensive flatland found in southern Belize narrows into a coastal plain, which gradually widens as one proceeds south. It is fringed on the east by the Belize Barrier Reef together with scores of cayes (small islands), and on the west by the verdant foothills of the Maya Mountains, which rise in ever-increasing contours. From the air, both borders form a picturesque frame around the coastal plain.

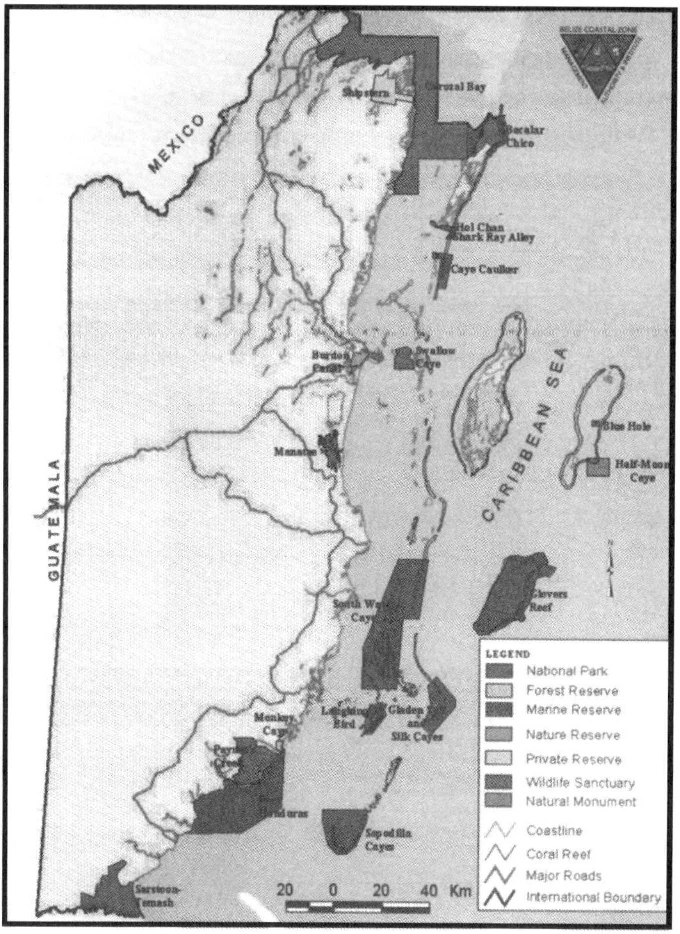

Figure 5
Protected areas of Belize

Tourism now contributes 18 per cent of the Belize GDP (Panting n.d., 37), with much of the industry focusing on marine resources as the primary drawing card. Fisheries contribute an additional 4.5 per cent. The combination of both sources of foreign exchange is taking root mainly in southern Belize. Shrimp aquaculture, which has mushroomed since the mid-1990s, is based there. In 2000, it generated US $28 million out of the total national export earnings of US$193 million (Palacio 2001). Before that, the artisanal fishery in southern Belize had long remained a productive industry, not only for Belizeans living there but also for those living as far north as near the Mexican border (see the study on Sarteneja in this volume). Incidentally, these figures do not take into account scores of poachers who come across from Guatemala and Honduras illegally.

To ascertain that there remains some compatibility between artisanal fishing and marine tourism, the Government of Belize declared almost 7 per cent of the 2.4 million hectares of national territorial seas to be under protected status in marine protected areas (MPAs) (Panting et al. n.d., 37). More of this extends along the southern coastline (see Figure 1) than the north. The rationale of MPAs is to limit fish exploitation and retain a healthy stock for both artisanal and sport fishing. Discussions with fishers reveal that even after only a few months, fish are returning to areas from which they had previously disappeared.

There is a disconnection, however, between the basically preservationist macro-level policy on MPAs and the survival of the 'small man' as artisanal fisherman (Brown 2003). If the techniques that fishers use have not been conducive to species preservation, there has also not been adequate support from the government and non-governmental organisations (NGOs) to assist them to upgrade their overall harvesting standards. Such a programme would review the techniques of harvesting, the seasonal movement of pelagic and other species, marketing, and providing value added. As well, this information would spread nationwide through an active and continuing education effort. Similarly, there would be a detailed review of past practices to assess their effectiveness and make recommendations on improvements. Right now, the small man is left to rely on his traditional knowledge and carry out his own experimentation. Palacio's technical-revitalisation project fits into this type of activity. While institutional support enabled him to get assistance from the Fisheries Department, others would not have been that fortunate.[2]

The primary gateway to southern Belize is the town of Dangriga. With a population of almost 8,500 according to the 2000 national census, it is the nucleus for government offices, banking, and other private-sector initiatives. Many of these services, along with the finances associated with them, pass through the town to other parts of the district, with little remaining in Dangriga itself. For example, this is what happens with respect to tourism. Tourists pass through the town to destinations along the coast or on the cayes. The result is an abiding economically depressed atmosphere that looms over the town. Notwithstanding the pall of gloom, Dangriga has the largest concentration of Garifuna people in the country. Among the ethnic groups represented in the town, 63 per cent are Garifuna. Their dedication to music, dance, painting, and other artistic expressions has earned the town the designation 'the culture capital of Belize'. This designation signifies that the industry still needs much attention if the artistic community in Dangriga and other parts of the country is to benefit.

At this time, cash remittances from the rest of the country and beyond, notably the United States, constitute a large proportion of the income in many households. Much income also filters through the informal economy in gambling, petty thievery, and the sale of cocaine and marijuana.[3]

With this socioeconomic background, we can now turn to the state of fishing within the town, with special focus on the Garifuna. Palacio's survey shows that on any one day over a period of a week in October 2003 there were between 200 and 300 pounds of fish for sale at the town market. When available, the fish most often sold are snapper, grunt, mackerel, jack, snook, tarpon, and barracuda. Fishers also sell at other spots in town, but Palacio was unable to get estimates of numbers or species.

Fish are caught by two types of fishers, while a third group concentrates primarily on catching lobster and conch. One category, comprising between 10 and 15 individuals, consists of men going out about 3 a.m. in their small dories, paddling 2 km from the beach, fishing for a few hours, and returning around 8 a.m. They call themselves 'longshore fishers'. Most are Garifuna men between the ages of 30 and 65 who use hook and line.

The second category of fishers catches larger quantities of fish. Because they use gill nets, they can time their arrival to coincide with the busiest periods in the market, usually between 7 and 9 a.m. They sell to middlemen, who then retail to buyers in the market. They may also sell in bulk to others who take the product out of town to sell. These are mainly recent Ladino immigrants from the neigbouring countries of Guatemala and Honduras, who came earlier as migrant labourers to work in the banana fields in the southern part of the Stann Creek District.[4] They travel in fibreglass boats powered by outboard motors. There are about five men in this category, and they work as family groups.

There is a third category of fishers, who catch mainly lobster and conch to sell to their cooperatives.[5] Occasionally they may go out to catch some scale fish, using mainly gill nets. Because their main source of income comes from selling to their institutions, they rarely serve the town market. There are about ten in this group, which consists of both Garifuna and non-Garifuna fishers.

Apart from the above groups that sell to market buyers, there are about ten other fishers who work mainly as tourist guides in the offshore cayes. Most of them are non-Garifuna, and they rarely sell to the town market.

In summary, the four categories of fishers total about 40 for Dangriga. The tour guides earn the most money, followed by the cooperative members, those who catch scale fish using gill nets, and finally the ones using hook and line. The Garifuna concentrate in the last category, which includes the largest number of intermittent fishers. They may go fishing if they need either fish or cash—but they may decide not to go if the weather is not promising. They are usually alone in their dories but fish within shouting distance of one other. They are friends and relatives who engage in fishing as one of several social activities among themselves.

The demand for fish within the Garifuna community in Dangriga is being met more consistently by non-Garifuna. The Garifuna fishers undoubtedly have access to other sources of cash. On the other hand, fish is traditionally a major part of their diet. They probably have more recipes using fish than the other ethnic groups. Tradition, among them, is giving way to the rule of supply and demand. Because chicken is more easily available in the town and at a cheaper price, this influences a change in diet and, hence, tradition.

This brief survey underlines the alienation that exists among the Garifuna from coastal resources relative to others within the same community. The solution is to demonstrate to the Garifuna that there can be an economic future in fishing. In fact, this was a major aim of Palacio's project. Such rehabilitation, however, goes beyond the limited demonstration effect within Palacio's project. Convincing the Garifuna that fishing represents a good living must be part and parcel of a deliberate and well-planned effort. In terms of CBCRM, fishing is one way that communities remain close to their coastal environment and learn to care for and manage it. The corollary is that non-use results in neglect.

Artisanal fishing has a long tradition among all coastal peoples of Belize—the Mestizo (a mixture of Hispanic and Maya) in the north, and the Creole (a mixture of Africans and Europeans) and Garifuna in the central and southern portions. Through centuries of inter-ethnic exchange they have learned a great deal from each other. Craig (1966) documents examples where the process takes place. Given these cross-cultural linkages, we need to ask to what extent the two methods that Palacio was reviving are truly Garifuna. The *maciwa* (crab trap, depicted in Figure 6) is used extensively throughout

Belize and beyond. It is not of Garifuna origin. In fact, the Garifuna traditionally used it to catch fish. In Palacio's study, it is being used mainly to catch crabs (*Callinecpes sapidus*).

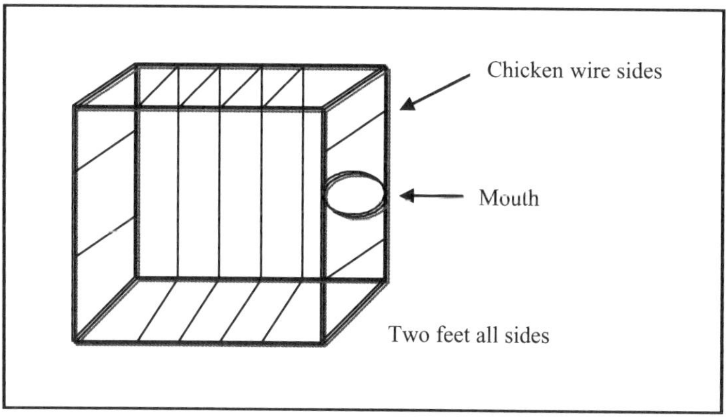

Figure 6
Crab trap

The *wamaredu* (Figure 7) is the other fishing method described in Palacio's study, and it may have some origins among the Garifuna. Information about it first attracted Palacio's attention while he was working on Phase I of the IDRC-CBCRM, during 2000 and 2001. He asked several older men about it, but only a few vaguely recollected using it and how it worked. The consensus was that it was a rectangular, crib-like structure, measuring about 2 by 2 m, which was planted at the mouth of rivers and creeks to catch fish. Informants could not add more details. Craig (1966, 79–80) mentions two structures that Mestizos use in northern Belize that are similar in structure and function to the *wamaredu*: the *rama*, and a heart-shaped weir originally imported from Canada.

The uncertainty about origins increased when we referred to the literature. The *wamaredu* falls into the category of weirs called set nets. There is a description of different kinds of set nets found in Japan (Inoue, Matsuoka, and Chopin 2000), where they have been used extensively.[6] Set nets are also similar to bag nets used in many parts of the world (NUFIC 2003).

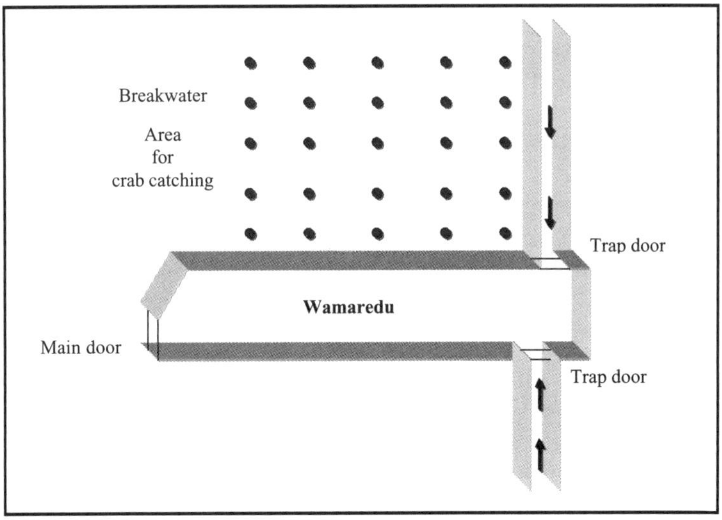

Figure 7
The *wamaredu*

It may be a moot point whether the *wamaredu* is of Garifuna origin. What is important in this discussion of technical revitalisation is that word about it came from these people. As we shall see later, workers in Dangriga figured out the components of the *wamaredu* using their own experiences about fish habits. During its construction, none of them mentioned that they were imitating something they had seen. The result, therefore, is tribute in part to recall, and partly to adjustments that they made while construction progressed. Ethnohistorical research on fishing methods in the areas of northeastern South America and Eastern Caribbean where the Garifuna originated may be helpful.

Livingston within Amatique Bay

In the review of territoriality in Livingston, Guatemala, we start with an overview of Amatique Bay, continue with the results of a recent study on the state of the fishery in the bay, and finish with a brief historical overview. We will show the significance of fishing among the Garifuna in town.

Amatique Bay is a major outlet for the drainage of the uplands of northwest Guatemala through three primary and navigable rivers—the Sarstoon, Rio Dulce, and the Motagua, together with tens of smaller rivers and creeks.

Several departments transport agricultural and industrial products via these rivers, destined for the two main ports located within Amatique Bay, Puerto Barrios, and Matias de Galvez. Imported goods, fish, and other products from the coast are conveyed inland on the return trips. Livingston has been a beneficiary of several opportunities for two-way trade.

The main contribution of Amatique Bay to the trade has been its ample fish products. The city of Puerto Barrios (estimated population 80,000), the town of Livingston (estimated population 12,000), and five smaller hamlets give the bay a combined population of just over 100,000 (Heyman and Graham 2000, 3). Hidalgo estimates that, of these, there are 3,000 fishers working within the 514 km^2 of the bay. Additionally, there are 67 shrimp trawlers. The scale of fishing we had previously observed in Dangriga was dwarfed by what takes place in Amatique Bay.

In response to overfishing and the steadily growing ecotourism industry, the government has declared protected areas along the Sarstoon as well as at Cerro San Gil and Punta Manabique (Heyman and Graham 2000, 31). Several hotels and small resorts are found in Livingston, along the coast as well as further inland along Lake Izabal. They advertise the undiscovered nature of the subregion—the forests, sea, inland waters, archaeology, and a mixture of contemporary ethnic groups made up of the Ladino, Maya K'ekchi, Garifuna, and others.

Heyman and Graham (2000) conducted a baseline survey of fishing in the bay that provides a larger context to what was taking place in Livingston. From their total sample of informants (42 boat captains), 11 came from Livingston. The survey revealed that 80 per cent of all the fishing gear being used was gill nets. The use of hook and line and of nets, such as cast nets and beach seine, was relatively minor.

The boats reflected the basically artisanal mode of most of the fishers. The most often used were small dugouts, many with outboards averaging 15 horsepower. Only about 11 per cent of the boats were fibreglass. Another 2 per cent were shrimp trawlers. The total annual value of the catch in the bay was about US$4 million, by far the largest proportion of which are sprats, which are dehydrated for sale further inland. Shrimp is the next most-captured species. Then follow several species of scale fish, including snook, mackerel, tarpon, and snapper.

With respect to legislation and the currency of regulations, the study found that the existing legislation was outdated and that fishers knew little about the regulations. Furthermore, the penalties, even when applied, were too small for the crime. The level of public education was minimal.

The Heyman and Graham survey did not isolate the Garifuna from fishers of other ethnic groups, which include Ladino, Maya K'ekchi, and some East Indians. However, it introduces the larger context that forms a backdrop to Hidalgo's study. It shows that the predominance of gill nets—even among smaller fishers using dugouts—is a major problem contributing to overfishing. So also the large-scale harvesting of sprats, which normally provide feed for larger fish. Finally, the weakness in legislation further confirms the lack of government intervention within an industry that is fast moving onto a path of self-destruction.

Hidalgo's historical overview of the Garifuna fishery presents a perspective of a community within Livingston that was intimately involved in systems of exploitation for roughly 200 years. The Garifuna did not exterminate the species; rather, they helped to increase the fish supply through the selectivity of their primary method of harvesting, the hook and line.

Hidalgo's reconstruction of the Garifuna fishery starts at the end of the nineteenth century, when people discovered that the reef patches were their *bajos* (fishing grounds) of choice. The discovery was so significant that often the first person to use a *bajo* gave his name to it. For example, there is one called after a Benguche, a popular surname among the Garifuna. Once the *bajos* had been found, they became meeting places where fishers in their dories would congregate and chat while fishing. At around the same time, the Garifuna found other fertile *bajos* in the delta of the Rio Dulce.

Because they were the first to explore the potential of Amatique Bay, they were able to fine-tune their fishing techniques to suit the type of weather they encountered and the species they wanted to catch. For example, they perfected the use of cast nets so they could catch sprats even in rough seas. They used them as baitfish, not for massive trading as is being done at this time.

The next phase in the fishing history of the Garifuna was the decade of the 1930s, when they started to combine group fishing with their earlier practice of one-man-per-dory. They used the beach seine to harvest large amounts of fish. The women processed them by salting and frying and subsequently taking them to sell in inland cities, reaching as far as the capital city. This type of family undertaking filtered through most of the Garifuna community, becoming its main source of livelihood.

The decline of the Garifuna fishing period came in the 1960s, when large numbers of men and women emigrated to the United States in search of jobs. Subsequently, many non-Garifuna people arrived from the Pacific coast, where they had also been fishers. They introduced their own fishing methods, which were more destructive than the previous practices of the Garifuna.

The final phase is Hidalgo's current project, where he is working with some fishers—Garifuna and non-Garifuna—to revindicate the sustainable practices that formerly took place in Amatique Bay under the domain of the Garifuna.

Ukupseni within Kuna Yala

Ukupseni is the name of the Kuna village where Coral did his fieldwork between 2002 and 2003. It is located in the *Comarca* (autonomous territory) of Kuna Yala (the Kuna name for their territory) along the northeastern Caribbean coast of Panama. The village straddles an island and a portion of the mainland, covering a total of 190 km^2. The island, which is home to 1,600 people, is 180 m from the mainland and connected to it by a walkway.

The mainland contains the major infrastructure that services the community, including the airstrip for light planes, the administrative environmental centre for Kuna Yala, and educational institutions. The village cemetery and agricultural plots are also on the mainland. Daily social interactions take place mainly on the island. Like the other islands in the *Comarca*, Ukupseni is coralline, interspersed with patches of sandy lowlands. Shrubs surround the beach, which gives way to primary rainforest further inland. An extended continental shelf heads east into the open sea.

Agriculture and fishing are the primary means of livelihood. Plantains and coconuts are the main crops, together with *molas* (colourful textiles decorated with art) made by women. Since 1923, the Kuna have enjoyed local government autonomy. There are two levels—the local community and Kuna Yala. The local congress is at the community level, and it assumes control over community affairs that are administrative, judicial, or related to economic production. Matters of health, education, and defense are reserved for the Panamanian state. At the level of Kuna Yala there is the general congress, whose members are selected from the local congresses. Its function is to act as intermediary between the local congresses and the state.

The Kuna are among Panama's poorest citizens. World Bank (2000) statistics indicate that 65 per cent of the Kuna population is poor, with 52 per cent at the level of extreme poverty. As many as 60 per cent of children younger than five are chronically malnourished. The infant mortality rate reaches 11.2 per cent, and this age group (from one to four years) has a malnutrition rate of almost 54 per cent. As many as 77.3 per cent are not going to primary school. Finally, only 7 per cent of the population has access to potable water.

As one would expect, such pervasive underdevelopment has led to mounting pressure from both the state and the private sector to modernise and develop Kuna Yala. Local congresses are targeted with requests for concessions for prospecting in mining and forestry. Consortia of tourism entrepreneurs are enticing, with the wealth that comes from the ample natural and cultural resources.

Given the local autonomy the Kuna enjoy, how are they responding to these pressures? More specifically, how have they been managing their natural resources in tandem with the diametrically opposed paradigm of the West? These are questions that Coral undertook to unravel. Unlike the focus in many studies of the IDRC-CBCRM where the resource is coastal, Coral's focus was on the complement of natural resources, given the small and circumscribed context of Kuna Yala as exemplified by Ukupseni.

The Kuna have certainly not been isolated: they have seen both sides of the development coin. Many have migrated to Panama City and other parts of Panama in search of jobs and improved welfare. Those remaining in Kuna Yala have seen the impact of unbridled development on their fragile physical environment. In addition, younger adults are less conversant than their elders with traditional lore, including the place names of farming zones.

In creating a broad conceptual orientation, Coral used interdisciplinary themes to reconstruct a model of natural resource management that corresponds to the Kuna. He calls it the Kuna Model of Natural Resource Management (MKGT is the Spanish initialism). In doing so he placed the Kuna model in opposition to the Western capitalist system. Coral admits that his reconstruction is the first attempt at documenting the Kuna, notwithstanding their historical reputation of intransigence toward Western encroachment (Howe 1988).

Coral's model is built on principles placed in the following sequence:

1. egocentricity;
2. equity;
3. balance;

4. control of production; and
5. Kuna cultural identity.

The Kuna world view places the universe within a structured space. The universe fits into eight stratigraphic levels, with each one accommodating specific components. Space, not time, is the measure of social relations. Cultural geographers have been grappling with similar forms of orientation by local communities in the study of landscape and seascape, as well as their cultural meanings (Demerrit 2000, 767–90). The second principle is equity. This dictates that all beings—living and non-living—have equal value within the universe. Unlike Western thinking, in which humankind assumes the apex over all things, among the Kuna men and women deserve no such ascription. The third principle is balance. All beings are kept in their place by charges of energy originating from the spirit world, which is the ultimate source of power. In Kuna mythology, the spirit world was created when the universe started. The fourth principle addresses the role of humankind in the state of universal balance. Men and women have specific functions. They are not to overdo, because this would put the universe into imbalance. This structure is so important that the local congress acts as regulatory authority on all means of economic production within the community. Finally, the smooth functioning of beings and forces is the main basis of Kuna cultural identity and autonomy. It is a primary commandment of the spirit world that Kuna maintain their world for the benefit of their survival as a nation as well as the integrity of their territory and autonomy. (We provide more details on the methods Coral used to arrive at these principles later on.)

Community Groups

Palacio's direct involvement was with the Buyei Juan Lambey Institute (BJLI), a community-based organisation registered with the government in 2001. It has an executive headed by a spiritual leader. The membership is loose, consisting of men and women on whom the executive can call as needed. Its main aim is to promote income generation through activities that entail the preservation of Garifuna spirituality. Palacio began interacting with them in 2000 when the group started working on a Garifuna Village Project, which was to be located near the beach on a site set aside for tourism development in Dangriga. Palacio helped with various tasks such as group mobilisation, which itself led to a crucial achievement: acquiring the land from the government for the Village Project. In laying the groundwork for its implementation, BJLI planned to build a kraal, in which to breed fish, a short distance from the beach. The fish would be part of the demonstration for the project and could also be served in the restaurant, which would be built on site. This was the beginning of what later turned out to be the revitalisation of the traditional *wamaredu* and *maciwa* methods of catching fish.

Palacio arrived at a division of labour and responsibilities with the BJLI executive with respect to the building and monitoring of the *wamaredu* and *maciwa*. He used project funds to pay for everything related to construction, as well as to pay for monitoring the structures. BJLI provided men and women to do the work and the monitoring; they also provided additional support as needed. After the initial enthusiasm at the beginning of construction, BJLI executive showed little initiative to pursue the agreement they had made regarding their contribution to the project. More often, they reacted to initiatives coming from Palacio instead of demonstrating dedication from being on-site owners of the project. (See below for a more detailed description of the field methods.)

Notwithstanding the proliferation of community organisations in Livingston, none focused on the plight of Garifuna fishers, who were being displaced by aggressive competitors. Through his NGO, the Foundation for Ecological Development (FUNDAECO-Costas), with his experience in community mobilisation, and with IDRC-CBCRM funding, Hidalgo was able to spearhead the formation of a new group called Balabala ('wheel' in Garifuna), composed of Garifuna and non-Garifuna members. As it gradually consolidated its formation, Balabala relied less on FUNDAECO-Costas.

During its gestation, Balabala was able to achieve some mileposts. They included incorporating into its membership a local person with legal training, who could advise on appropriate methods of advocacy. They have negotiated an agreement with some non-Garifuna fishers to limit the destructiveness of their fishing methods. Also, they positioned their president to become a spokesperson for the National Federation of Artisanal Fishers (FENAPESCA). Among others, significant achievements included offering a course in co-management for four of their executive, and integrating older fishers to be councillors of the organisation. As the project progressed to the point of planning the municipal reserve around one of the reef patches that the Garifuna traditionally used, Hidalgo realised that another group should be formed, to consist of Garifuna and non-Garifuna fishers. Its task, however, was to lay the guidelines for the reserve and work against impediments toward its acceptance. Hidalgo adds that the deliberate inclusion of non-Garifuna in both groups was a strategy to speed the pace of interaction between them, thereby limiting the potential for conflict. Besides working with groups, Hidalgo held several interviews with women fish vendors, among other informants.

Coral's first responsibility was to request from the Ukupseni local congress permission to stay in the village so he could do the study. He planned on seven groups to provide data via a series of workshops. These consisted of people engaging in various types of livelihood including *botánicos* (a person who knows about the diseases of plants and animals and can provide cures), hunters, farmers, fishers, divers, and students. The predominance of male-dominated occupations was congruent with the Kuna custom that as a male, Coral should interact only with male subjects. Coral asked three female German exchange students who happened to be on-island to administer some interviews and keep a daily log of activities so he could capture women's perspectives on their occupations. The total number of subjects was 76, 52 of whom were men. In narrowing his sample, Coral used the following criteria, under the influence of the Kuna belief on the social nature of production. The person had to be dedicating roughly 80 per cent of his working time to his occupation, and had to be maximising the involvement of his family and other community members. On this basis, Coral discovered that the *botánicos* and divers were the most exclusive occupations, followed by hunters, fishers, and students. The least exclusive were farmers.

Methods

There are two main parts of the *wamaredu* complex, as shown in Figure 7. The one located furthest from the beach is the breakwater area, followed by the actual *wamaredu* structure. The breakwater consists of several *botan* (*Sabal mauritiiformis*) posts implanted into the seabed to break the force of the waves. Palacio's team placed the *maciwa* in this area, because he wanted to accentuate the area's biodiversity. Crabs would attract their own microbes, which would in turn attract others that the fish in the *wamaredu* would eat. The *wamaredu* enclosure has two parts: the first is the funnel the Garifuna call *leilei*, leading from the sea as well as the land. The other is the box, separated from the funnel by trapdoors. The principle underlying fish breeding within the *wamaredu* is that microbes grow by attaching themselves to the structure. In turn, they attract fish at higher levels of the food chain. (*Wamaredu* comes from the word *wamúrebedu*, which means 'fungus' and is the name for the algae that forms on wooden posts within a few weeks of being in the sea.)

TABLE 3
OBJECTIVES AND METHODS FOR THE STUDY OF CULTURAL REVITALISATION, TERRITORIALITY, AND SYMBOLISM

Topic	Objectives	Methods
Cultural revitalisation	1. Building *wamaredu* ▪ planning ▪ implementation ▪ evaluation	Construction using wood and wire ▪ drawing working sketch ▪ modifying sketch to meet problems from wave action ▪ keeping records of the catch
	2. Making *maciwa* to catch crabs	Building 20 using chicken wire
	3. Capacity building for BJLI	Workshops Working closely with BJLI on Garifuna Village Project
	4. Mobilising intersectoral validation	Involving Fisheries Department, local high school, University of West Indies School of Sciences (UWISCS)
Territoriality	1. Oral history of fishing	Discussions with elders
	2. Identifying fishing sites	Field visits and interviews
	3. Placing sites on GPS	GPS methods
	4. Assessing ecological status	Scuba diving and observation
	5. Consolidating a fisher group community-based organisation (CBO)	Workshops and discussion
	6. Mobilising 'special fishing zone' status	Negotiations with several stakeholders
Symbolism	1. Selecting sample of 76 informants	Fine-tuning criteria and eliciting participation
	2. Drafting mental sketches	Mental mapping
	3. Attributing values to territoriality	Semantic categorisation
	4. Participatory transects	Accompanying informants on walks
	5. Record of transit	Recording data on pre-arranged forms
	6. Diary of women's activities	Collected by colleagues
	7. Ethnographic sketches	

Table 3 outlines the procedures Palacio's team undertook. The first part of the field operations was to acquire the materials to be used. They include *botan* posts, chicken wire made from plastic (and not galvanised) to limit corrosion from the sea, tying wire, and felt. The chicken wire is for the walls of the structure and is useful because it is permeable as well as flexible, so it can bend with the waves. The felt is attached to the chicken wire and is an added attraction for the microbes, which cling to its fibres. When building the box part of the structure, Palacio's team started ambitiously, with a dimension of 10 m wide by 20 m long by 2 m high. They soon discovered that it was too big, cumbersome, and easily destroyed by the force of waves. The weakness was a result of the fact that the support posts had been driven manually into the seabed only to a depth of about 0.5 m. After a few weeks, we limited the size the size to 3 by 2 m, which proved more manageable. Even then, daily monitoring was required to carry out minor repairs as needed.

Within a period of six weeks, the microbes on the *botan* were clearly visible and small fish were nibbling them. After an additional six weeks, the algae were reaching some 3 cm in height, and a few eels were swimming around, together with snappers and grunts. The numbers steadily increased over the nine-month life of the project.

The catch of crabs from the breakwater was much greater than the fish catch. Palacio's team made ten traps, which they baited with small, bony pieces of meat. Within one hour, one trap might catch up to three crabs.

Table 3 has a list of the several field methods that Hidalgo implemented. As in Palacio's case, there were operations of a more technical nature and others that were more social. The former included placing fishing sites on GPS and assessing their levels of fertility and overall ecological status, so as to substantiate allegations that they were being denuded. We have already discussed the social methods, which included doing oral history and engaging in group mobilisation.

The list of objectives and methods Coral used are in Table 3. The battery of tests he used included mental imagery and semantic categorisation from clinical psychology; participatory transects and transit recording from cultural geography; and daily diaries with observations, derived from ethnography. A brief summary of Coral's results follows.

The subjects demonstrated strong levels of cognitive association with specific geographic features, such as the coastline and the sources of their livelihood—the sea for divers and fishers and land for farmers. Furthermore, there are cultural values associated with specific geographic features. For example, land has a southward orientation and water a northward one. Coral interprets this as the centrality of the villagers' affinity to the island, in contrast to the hierarchical Western orientation from the village to the town and ultimately the country. Finally, by attaching themselves to certain land forms, like the waterfall, spirits limit the movement of villagers. Hunters and *botanicos* were most aware of the direct intervention of spirits in daily transactions.

The data forthcoming from the women's ethnographic sketches was especially significant in terms of gender recognition. The women have a relatively high social value, not only because the Kuna are traditionally matrilineal but also because of their dedication to *mola* production. Through this ancient art, women transmit intricate information about Kuna mythology. Their function of socialising the children in this knowledge adds an even higher dimension to their importance.

Contributions to CBCRM

In the discussion on Dangriga as the setting for Palacio's study, we noted that Dangriga represented the end phase of Garifuna alienation from the type of artisanal fishery they had traditionally practised. We argued that it was crucial to break the chain of alienation that had its grip upon the Garifuna, which consistently forced them away from the sea as their main form of livelihood. We used the term 'rehabilitation' to describe the complex activities that needed to be put in place. The revitalisation exercise can be described as a form of self-initiated rehabilitation in only two methods of harvesting fish. The advantage of both methods is that they create opportunities to harvest fish consistently, rather than temporarily luring them with the bait on hook and line. The *wamaredu* especially has to have a programme of husbandry that monitors the state of the structure as well as doing the necessary repairs on it, to maximise the catch.

It was interesting to observe some of the changes that accompanied the *wamaredu* experiment by the beach in Dangriga—by-products of the exercise. Several birds came to perch on the posts, as if they had been waiting for such an opportunity to pass time there. Townsfolk stopped to observe them, commenting that there were some species they had not seen for a long time. There was a noticeable extension of the area of the beach behind the *wamaredu*. It showed that the breakwater and the *wamaredu* had lessened the erosion of the beach. The return of the birds and the lessening of beach erosion came as lessons in re-learning the beach ecosystem, which is a necessary step toward its sustainable management.

The inability to engage in the kind of rehabilitation we have described results in a vacuum in the stewardship of a vital resource. Precisely this kind of vacuum occurred in the waters of Livingston as a result of the Garifuna emigration, which attracted other kinds of fishers who introduced more destructive methods. This process is being repeated in Dangriga. Again the Garifuna are moving away from fishing, as others are taking over.

To what extent was the *wamaredu* successful in attracting fish for breeding? It was moderately successful. If Palacio's team had been able to provide the level of monitoring it demanded, it would have been even more successful. If there had been a marine biological feasibility study of the overall project beforehand, it would have been possible to plan a better implementation. Palacio adds that, given the little bit that his team was able to provide to the exercise, he was pleasantly surprised with the potential it demonstrated, and that the team is in a better position now to repeat the project. The experiment shows even greater potential with respect to crabs.

Territoriality is indispensable to the use of coastal resources and, by extension, to CBCRM. The type of territoriality that fishers in Belize and Guatemala are forced to live with is the MPA. On the whole, fishers have been suspicious of—if not hostile to—MPAs, because of their methods of imposition. If fishers were told that MPAs are another dimension to their own territoriality, their response would be far more favourable.

Hidalgo's study has helped in the understanding of two levels of territoriality. One level is the general zone. In the case of Livingston, it is the sea in front of the town, which villagers refer to as theirs. Within this area, they have used their own transportation for generations –dugout, paddle, and two or three sets of sails. They also know the second level of their territoriality, the reef patches where they do their fishing, where they practise another kind of traditional technology. This is the use of the paddle to determine the location of rocks on the seabed. By placing the paddle to the ear one can hear certain crackling sounds that are emitted by submerged reefs. These are only two of several traditions that are associated with territoriality.

Hidalgo's methods have enriched another aspect of CBCRM, namely mitigating the chances of conflict between competing users of the same marine environment. He sought to have fishers from the two opposing sides engage in dialogue and even join the same organisations. That way they could re-orient their vision to the common resource they all share and for whose preservation they should cooperate.

The studies of Palacio and Hidalgo have focused primarily on one dimension of management, namely the social world with its two components—how people reclaim technology and territoriality. The physical world—the coast and a few kilometres in the open sea—has provided a backdrop to their study. There is a third world, the cultural world, to which they have not paid too much attention, notwithstanding brief references to inter-ethnic relations and the culture of alienation from the sea. Coral's study combined the three worlds—social, cultural, and physical—and placed them as interrelated elements in the management of natural resources. He did so in attempting to reconstruct how the Kuna have been able to regulate their behaviour to limit environmental degradation. He concludes with what could be termed 'the Kuna alternative' to CBCRM: the Kuna model of natural resource management, which is depicted in Figure 8.

The spirit world is the ultimate authority in regulating all things in the Kuna universe. Spirits identify the cultural norms of behaviour and the Kuna ideology. They also regulate the social structure of the community through the local congress. Sanctions that apply to the breaking of Kuna regulations come through the local congress. Should the infraction be major, the spirits can intervene directly, by inflicting large-scale damage on the community itself. The reward that the community reaps by following the regulations is harmony among all species, including humankind. Environmental integrity is a major tenet of Kuna life.

As the field of social sciences delves deeper into the application of CBCRM, more elements that need attention make their way to the surface. In our study we can identify three examples. One is the question of the ownership of fishery technology, especially in the efforts of revitalisation, as Palacio addressed. We can see that this question is not that significant in territorial revindication because of the fixity of geographical location. Fishery technologies are prime examples of extensive intercultural borrowing. They no doubt

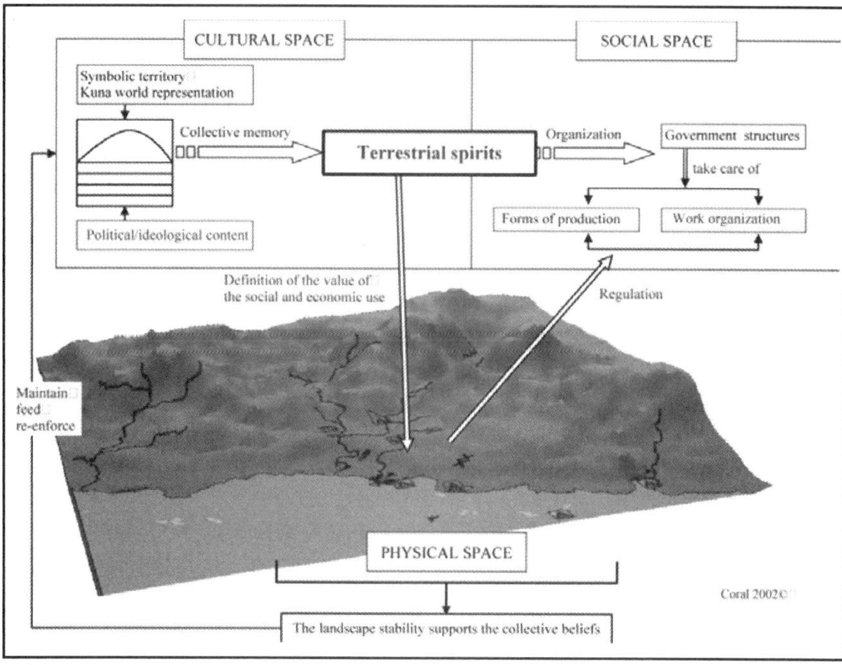

Figure 8
The Kuna model of natural resource management

provide challenges to the emerging field of intellectual and cultural property rights among indigenous peoples.

The second example is more mundane and has to do with field methods. How does the researcher maintain a synergy with his community group that results in a flow of enthusiasm as the project progresses? For Palacio, the waning interest BJLI demonstrated in his project was one of the discouraging aspects of fieldwork. Undoubtedly Hidalgo and Coral experienced similar periods.

Finally, community-based fieldwork has its own trajectory that needs to be captured so as to reveal how field counterparts think. The Garifuna Village Project of BJLI represents an incredible effort by a community group to bridge the gap between artisanal fishing and tourism. This background problem, which Palacio identified earlier in this chapter, is common in underdeveloped communities. Indeed, such suggestions on inclusion need to be studied in greater detail, especially if they will result in lessening the marginalisation of artisanal fishers.

Conclusion

Both the Kuna and the Garifuna have experienced overwhelming transformations in the face of cataclysmic impositions from the West. Notwithstanding this, we can detect aspects of their culture grounded in the inviolability that is traditionally found in the bond between tribal peoples and their natural resources. The field of CBCRM is the beneficiary of this revelation, which is coming from the Kuna and Garifuna. In the West, immediate cash value is the primary indicator of natural resource use. For the Garifuna, immediate cash value is sacrificed for the prudent use of the ocean through traditional tenure and technology. For the Kuna, natural resources are valued as an extension of the community's well-being.

Indigenous peoples would argue that it is the Western misconception on the ultimate value of natural resource use that relegates them to poverty. From this chapter we can begin to appreciate why indigenous peoples always make up the poor within Western societies. More than this, it explains why the indigenous peoples themselves do not consider themselves as the poor. A spotlight on indigenous peoples and CBCRM throws light on this dilemma.

Acknowledgements

Joseph Palacio would like to thank several people in Dangriga who provided information; the Buyei Juan Lambey Institute; staff at the University of the West Indies School of Continuing Studies in Belize; Ms B. Wade, Mr R. Carcamo, and other staff of the Fisheries Department; Mr F. Humphreys, the principal of Ecumenical High School; Dr Hugh Saul and staff at CARICOM Fisheries Unit in Belize City; and Dr Yvan Breton of Laval University.

Notes

1. This study falls within the International Development Research Council's community-based coastal resource management programme for the Caribbean.
2. With the generous assistance of Ms B. Wade and her staff at the Fisheries Department, Palacio learned how to identify and measure fish found in the *wamaredu*.
3. A survey of criminal records shows a higher overall rate for Dangriga than for towns in Belize with a larger population (Palacio 2003).

4. Woods, Perry, and Steagall (1997, 63–88) documented the large-scale inflow of immigrants into Belize within the past 20 years.
5. In Belize, cooperatives dominate artisanal fishing that targets lobster and conch. Because of the high returns from sales for their products, men belonging to cooperatives do not usually sell at the local market.
6. Palacio is grateful to Dr Milton Haughton of CARICOM Fisheries for this information.

References

Bavinck, M. 2001. *Marine resource management—conflict and regulation in the fisheries of the Coromandel coast.* New Delhi: Sage Publications.

Bray, D.B. 2000. Adaptive management, organizations, and common property management: Perspective from community forests of Quintana Roo, Mexico. Paper presented at the 8th Biennial Conference of the International Association for the Study of Common Property, Bloomington, Indiana, May 31–June 4.

Brown, D.A.V. 2003. A view from the ground: Competing discourses on impoverishment and the coastal environment in Belize. Paper presented at the Annual Conference of the Society for Caribbean Studies, Bristol, July 7-9, 2003.

Craig, A.K. 1966. Geography of fishing in British Honduras. Coastal Studies Series, no. 14. Baton Rouge: Louisiana State University Press.

Dakin, S. 2000. There is more to landscape than meets the eye: Towards more inclusive landscape assessment in resource and environmental management. *Canadian Geographer* 47(2): 215–40.

England, N.C. 2003. A framework for the practical application of the concepts of critical natural capital and strong sustainability. *Ecological Economics* 44: 165–85.

Ferrer, E.M., L. Poloton-de la Cruz, and M.A. Domingo. 1996. *Seeds of hope.* Quezon City: University of Philippines.

———. 2001. *Hope takes root.* Ottawa: CBCRM Resource Center.

Heyman, W., and R. Graham. 2000. *La voz de los pescadores de la costa atlantica de Guatemala.* Guatemala City: FUNDAECO and TIDE.

Howe, J. 1998. *A people who would not kneel: Panama, the United States, and the San Blas Kuna.* Washington, DC: Smithsonian Institution Press.

Inoue, Y., T. Matsuoka, and F. Chopin. 2002. Technical guide for set net fishing. International Set Net Fishing Summit in Himi, Japan, Iberaki. National Research for Fisheries Engineering. Fisheries Research Agency.

Johannes, R. 2000. The renaissance of community-based marine resources management in Oceana. *Annual Review of Ecology and Systematics* 33: 317–40.

Laviolette, P. 2000. Landscaping death—resting places for Cornish identity. *Journal of Material Culture* 8(2): 215–40.

NUFIC (Netherlands Organization for International Cooperation in Higher Education). 2003. Bag-net fishing. Indigenous Knowledge Worldwide, April 2003. www.ik-pages.net/ikww/200304IKWW.pdf.

Palacio, J.O. 2001. Past and current methods of CBCRM in the southern coast of Belize—final report to the IDRC-CBCRM.

———. 2003. Social deterioration and cultural capital among the Garifuna at the beginning of the 20th century. Paper delivered at the Plenary of the Caribbean Studies Association meeting, Belize City, 2003.

Pantin, D. N.D. People and the Caribbean coast—feasibility of alternative sustainable coastal resource-base enhanced livelihood strategies. St Augustine: University of the West Indies.

Wolf, E. 1982. *Europe and the people without history.* Berkeley: University of California Press.

Woods, L.A., J.M. Perry, and J.W. Steagall. 1997. The composition of distribution of ethnic groups in Belize: Immigration and emigration patterns, 1980–1991. *Latin American Research Review* 32(3): 63–88.

4

Communities and Stakeholders in Marine Protected Areas in the Caribbean

Julia Fraga Berdugo, Yvonne Arias, and Jorge Ángulo

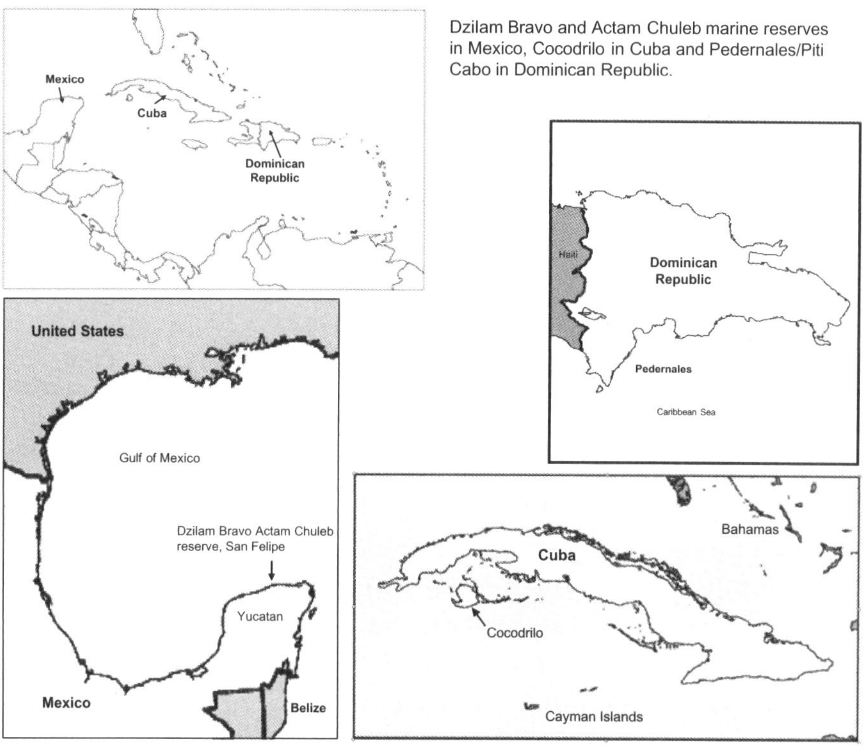

Figure 9
Location of selected communities

This chapter on communities and stakeholders in marine protected areas (MPAs) presents the results of research into Caribbean coastal resource management from an ethnographic and a pan-Caribbean perspective. Three case studies in Mexico, the Dominican Republic, and Cuba help reveal key elements that demonstrate the heterogeneity of this geographic area. We found a gradient with respect to the management approaches used by each country, which shifts from a top-down approach in the Dominican Republic and Cuba to a bottom-up approach in Mexico.

This chapter also examines community dynamics with respect to different categories of management for natural protected areas, as well as issues surrounding the environmental values of Caribbean communities.

TABLE 4
MAIN FEATURES OF THE SELECTED COMMUNITIES

	Cocodrilo	San Felipe	Piti Cabo-Pedernales
Country	Cuba	Mexico	Dominican Republic
Location	Isla de la Juventud 15 km from Punta Frances marine park	Northeast coast of Yucatan	Parque Nacional Jaragua, southeast part of the country
Population	308	1,832	650, located in various small fishing stations
Economy	Artisanal fishing, small agriculture, and woodcutting	Fishing and tourism	Artisanal fishing with seasonal migration
Other	Scuba diving from cruisers in the area	Creation of local marine reserve in 1995	Communities without legal status in the park

Approximately 60 per cent of the people of Latin America and the Caribbean live in coastal areas, where their increasing population is causing serious problems. The Caribbean has been listed as one of the world's four or five hot spots by Conservation International, and five of the 200 ecoregions classified by the World Wildlife Fund (WWF) as priorities for world conservation efforts are located in this region.

The establishment of protected areas in the Caribbean dates back more than 200 years, with the 1765 creation of the Main Ridge Reserve in Tobago. Jamaica established its first marine area in 1907 (Insular Caribbean WCPA Report to the World Parks Congress, Durban, 2003).[1] Currently, the region has more than 400 protected areas, representing more than 15 per cent of its surface area. There are roughly 300 marine areas (a common island asset), among which 25 are marine reserves. These play a crucial, invaluable role in conserving coastal marine biodiversity resources, and in ensuring their use by local and regional residents.

Mexico's conservation policy was based on creating and strengthening natural protected areas. It emerged in the 1980s and 1990s (Halfter 1981; McNeely, Harrison, and Dingwall 1994; Barzetti 1993; SEMARNAP 1997), reflecting the trend towards environmentalism and conservation in the West. These protected areas were created and expanded during the past eight decades, in a clearly top-down approach that was started, primarily, through government initiatives, as noted by Gómez-Pompa and Dirzo (1995). During the 1990s, it became necessary to reclassify natural protected areas that had been artificially created and which were not operational (Garrido 1991; Pérez-Gil 1993; INE-SEMARNAP 1995–2000). Moreover, such areas exhibited the vicious circle represented by lack of financing, lack of community involvement in conservation strategies, and lack of trained personnel, along with many other shortcomings.

San Felipe

In Mexico, creating protected areas was justified as a way of halting ecological deterioration of the country's most representative ecosystems, safeguarding ecological capital for national development, and ensuring that the areas could be handed down to future generations. The Ecological Balance Act (Ley General de Equilibrio Ecológico, LGEEPA) was passed in 1988. Its article 45 calls for the establishment of natural protected areas.[2]

> These areas constitute a geographic network for conservation and sustainable development initiatives that are becoming strategic assets for Mexico, and with new methodologies and scientific knowledge the value of the goods and services they generate can be estimated in economic terms, and elements of judgment can be derived for guiding private and public decisions affecting conservation. (INE-SEMARNAP 1995–2000, 5)

In 2002, Mexico had 444 natural protected areas, 60 per cent of which contained aquatic habitats and 40 per cent land habitats. MPAs have been growing in number since the 1990s, under various categories of management.[3] There are some discrepancies in the number of MPAs reported in Mexico.[4] All of these marine areas were proposed through outside initiatives such as environmental non-governmental organisations (NGOs), scientists, and government natural-resource administrators. Their creation was also determined on the basis of biological and economic considerations relating to fisheries management.[5]

Cocodrilo

In Cuba, the creation of terrestrial and marine protected areas is a key element in the National Environment Strategy (Ministry of Science, Technology and Environment, 1997). In July 1997 the government adopted the Environment Act, Law 81, reflecting the national interest in protecting the environment and establishing general objectives for what has come to be known as the National System of Protected Areas (SNAP). It represents the culmination of a participatory process that sought to find a strategic working tool through which future actions could be channelled. The goal was to preserve the most significant values of Cuba's natural heritage and, in particular, its biodiversity, within designated protected areas (National Centre for Protected Areas 2002).

The system now has 263 identified protected areas, of which 35 have been officially approved and 23 are at an advanced stage of processing. The remainder remain at the proposal stage. Once the system is fully established, 41 per cent of the national territory, including the island's offshore shelf, will be protected under various management categories, consistent with the development objectives of each region (National Centre for Protected Areas 2002).

As part of this system, there is a proposal to create a Managed Resource Protected Area (APRM) in the southern portion of the Isla de la Juventud. APRMs represent a management category within SNAP. The objective is to protect and maintain biological diversity and simultaneously to provide a sustainable flow of natural goods and services to meet local and national needs (Decree Law 201 on the National System of Protected Areas, December 23, 1999, Council of State). APRMs are supposed to embrace other, and more strictly defined, protected areas such as natural reserves, national parks, and ecological reserves. Thus, the Punta Frances National Marine Park (PNMPF) examined in this case study constitutes an integral part of the APRM on the Isle of Youth.

Petit Cabo-Pedernales

In the Dominican Republic, key dates in the protection of natural areas include 1919 (executive order), 1928 (ban), 1933 (national park), 1966 (scientific reserve and natural monument), 1967 (forest preserve), and 1976 (natural scientific reserve). In 1977, a national historic park was declared and a year later an archaeological zone established. In 1986, the first scenic route was designated, and in 1992 and 1993 the categories of ecological park and anthropological reserve, respectively, appeared. The natural monument, wildlife refuge, and refuge categories came into use in 1995. In 1996, a scientific reserve was declared. Since that year, other categories have been declared, including an anthropological reserve, a biosphere reserve, a biological reserve, a national recreation area, an ecological corridor, and a natural area.

On November 8, 1974, Law 67 was adopted, creating the National Parks Directorate as the senior body overseeing the Dominican Republic's protected areas. On August 18, 2000, Law 64–00, the Environment and Natural Resources Act, was promulgated and the Ministry of Environment and Natural Resources created. Although many areas were created by presidential decree, Law 64–00 includes all the areas; as a direct result, all automatically became protected by law.

The National System of Protected Areas currently contains a variety of ecosystems divided among different management categories, many of which are inconsistent with recommendations of the International Union for the Nature Conservation (IUCN). However, draft legislation for a Protected Areas Act proposes significant changes to categories and areas. Within the Ministry, the Protected Areas and Biodiversity Department (formerly the National Parks Directorate) has direct responsibility.

The preceding paragraphs outline historical developments in the three countries on the legal and management fronts. Table 5 summarises the sociodemographic and economic features of each community studied, as an aid to appreciating the approach taken in each case and, above all, addressing the following three concerns:

1. To what extent does the community structure permit management of a protected area?

2. To what extent are socioenvironmental research results accepted by our governments as the basis for effective management?
3. Does the category assigned to a protected area bear any relationship to the community that uses the area?

TABLE 5
SOCIAL ORGANISATION OF THE COMMUNITIES UNDER STUDY

Socioeconomic characteristics	Mexico San Felipe	Cuba Cocodrilo	Dominican Republic Pedernales, Piti-Cabo
No. of fishers	621	23	500
Main activities	Artisanal fishing, livestock, and incipient tourism	Fishing and farming	Fishing
Emigration	Low to moderate	Very low	Medium
Immigration	High	None	Highly seasonal
Education	Primary and secondary	Primary, secondary, and higher	Majority unschooled
Health services	Two centres: Ministry of Health and Assistance (SSA) and Mexican Institute of Social Security (IMSS)	A family clinic	None
Religion	Catholic	Catholic	Catholic
Family relationships	Strong family ties (same surnames)	Strong ties	Weak ties
Ethnic group	Mestizo	Mestizo	Mestizo
Role of women	Collecting squid for bait	Services and administration	Processing the catch
Local organisations	Fishing cooperatives (3)	People's councils	None
Main problems	Partisan rivalry between National Action Party (PAN) and Revolutionary Institutional party (PRI), break-up of the cooperative (two sections A and B), crisis in the fishery vs. low emigration of young people to the Mayan Riviera and Cancún	Substandard housing, poor transportation, few employment opportunities, little contact with the outside world because of geographic isolation	Precarious living conditions, no basic services of any kind, broken families, few economic alternatives, overlapping of official functions

THE ACTAN CHULEB MARINE RESERVE IN MEXICO (Julia Fraga Berdugo, Jorge Eúan-Ávila, Silvia Salas Marquez, and Ratana Chuenpagdee)

This case study of the Actan Chuleb Marine Reserve describes a local initiative for the conservation of fishery resources that has now been in place for 10 years, and which has seen repeated intervention by local and outside stakeholders with varying interests and motivations. The process reveals how the state serves to try to promote conservation through legislation (the Ecological Balance Act). However, the state has been incapable of handling management at the local level. The result is that the community of San Felipe asserted its own collaborative management of the resource. The Actan Chuleb Marine Reserve (Actan Chuleb is a Mayan term for a species of marine bird) is perhaps the only example in Mexico of a reserve established and managed by a local community. In this case, a group of 30 traditional fishers established a marine area of 30 km^2, located 5 km from the port and village of San Felipe, with its 1,832 inhabitants. The port of San Felipe is on the northeast shore of Yucatan

San Felipe: Shifting patterns of community use of coastal resources

Every human community lives face to face with nature in a manner mediated by symbolic, cultural, economic, and political dimensions. Looking into the mirror of the past, we can identify resources and ecosystems that were transformed by the activities of coastal inhabitants and by the models of capitalist economic growth in two areas: the terrestrial and the marine. San Felipe has followed the spiral of socioeconomic development based on exploitation of its coastal resources since the twentieth century. These have evolved from subsistence farming to extensive ranching. Since the 1970s, there has been a concentrated effort to build a commercial fishery. Currently, the fishing effort has been combined with ranching. The twenty-first century is witnessing a sudden search for alternatives to the traditional fishery. This is because the fishing grounds are shrinking, and the coastal landscape—with its beaches, estuaries, and marine wildlife—is now viewed as the most promising alternative for the local economy.

In addition to this historical approach to understanding the use and management of the coastal resources of San Felipe, we must not overlook the internal social fabric that underlies the interaction of inhabitants with resources and ecosystems. That social fabric explains the current conditions of participation, the initiatives for protecting resources, and the potential for community-based management of marine resources (Chuenpagdee, Fraga Berdugo, and Eúan-Ávila 2002, 2004).

San Felipe has two social characteristics that must be remembered: close family relationships and the general acceptance of the Catholic religion. The first is the product of its geographic isolation during the first 50 years of the twentieth century, when its domestic economy was based on self-consumption of locally grown crops—corn, grasses, and tubers. Farming yielded to extensive livestock ranching in the 1950s, which is currently the second most important economic activity after the artisanal fishery. The fishery received a boost in 1970 with the establishment of the fishing cooperative known as the Authentic Fishermen of San Felipe. Fishing sparked the community's economic development, expanded communications with the outside world, drew *campesinos* into fishing, and produced technological innovations in fishing methods, boats, and port infrastructure. At the same time, new fishing organisations appeared, and the government established a greater presence to administer the fishery resources.

Other factors affect the community and its interrelationships and culture. Marriage with outsiders has diversified social and family relationships. The Catholic religion not only has dominated behaviour but also has constituted the focal point of community and working life. When farming was the main activity, people turned to a fusion of Mayan gods and Christian images to appeal for better yields. When farming was replaced by livestock, Christian figures were seen as intermediaries between the ranch owners and the yield from their herds. Now that fishing is the principal activity, the Christian figures have become the main protectors, guardians, and harbingers of good luck to fishers.

Fishing brought with it growing numbers of people who are devoted to this activity. This sparked a net demographic growth (immigration minus the difference between deaths and births). San Felipe's population rose from 300 in 1950 to 1,254 in 1980, and to 1,832 in 2000 (CONAPO-CINVESTAV 1987; Fraga Berdugo1992; INEGI 2000).

These successive broad stages in socioeconomic development (subsistence farming, extensive ranching, artisanal fishing, and regional tourism) plus the internal characteristics of family and religious bonds explain another fundamental feature of this community. This is its ability to organise self-management based on the fishing cooperative, the municipality (and its president), and the Fuerzas Vivas, a type of village council formed by the leaders of local producers' organisations. Such self-management has made it possible to attract investments to improve community infrastructure and social welfare (construction of a church, a school, a sports field, and a health clinic, paint for house fronts, street cleaning, etc.).

In 1990, this self-management capacity led to the creation of the marine reserve. Initially referred to as the 'area for hard times in the fishery', it was subsequently renamed 'the natural fish nursery', and then the 'fish sanctuary'. Finally, it took the name by which it is known today—the Actan Chuleb Marine Reserve—as a result of an official municipal decree signed by the Fuerzas Vivas in 1995 and 1997. These different categories of local use and management reflect the progressive changes that took place in the intergenerational interactions within the community and in the relations with outsiders. Older fishers use the first two terms, while the younger fishers and NGO staff refer to the more recent one.

Actan Chuleb Marine Reserve: A 10-year local initiative

MPAs were being established elsewhere in the 1990s with a clearly top-down focus. However, as we noted earlier, through their own local initiative, fishers of San Felipe created a marine zone of 30 km^2 that contains no land portion (no dunes or mangrove swamps), located 5 km from the port, with its own rules and penalties.

Creation of the reserve was made possible by an institutional arrangement[6] peculiar to San Felipe, reflected in a community-based organisational structure. It was the result of an initiative of the fishing cooperative, with the support of the municipal government and the Fuerzas Vivas committee, which has the power to take decisions on any community matter. It also reflects a new concept of the coastal landscape, motivated by scarcity—the need to conserve fishing resources, especially those of high commercial value such as lobster—and market incentives (Fraga Berdugo 2002). People accepted the conservation argument without discarding their local knowledge and experience. On the basis of traditional knowledge, the boundaries of the reserve were initially set at the line of submerged vegetation, or 'dry grass' as it is known, in an area protected from marine currents and wave action. Here, fish species seek shelter for feeding and spawning. Therefore, boundaries of the reserve were based on physical and biological components of the environment (Fraga Berdugo, Euán and Chuenpagdee 2001).

The establishment and local management of the reserve, which exhibits the features of collaborative management between users and the local authorities, is questioned by some. On the external front, it has no recognition from the state or federal governments, because it is located in the Bocas de Dzilam State Reserve, created in 1989. It is also very close to the western boundary of the Ria Lagartos Biosphere Reserve (Fraga Berdugo 2001). While the reserve is not recognised in law or in the management plan for the state reserve, it is considered an area of restricted use, managed by the community of San Felipe. The community argues for its right to establish and manage the reserve and to receive support, on the grounds that the reserve is the result of a collective decision. The marine reserve relies on local conservation control, based on a reinterpretation of the landscape, which contrasts with the dominant view (Nigh 2001). Thus, a confrontation exists between two interpretations of the same landscape. The local one regards it as a marine reserve, while the official one treats it as a restricted area within another reserve, according to the Management Plan of the Dzilam Bravo State Reserve (Biocenosis1999).

The reserve is questioned within the community because the local administration has not taken into account all the stakeholders. In particular, independent fishers feel excluded from the decision-making process. Female fishers who have organised a cooperative are also demanding a seat at the table for taking decisions about the reserve, such as those relating to enforcement patrols. While the independent fishers do not openly challenge the reserve, in practice some of them breach its management rules.[7] During the 10 years of the reserve's existence, stakeholders have questioned the shift of focus from community to monetary interests. There was a clearer community interest in the first years of its establishment (1990 to 1998), when those responsible for patrolling the reserve kept the population informed of their actions. At that stage, both men and women questioned and criticised decisions on any matter affecting the reserve. In contrast, according to a fisher who was a former reserve warden, since 1999 the main concern has been money for maintaining the reserve.

This shift reflects the flood of donations that the fishing cooperative received from two sources, the United Nations Development Programme (UNDP) and the Nature Conservancy Fund, for its conservation and enforcement work in the marine area between 1997 and 2000.

The foregoing reflects the complexity and the temporal and contextual variability of institutional arrangements among the different stakeholders, inasmuch as they involve questioning and negotiation of different interpretations of the landscape and environmental entitlements (Leach, Mearns and Scoones 1999). In the eyes of outsiders, San Felipe seems a relatively homogeneous community that, as a whole, maintains control over the reserve. However, when seen from within, there is a division between members of the fishing cooperative and the independent fishers, and between those who support the community interest and those who give priority to the monetary interest in conserving the area. At the same time, the two sources of power within the community, the municipal government and the cooperative, are moving at different levels of intervention to ensure sound management of the reserve. They are basing this upon the family ties among their representatives, who change every three years. The 'mercantilisation' of conservation (Rist 1996) through the Actan Chuleb Marine Reserve is a symptom of the current disagreement among the inhabitants of San Felipe.

The state and San Felipe

Through the Ecological Balance Act, the federal and state governments regulate and administer protected natural areas, including those in the Ria Lagartos Biosphere Reserve and the Dzilam Bravo State Reserve, in which the Actan Chuleb Marine Reserve is located.

The two reserves have management plans with similar consequences in social terms. Both regard San Felipe's inhabitants as a problem since they see the bigger reserves as inadequate for the management of their local resources. However, at the same time, they are potential stakeholders or clients for environmental education and ecotourism activities, which are promoted within the larger reserves (see the management plans of the two reserves). In its current unofficial version (Duhne 2000), the Dzilam Bravo management plan recognises the local initiative to establish the marine area and its zoning as a restricted use area. The programmatic plan for the Actan Chuleb Reserve (1998), drafted by the fishers' wardens under the supervision of the Research Centre on Natural Resources (CIRNAC), a Mexican NGO, establishes rules for the marine reserve (Ortiz, Ortiz and Hirose, 1998).

Those rules include a prohibition on all types of commercial fishing and any type of fish farming or use of fish tanks. They prohibit the sunken hook-and-line techniques that poachers use, where the penalty is confiscation of the entire catch. Fishing is not permitted in the main channels linking the reserve to the sea. The catching of various species of fish, such as sharks and wreckfish, in the reserve is prohibited, and the penalty is confiscation of catch plus a fine of 5,000 pesos. Before any species of sea cucumber can be taken, studies must be submitted showing its life cycle, population, distribution, and relationship to the environment, and the environmental impact of taking it. Mexican official standards must be respected, against the applicable penalties. Citizens are required to inform the authorities of any irregularity in the reserve.

Failure to comply with these rules, which were established to protect against the exploitation of the reserve's species, is punishable with suspension of fishing licences. People caught in the act of destroying or harming the zones or areas earmarked for study, conservation, and reproduction are punished. People who enter designated zones for manatees will be punished. In fact, this zone can be entered only with permission from the reserve authorities. Diving is allowed only for viewing the species and must not disturb them, and it may be practised only when the administration considers it appropriate.

While these rules exist in the Programmatic Plan for the Fish Sanctuary (1998), a copy of which was sent to the State Ministry of Ecology in 2000, the initiative has no official backing. From an interview with a municipal president, we learned that the cooperative and the municipality have no enforcement powers, since they would be operating outside the law. On seven occasions, the local government has fined poachers fishing in the reserve, because the cooperative transferred this responsibility to the municipality under the cover of a community agreement. Yet the power of the municipal authorities is slipping from their hands with each change of administration (every three years the executive and councillors change). In addition, depending on the family relationships between the executive and council representatives, there may be little inclination to enforce proper management of the marine reserve. Another obstacle to sound management of the reserve is the fact that in 2003 the fishing cooperative was split into two sections for reasons of partisan political rivalries and other internal considerations.

Change at the state government level is another obstacle to collaborative management of the marine reserve, because it allows for no continuity in the process, and incoming representatives are unfamiliar with the social issues at stake in protected areas.

Discussion and outlook

How can we summarise the 10-year history of this local initiative for a protected marine area? We may distinguish three broad stages in this initiative, which are closely linked to the internal characteristics of the community and to external institutional relations. The first stage was that of the reserve's establishment (1990–95) without any external involvement or financing. The second stage covers the high point of the reserve's history (1995–2001), a period marked by strong municipal government support and good relations with the fishing cooperative. At that time, family ties were very close between the two representatives of these institutions. This period witnessed community recognition of collective benefits, the search for external funding for enforcement activities, and visible returns through the restocking of marine species. The stagnation stage (2002–04) has seen disorganisation in the cooperative in charge of management (for example, this was the first time a reserve was being divided into two sections), the arrival of poachers who lay out their nets by night, a lack of understanding among the two key authorities in the community (the municipal president and the president of the fishing cooperative), and the failure of the Fuerzas Vivas to make successful trade-offs.

The local benefits of control over the reserve and the need to maintain it are accepted by fishers of the cooperative, who account for 80 per cent of the permanent fishing population in the area. However, these people are also faced with new circumstances. They have to ready the reserve to receive sport-fishing tourists, now that hotel owners, primarily in Cancún, have made arrangements to assure a steady stream of visitors. Here again, the focus is shifting from a community interest to a monetary interest in conservation, according to local informants.

In June 2003, a start was made at decentralising control over the reserve through the proposed Marine Reserve Committee. In March 2004, that committee, consisting of two representatives of each of the community's producer organisations, obtained registration as an NGO. This process has been supported by the municipality but not by the cooperative itself, because there are two camps within the cooperative: those who approve decentralisation and those, essentially the directors, who do not. Faced with this situation, we must take account of the following elements for a more in-depth analysis of the future outlook for the reserve:

- a still incomplete process of decentralising the reserve (cooperative versus community);
- recognition of the area's tourism potential if it is maintained as a marine reserve;
- the demand for participation by other stakeholders (independent fishers and members of the women's cooperative) in patrolling the reserve;
- the need for financing for alternative activities to fishing; and
- the demand for a new representative structure, despite the new committee created in 2003.

Governments—municipal, state, and federal—are facing diverse situations and interests with respect to protection and conservation of resources. In the particular case of the marine reserve, the problem is appreciated from different perspectives. Some are short-term, and there are conflicting interpretations and perceptions of the laws that have been issued.

When examining natural protected areas, this Mexican case reflects the need to take account of the social relationships existing between the inhabitants of the communities and the different interests relating to use and management of resources. In the following paragraphs, we shall examine a case in Cuba and the similarities and unique features that exist there, given the social and political structure of the island.

COMMUNITY AND MARINE PARK ON THE ISLA DE LA JUVENTUD, CUBA
(Jorge Ángulo, Rodney Borrego, and Reynaldo Borrego)

In Cuba, our area of study was the National Marine Park of Punta Frances (PNMPF), located on the Isla de la Juventud. This area has been designated for recreational scuba diving since 1976, when it was placed under a special regime of use and protection by the Ministry of Fisheries (MIP). Adjacent to the Park is the coastal community of Cocodrilo, founded at the beginning of the last century. It has remained in splendid isolation since then because of its geographic location.

The objective of this study was to evaluate the real and potential benefits the park brings to the community. To this end, we worked with secondary information sources and qualitative interviews involving community members, including the president of the community, the official historian, and the general public, in addition to various government representatives of the zone. Through these interviews, we were able to ascertain that under the current conditions in the community of Cocodrilo, the people feel no sense of ownership over the resources of the PNMPF. In addition, they receive no direct benefits from it of any kind. We propose some possible routes for resolving this problem.

Isla de la Juventud

Since 1976, the area around Punta Frances has been a national marine park, with management category APRM (managed resource protected area). It has been used for tourism purposes by the Ministry of Tourism; therefore it has been subject to special conditions governing its use and protection. The region contains special natural features that make it one of the principal tourist destinations in the country for observational scuba diving (Gonzalez-Sanson, Breton, andOvares, 2002).

Although this marine area has been subject to some form of protection for a long time, it is not legally recognised as a national marine park. Instead it is a 'zone under special use and protection' (Resolution 560 of the Ministry of Fisheries, December 24, 1996). That resolution merely regulates commercial and sport fishing activities, while other primarily tourism-related activities conducted in the zone fall outside its purview. This has led to conflicts between park uses and users that have become very evident in recent years, and there are fears that the environmental impact will increase in the near future. This means that it is essential to take specific measures to protect the integrity of the marine and land ecosystems in the zone and assure proper management of this MPA as an instrument for conservation and rational use of coastal resources (Bohnsack 1993; Bohnsack and Ault 1996; UNEP 1996; Agardy 1997; Mascia 1999).

Community of Cocodrilo

One of the most interesting aspects of this research project was the coastal community of Cocodrilo, which stands isolated on the southwestern shore of the Isla de la Juventud, approximately 20 km from the PNMPF and 100 km from Nueva Gerona, the municipal capital (see Table 4). Cocodrilo was established at the beginning of the twentieth century with the arrival of fortune seekers from Jamaica and the Cayman Islands, and it remains the only human settlement on the southern portion of the island. Thus, it is socially isolated. One of the first settlers was Atkins Jackson, who came there with his family. The place was originally known as Jacksonville, but the name was changed to Cocodrilo (crocodile). For many years the village was inhabited by English-speaking people who introduced their customs and their culture, and who lived essentially from catching fish and sea turtles and exploiting the land. Some examples of these early settlers' typical architecture and their subsistence economy are still preserved.

The community currently has a population of 308: 135 females and 173 males. The working-age population numbers 174 (90 men and 84 women). Of these, 106 are actively employed, representing 60 per cent of the workforce. The community includes 93 children and adolescents. Although the employment level is high, it is still a struggle to strengthen people's working links. Attempts are being made to develop new sources of employment. It is the women who are most affected by unemployment. A total of 34 women are working, representing only 19 per cent of the working-age population (Tenenbaum, Jeréz, Pillar, Portilla and Cruz 1998; National Centre for Protected Areas 2001).

The community is represented within the Cuban system of government through the People's Council of Cocodrilo. It is chaired by a delegate who is elected democratically from among the inhabitants of the zone, and who is responsible for representing the community and conducting all dealings with the government. Therefore, the president of the council is closely involved in all aspects of efforts to achieve social and economic development. As well, there are a number of political and mass-action organisations that effectively unite collective efforts and guarantee proper use of the material and financial resources received from the territorial government. These organisations include the Federation of Cuban Women, the neighbourhood

Committee for Defence of the Revolution, the Union of Young Communists, and the children's Pioneers Organisation. In their dealings with the government, community delegates are held accountable to the voters for their performance. Public meetings are held at which people set out the basic problems of the community and demand or propose solutions. The majority of the population thinks highly of this form of government, on the whole, as was made clear during our interviews. The country's difficult economic situation is an obstacle to achieving improvements in the community over the short term.

Farming and fishing are the principal sources of employment; other opportunities include forestry and the production of charcoal, as well as plant and wildlife conservation. Farming output has improved since the farming cooperative was revived; this has brought about a notable increase in the food supply for the community. Efforts are being made to establish a goat farm to increase the supply of fresh milk and meat. There is a fishing cooperative, which constitutes the principal source of employment in the community. The catch has remained quite stable despite the deteriorated state of the boats and the lack of electricity and drinking water in the cooperative's facilities. The men fish in pairs, setting out in the morning and returning at dusk. Because of the condition of the boats, fishers see very little possibility of moving to better fishing grounds. The methods used to catch fish include hook and line, drift nets, fish cages, and paternoster lines; turtles are taken with nets.

The entire catch is purchased by the cooperative directly from the fishers at prices established nationwide by the MIP. The payment scheme for fish provides fishers with a bonus in freely convertible currency (US dollars), which amounts to 20 per cent of the value of the catch. This payment mechanism operates nationwide and could promote community development. However, being the only human settlement on the south shore of the island, Cocodrilo is an isolated entity and so receives a high state subsidy in staple products. If working conditions could be improved (for instance, through better boats and refrigerated storage facilities), the fishing families of Cocodrilo could see their purchasing power increase significantly, and their economic well-being would rise accordingly.

An important element in this community, and one that merits special mention, is the fact that turtles are being caught. International regulations are in place that prohibit the fishing and marketing of these endangered species. In fact, Cocodrilo is the only place in Cuba, and among the few places in the Caribbean, where it is permitted to take turtles, which are consumed locally as a traditional food. In the case of the hawksbill or Carey turtle (*Eretmochelys imbricata*), both its meat and its shell are used. The shells are graded, tagged, and shipped to Havana for storage with a view to future marketing, if approval can be secured from the Convention on International Trade in Endangered Species (CITES). The fishers receive 110 Cuban pesos per ton of loggerhead or caguama turtle (*Caretta caretta*), 200 pesos per ton of green turtle (*Chelonia mydas*) and 590 pesos per ton of hawksbill. The fishers do not receive any US dollar bonus for turtles.

The community has a sea turtle nursery that belongs to the MIP and is the only one of its kind in the country. Its objective is to contribute to conservation of the species by reducing natural mortality in the early stages of development. Newly hatched turtles are collected on nearby beaches and transferred to the nursery where they are kept in tanks until they are three years old. During this time, they receive special care until they are released to the wild. The facility provides employment for local inhabitants, and is considered a potential tourist attraction that could draw visitors to the community.

Because of the high priority that Cuba places on public health and education, the inhabitants enjoy free and full access to these services. This is no doubt a very favourable element for the community's development, since basic living needs are covered by the Cuban Government.

There are three nearby electric generating plants. Current average consumption is 13 kilowatt-hour, and in November of last year, service became available 24 hours a day. Previously there was power for only nine hours a day during the week and 12 hours a day on weekends. Much is made of the use of alternative energy sources. In this case, the family medical clinic and the school are powered with photovoltaic panels, guaranteeing that medical and educational services are always available.

Discussion and outlook

One of the most widely used arguments for creating MPAs around the world is that it will produce both direct and indirect benefits to coastal communities (Russ and Alcala 1994; Kelleher, Bleakley and Wells 1995; Lauck, Clarke, Mangel and Munro 1998; Boersma and Parrish 1999; Suman,

Shivlani and Milon 1999; Hatcher 1999; Nowlis and Roberts 1999; Roberts, Bohnsack, Gell Hawkins and Goodridge 2001). Yet there are few practical examples to support such an argument. The case at hand represents a practical example that does not in fact fit with the initial hypothesis.

Before 1976, the Punta Frances area was used freely and without restrictions by the community of Cocodrilo, whose members took advantage of its opportunities for recreation and enjoyment. The area's natural beauty attracted local visitors and outsiders who, despite the poor state of the access road, would come for camping. Another use, although on a much smaller scale, was fishing, because the entire island shelf is very rich in species of commercial interest. Punta Frances was also famous as a highly productive breeding ground for pelagic species.

In 1976, limits were placed on access to Punta Frances with a view to conserving the area and devoting it to tourism uses. This decision was made because the area's superb natural features made it one of the country's best destinations for recreational scuba diving. With the decision to preserve the area, fishing was banned, and this affected fishers not only from Cocodrilo but also from other provinces who relied on this fishing ground. The situation resulted in a sharp dispute between the International Scuba Diving Centre of the Colony Hotel (the agency responsible for tourism operations in the area) and the MIP.

During the 1980s this dispute was exacerbated to the point where an accord had to be struck between the parties. To this end the MIP issued Resolution 273/85 which, while it placed partial limits on fishing activity, did not resolve the problem, because it allowed the use of unselective mass-catch techniques in areas adjacent to Punta Frances. In 1995, international diving groups and individuals issued a call for more effective protection of the zone. It was then decided that the Ministry of Science, Technology and Environment (CITMA) should take over the matter and create a multidisciplinary group to analyse and resolve the problem. As a result of CITMA's efforts, the following was agreed:

- to recommend to the National Centre for Protected Areas (CNAP) and the Environment Unit (UMA) of the Isla de la Juventud the creation of the PNMPF and adoption of an operations management plan;

- to have the MIP revise its fishery regulations for the area;
- to have the Ministry of Tourism publish diving regulations for the area; and
- to make the UMA responsible for drawing up a set of regulations for the area and enforcing them.

All of these agreements have been fulfilled except for the first, which is still at the government approval stage. As noted earlier, the zone is legally recognised in MIP Resolution 560/1996.

Despite good intentions and interest in resolving the problem, there is a critical element missing that leaps to view. In the make-up of the multidisciplinary team created by the CITMA, there was no direct representation from the community of Cocodrilo, meaning that its interests in the area were not considered. This oversight contributed to the current feeling of indifference towards the park among the inhabitants of Cocodrilo.

Indeed, from the interviews we conducted, we can say there is no significant interaction between the PNMPF and the community of Cocodrilo. On the contrary, local residents referred to it as a 'no-go zone' where all access is banned, and from which they derive no benefit of any kind. We heard expressions like 'I didn't know that was a park', 'I have no interest in visiting it', and 'I don't see that it's going to bring us any benefits.' If this situation is to be reversed, these views must be taken into account by those who have to make decisions about the local and regional environments.

Another interesting aspect that emerged from interviews was that the local inhabitants recognised that their limited vocational training was a major obstacle to finding employment in the park. Currently, there are only three people with post-secondary education in the community, one of whom used to work in the park but no longer does so. Nonetheless, on several occasions people have been brought in from other places to do work that could just as well be performed by inhabitants of Cocodrilo.

Although there is a pronounced indifference towards the park among local inhabitants, some of them can see potential benefits for the community. These are both economic and non-economic. Economic benefits include the possibility of jobs, the provision of goods and services to tourists visiting the park, and fishery benefits through the use of resources from the open sea that are not covered by Cuba's fisheries regulations. As mentioned,

Punta Frances contains splendid fishing areas for pelagic species. Non-economic benefits include the establishment of relationships with new people from other places, thereby increasing cultural cross-fertilisation (this is especially important, given the community's historic isolation) as well as raising local people's cultural awareness, and the strengthening of their sense of ownership and custody over the natural treasures of the PNMPF. Such exposure will reinforce traditional values and pride in their history and culture among community inhabitants, and will help them transmit these to other places and people. In this connection, we could see that the inhabitants were very proud that their community was free of social problems such as drugs, prostitution, and crime. Many pointed out that people in the community leave their doors unlocked.

It was also interesting to note the consensus among community members that the current system of government is the best one for resolving the problems currently affecting them. Most of the people we interviewed called for making better use of existing tools. They referred to those political and mass-action organisations which they felt could focus efforts on reducing tensions between the park and the community. One option that emerged from this project was the creation of a pro-nature group in Cocodrilo. Funding for it was received from the Cuban NGO Pro-Naturaleza, and it is hoped that the group will serve as a catalyst for reconciling the PNMPF and the community of Cocodrilo.

In conclusion, under current circumstances, the community of Cocodrilo feels no sense of ownership over the resources of the PNMPF, and receives no direct benefits of any kind from the park. We believe that the decision to protect this marine area should have been worked out in consultation with the community, given its interests in the area. Had this been done, today the community of Cocodrilo would enjoy better living conditions and could set a good example for other coastal communities in the Caribbean in terms of the benefits of establishing an MPA.

FISHING COMMUNITIES IN THE JARAGUA NATIONAL PARK, DOMINICAN REPUBLIC
(Yvonne Arias, Ernst Rupp, Jeannette Mateo, Víctor Gómez, and Milton Haughton)

This case study focuses on the socioeconomic characteristics of local stakeholders and of the fishing activity itself, which relates primarily to the species *Strombus gigas,* the pink or queen conch (known locally as 'lambí'), in the Jaragua National Park. Our study looks at existing legal mechanisms, threats, characteristics of the park, some features of the fishing communities, and the outlook for management of the coastal marine zone. We used interviews with fishers, conch merchants, and women who are involved in the conch business, as well as the authorities and key stakeholders in the fishery. We evaluated levels of knowledge about the conch and perceptions about the institutional setting surrounding the fishery. We administered a total of 79 questionnaires to collect socioeconomic data and information on the fishery.

Jaragua National Park

The zone where the Jaragua National Park is located was formerly known as the Cacicazgo of Xaraguá, which was ruled by the Cacique (or 'strongman') Guarocuya, who was one of the most important leaders of the Taino. The area was used for the fishing of conch, among other resources. Vestiges of this activity can be seen in the thousands of shells in the *concheros,* conch deposits. A particular feature of the *concheros* is the circular opening in each shell, through which the meat was extracted.

The zone has always been considered of high conservation value because of its biological diversity, because it is a refuge for endangered species, and because its fishery holds great scientific and commercial interest. It is also a strategic military zone, with a navy base on Beata Island. With its great concentration of seagulls, the island of Alto Velo was once a major source of guano, which was extracted and exported. The geological features of the park are such that there are no significant human settlements, for the thickness of the vegetation and the poor quality of the soil made it inhospitable to humans. Therefore, the forest cover of the protected area is intact and in a very good state of conservation.

The park was established on August 11, 1983, via Presidential Decree 1315. All the technical steps necessary to its establishment were taken, in terms of surveying its natural, cultural, and economic resources. Social conflicts were identified using a multisectoral and interdisciplinary participatory approach. Since its creation in 1983, it has faced continuous threats from proposed subdivision of its lands, primarily along the coastal area, to meet private demands of the tourist industry. The park is located in the southwestern part of the Dominican Republic, in the Enriquillo region in the province of Pedernales, with geographic coordinates 17.47° N to 17.97° N and 71.27° W to 71.73° W. It has a total area of 1,374 km^2, of which the coastal marine zone embraces 905 km^2. This circumstance makes it one of the largest protected areas in the Caribbean. It occupies the southern portion of the Barahona Peninsula, and includes within its boundaries the islands of Beata and Alto Velo, as well as the Los Frailes and Piedra Negra cays.

Along with its buffer zone, Jaragua National Park constitutes one of the few remaining areas of pristine Antillean wild lands, particularly those occurring in arid and coastal-marine ecosystems. The park protects a unique sample of numerous ecosystems belonging to important biogeographic provinces of Hispaniola, which have served as centres of plant and animal speciation and dissemination for the Antilles. It possesses twelve types of terrestrial plant associations. Its ecosystems include beaches, rocky coastlines, wetlands, seagrass meadows, coral reefs, cays, and islands. The park's unique flora and fauna present high levels of endemism, at both the species and the higher taxa levels.

The pristine white sandy beaches, such as those of the Bahia de las Agilas and Trudillé, and the wetlands offer incomparable scenic vistas, as do the rocky cliffs along the mainland and on Beata Island. The park represents one of the most significant habitats for *in situ* conservation of biodiversity in the Caribbean. It represents the only protected portion of coastal marine lowlands of the 'South Paleoisland,' an ancient division of Hispaniola. Some of the most extensive and best-preserved seagrass meadows of the region are found within this park's marine ecosystems. These support several wildlife species that are threatened or of commercial importance. In other words, the best-preserved reefs in the Caribbean are to be found in its waters.[8]

Research techniques

This study focused on fishing communities and their activities, primarily conch harvesting, at five fishery sites in the Jaragua National Park. We conducted interviews with fishers, conch merchants, and women involved in the conch business, as well as with the authorities and key stakeholders in the fishery. We evaluated levels of knowledge about the conch and perceptions about the institutional framework that governs the fishery.

To collect socioeconomic data and information on the fishery, we conducted a total of 79 semi-structured interviews with conch fishers in five communities in or adjacent to the Jaragua National Park: Pedernales, La Cueva, Trudillé, Piti Cabo, and Beata Island. These interviews were conducted between September 2002 and April 2003. Using the key-informant interview technique, we interviewed the six biggest conch merchants in the community of Pedernales, the main port of departure for fishing in the zone. We performed a strengths, weaknesses, opportunities, and threats (SWOT) analysis with a focus group consisting of ten people, including the major conch merchants and fishers. We interviewed seven women –the only females involved directly in the conch business—between January and May 2003, in the communities of Manuel Goya, La Cueva, La Colonia, and Trudillé.

The park's fishing communities

One feature of the communities that are economically involved in the park is that they are located both within the park and in its immediate vicinity. As explained earlier in this chapter, this meant we had to adopt a flexible notion of what constitutes a community, since most of the settlements consist of fishing camps that have no real legal status. Pedernales, the major permanent marketing point for park products, stands on the frontier with Haiti, and La Cueva, Trudillé, Beata Island, and Piti Cabo are secondary points with seasonally shifting populations.

The fishers lead a very precarious existence, with no basic services of any kind, living in dwellings made of palm fronds, with sand floors. Because it is impossible to live as a family unit within the park, fishers are separated from their families, which are generally headed by the mother and dwell in villages far from the fishing encampments. More than half of the fishers are single and they move from one camp to another, depending on the fishing prospects. Family settlement is strictly prohibited on Beata Island, which is considered a strategic military site and has a permanent naval base.

Most of the conch fishers are between the ages of 20 and 40 years, and about half have no primary education. Nearly all are self-taught divers who previously worked at lowlier occupations as cleaners, porters, cooks, and fishing crew.

Conch fishing generally involves diving, with or without air tanks. The necessary equipment includes a harpoon, a mask, flippers, a sack, a hook, and a diaphragm for scuba diving or a snorkel for skin diving (Tejeda 1995). The compressor used in conch fishing is of the kind built for painting automobiles. The divers generally descend from boats made of fibreglass. Most fishers claim they are aware of the risks of scuba diving and have experienced the bends, or know of others who have suffered decompression accidents. However, these incidents do not seem to be tabulated, and other accidents, such as compressor failure or attacks by sea creatures, are rare.

The Enriquillo region is considered one of the most biologically diverse in Hispaniola. Like the park, it is located in the province of Pedernales—the most desperately poor province in the country. A fisherman's net income varies greatly from one year or fishing season to the next. In all cases, proceeds are shared between the fisher and his helper, in more or less fixed proportions. Nonetheless, fishers feel that despite the risks inherent in their livelihood, they earn more and enjoy greater independence than do the poverty-stricken people in the communities from which they come.

Discussion and outlook

At least in legal terms, the coastal marine resources of the Dominican Republic are in the midst of a period of transition that threatens them with a fragmentation which has no scientific basis.

Governance is highly complex, because so many government institutions are involved: the Ministry of Environment and Natural Resources (Departments of Protected Areas and Biodiversity, and Coastal Marine Resources), the armed forces (the Navy), which field the park wardens and inspectors, and other authorities such as the local mayors. The resulting overlap of functions and lack of coordination, coupled with the scarcity of human, logistic, and economic resources, provides no guarantee of effective management.

Among the elements that must be taken into account in planning for effective management are the growing number of fishers (estimated in 1997 at 500, associated with 20 fishing stations), encroachment into conch breeding areas, health risks facing the fishers, their lack of experience in other fields, the absence of alternatives, the low degree of involvement of key stakeholders in management decisions, the failure of fishers to form cooperatives or associations, and the lack of systematic records that would allow lessons to be drawn from previous experience.

The proposals emanated from studies conducted during the 1990s associated with Artisanal Fishery (PROPESCAR), along with several projects under the authority of the Coastal Marine Biodiversity Conservation, which included the Global Environment Facility (GEF) and UNDP. As well, results from other scientific studies could provide valuable input for the planning and management of the resource—provided that the opinions of local merchants and fishers are considered. These local people must be involved in designing a permanent mechanism for exchanging high-quality information as the basis for managing and settling disputes.

Conclusion

This summary of the three cases proves that communities play varying roles in the management and conservation of MPAs. This concluding summation offers the reader an opportunity to consider the questions posed earlier, in the comparative table of the three countries, and to delve further into what is becoming a crucial issue in the Caribbean.

The three case studies used different levels of analysis to portray the community dynamics that must be taken into account in any relationship between people and natural protected areas. The social, cultural, economic, demographic, and political characteristics of the communities are in constant flux. Social changes often come swiftly, and any management plan that proposes a protected area must allow for flexibility in deciding the proper use of the area under protection.

It is essential to take into account the characteristics of the communities before attempting any management activity, bearing in mind that the Caribbean is the setting for many economic and ecological interests in the conservation of marine and coastal resources. The wealth of landscapes, wildlife, and biological diversity make the Caribbean a priority region for pooling efforts to achieve economic development that is compatible with the conservation of coastal resources.

These three case studies show that tourism is slowly displacing fishing as a source of livelihood. In the case of San Felipe, the Actan Chuleb Marine Reserve, which was established for conservation purposes by the fishers themselves and where taking is either banned or conditional, is becoming an area of tourism interest, primarily for sport fishing. In the Cuban case, the tourism interest is much more evident and has a longer history than in San Felipe. However, in contrast to San Felipe, the community of Cocodrilo receives no direct benefits from being a protected area. The Jaragua Marine Park in the Dominican Republic was created in 1983 with a view to incipient tourism. However, today its management is focused on attracting an 'outside' or tourist clientele with no benefits for the local users, since they do not even have the legal right to establish permanent communities within the park.

As these three case studies show, Caribbean communities exhibit great heterogeneity: the populations are different in their ethnic composition and their size, and also in the role that stakeholders play with others on the business and government fronts.

The fishers of Cuba are dependent on the central government for their use of and access to fishery resources, and they rely on a cooperative to sell their output at preferential prices. Fishers in the Dominican Republic and in Mexico are highly dependent on one or a few private merchants. The relationship between fishing and MPAs must take account of the varying size of those areas and the timing of the decree establishing them. In the case of Actan Chuleb Marine Reserve, which was created in 1995 with only 30 km^2 set aside, people feel that the zone is highly productive because it is a natural spawning ground for fish. As well, by setting and enforcing their own rules they have gradually turned the zone into a place that works to their benefit. By contrast, in both Cuba (where the reserve dates from 1996) and the Dominican Republic (where a national park was created in 1983 and a biosphere reserve in 2002), the relationship is more diffuse, and actually foreign to the objectives of conservation.

This area of study is very vulnerable to social conflicts over the use of and access to resources and land. Part of the vulnerability stems from the mobility of the local population in search of the means of subsistence, especially in

Jaragua, because it is in a frontier zone. Against this backdrop, the legality of conservation efforts (management plans and land-use ordinances) is a point of potential conflict, particularly if stakeholders are excluded from taking decisions for collaborative management of the resources. The technical viewpoint continues to prevail in ecological planning, even in the Cuban case. The three countries are caught up in the international conservation movement, which has a clear top-down focus, and although Cuba has a community participation model, it is not being applied to conservation policy in protected areas. We can see this in the case of the Punta Frances Marine Park, where local people indicated that they did not know it was a park and that they saw no benefits accruing to them from its status as a park.

Another element that emerges from these case studies is that the protected areas exist only on paper: there is no assured financing or any involvement of local residents in their management plans. In San Felipe, the intent was to create a marine area without government involvement, subjecting it to community rules. However, there was little hope of success because the state is responsible for conservation. Thus, conservation is in the hands of outside agents who are unable to forge a clear understanding between local users and the administrators of the resources. In our interviews in June 2004, the state government authorities proposed that this marine area should be decreed a 'core zone' of the Dzilam Bravo State Reserve, created in 1989. This term and the 'restricted use area' term (previously proposed) are in conflict because their scope is not understood and because they represent a legal notion that clashes with the daily concerns of stakeholders.

One of the clearest trends that we observed in the case studies is that marketing of these areas for tourism is outside the control of the local communities. With this 'invasion' of uses for a mobile market, there is no guarantee that the Caribbean communities will rebound. They will never again be the same, whatever the ability of their inhabitants to perform the economic activities that the global market is imposing on them.

Notes

1. The first marine protected area in the United States was Fort Jefferson National Monument in Florida, established in 1935.
2. These are areas set aside to preserve representative natural environments; to ensure sustainable use of ecosystems; to provide a suitable field for scientific

research; to generate, retrieve, and disseminate traditional knowledge and practices for sustainable use of ecosystems; and to protect the natural surroundings of zones, monuments, and archaeological sites of historic or artistic interest.

3. Articles 5 and 7 of LGEEPA established eight management categories for protected areas: biosphere reserves, national parks, natural monuments, natural resource protection areas, flora and fauna protection areas, sanctuaries, state parks and reserves, and urban ecological preservation zones.
4. The Environment Ministry lists 22 biosphere reserves, 33 national parks, 4 natural monuments, 2 natural resource protection zones, 26 flora and fauna protection areas, 17 sanctuaries, and a significant number of state reserves and urban preservation areas (www.semarnat.gob.mx).
5. The Yucatán Peninsula is home to a number of Natural Protected Areas. Seven biosphere reserves were decreed between 1986 and 2000: Reefs of Sian Ka'an, Banco Chinchorro, Calakmul, Ría Celestún, Ría Lagartos, Los Petenes, and Reserve of Sian Ka'an. Six national parks were decreed between 1987 and 2000: Arrecife Alacranes, Arrecifes de Cozumel, Costa Occidental de Isla Mujeres, Punta Cancún y Punta Nizuc, Arrecife de Xcalak, Arrecife de Puerto Morelos, and Parque Nacional de Dzibichaltún. Two flora and fauna areas were decreed in 1994: Laguna de Términos and Yum Balám. Two sanctuaries were created on October 26, 1986: a beach adjacent to Rio Lagartos Playa, and Isla Contoy Beach.
6. We understand institutions as 'regularised social patterns' that emerge from a set of structures or rules in use (Leach, Mearns and Scoones 1999).
7. During our interviews in April 2004, local stakeholders declared that there was a growing lack of interest in patrolling the reserve, compared to the early 1990s. 'Now there is fishing in the reserve and it's not like it was when people took care of it. Then there was conservation, now the only interest is money.'
8. The National System of Protected Areas is currently covered by the framework of Law 64–00. The Sectoral Law on Protected Areas was submitted by the Ministry of Environment and Natural Resources to the National Congress in 2002. In April 2004 the Senate, responding to demands that marine coastal areas should be used for conventional tourism, approved amendments to the Draft Sectoral Law on Protected Areas to exclude major coastal areas of the national parks. That bill is currently under debate, following observations from the executive branch, and the coastal zones of these two national parks thus remain at risk.

References

Agardy, T.S. 1997. *Marine protected areas and ocean conservation.* Austin: R.G. Tandes and Academic Press.

Barzetti, V. 1993. *Parks and progress.* Washington, DC: IUCN-IDB.

Biocenosis, A.C. 1999. *Plan de manejo de la reserva ecológica Dzilám Bravo.* Mérida, Mexico: Secretaria de Ecología del Gobierno del Estado de Yucatan.

Boersma, P.D., and J.K. Parrish. 1999. Limiting abuse: Marine protected areas, a limited solution. *Ecological Economics* 31: 287–304.

Bohnsack, J.A. 1993. Marine reserves: They enhance fisheries, reduce conflicts, and protect resources. *Oceanus* 36: 63–71.

Bohnsack, J.A., and J.S. Ault. 1996. Management strategies to conserve marine biodiversity. *Oceanography* 9(1): 73–82.

Chuenpagdee, Ratana., J. Fraga Berdugo, and J. Eúan-Ávila. 2002. Community perspectives toward a marine reserve: A case study of San Felipe, Yucatán, México. *Coastal Management* 30: 183–91.

———. 2004. Progressing toward co-management through participatory research. *Society and Natural Resources* 17: 147–61.

CONAPO-CINVESTAV. 1987. *Sistema de ciudades de Yucatán.* Mérida, Mexico: Yucatán Centro de Investigación y Estudios Avanzados del IPN, Unidad Mérida.

Cuba. Resolution 560. 1996. Declaring the Punta Francés area a 'Zone under Special Use and Protection'. December 24, 1996. Ministry of Fisheries.

———. Decree Law 201, on the National System of Protected Areas. December 23, 1999. Council of State of the Republic of Cuba.

Duhne, E. 2000. *Plan de manejo de la Reserva Ecológica Dzilám Bravo.* Mérida, Mexico: Secretaria de Ecología del Gobierno de Yucatán.

Eúan-Ávila J., J. Fraga Berdugo, et al. 2001. La reserva marina Actan Chuleb. Informe final del proyecto al IDRC, Fase 1. Mérida, Mexico: CINVESTAV.

Fraga Berdugo, J. 1992. El proceso de migración hacia la costa de Yucatán. In-house working paper on research project sponsored by the Asociación Mexicana de Estudios de Población and CINVESTAV. Unidad Mérida.

Fraga Berdugo, J., Euán, J. Torres, R. y Chuenpagdee, R. 2001. Reporte Final del Proyecto Manejo Comunitario de una Reserva Marina Protegida en San Felipe, Yucatán, México. Presentado al International Development Research Center, International Ocean Institute, CARICOM Fisheries Unit y Université Laval. Mérida, Yucatán (no publicado).

Fraga Berdugo, J., et al. 2002. Manejo comunitario de una reserva marina en San Felipe, México. In *Balance entre población y recursos. Investigación interdisciplinaria y manejo de areas costeras en el Gran Caribe.* IOI-CFU-LAVAL-IDRC. Heredia, Costa Rica: Editorial Fundación. UNA.

Garrido, D. 1991. *Diario de Yucatán*: Conflicto eterno: areas protegidas versus comunidades, 9 de Junio.

Gómez-Pompa, A., and R. Dirzo. 1995. Proyecto sobre las Areas Naturales Protegidas de México. Mexico City. Draft of an in-house working paper, SEMARNAP–University of California. Riverside-Centro de Ecología. UNAM.

González-Sansón, G., et al. 2002. Investigación orientada al establecimiento de un plan de manejo en el Parque Nacional Marino de Punta Francés, Cuba.

In *Balance entre población y recursos: investigación interdisciplinaria y manejo de áreas costeras en el Gran Caribe*. IOI-CFU-LAVAL-IDRC. Heredia, Costa Rica: Editorial Fundación UNA.

Halfter, G. 1981. The Paopimi Biosphere Reserve: Local participation in conservation and development. *Ambio* 10(2–3): 93–96.

Hatcher, B.G. 1999. Varieties of science for coral reef management. *Coral Reefs* 18: 305.

INEGI (Instituto Nacional de Geografía e Informática). 2000. Population and Housing Census. Mexico City.

INE-SEMARNAP. 1995-2000. Programa nacional de Areas Naturales Protegidas de México. México: Distrito Federal.

Kelleher, G., Bleakley, C., Wells, Sue 1995. *A Global representative system of marine protected areas*. Canberra: ACT, Australia; Washington, D.C.; Gland: Great Barrier Reef Marine Park Authority; World Bank; World Conservation Union..

Lauck, T., Clark, C., Mangel, M., and Munro, G. 1998. Implementing the precautionary principle in fisheries management through marine reserves. *Ecological Applications* 8(1): S72–S78.

Leach, M. Mearns, R. y Scoones, I. 1999. Environmental entitlements: Dynamics and institutions in community-based natural resource management. *World Development* 27: 225–47.

Mascia, B.B. 1999. Governance of marine protected areas in the Wider Caribbean: Preliminary results of an international mail survey. *Coastal Management* 27: 391–402.

Mexico. General Law on Ecological Balance and Protection of the Environment (LGEEPA). 1988. Mexico City (with amendments), January 7, 2000.

McNeely J., J. Harrison, and P. Dingwall. 1994. *Protecting nature*. Regional Reviews of Protected Areas. London, UK: UICN.

Municipio de San Felipe y Fuerzas Vivas del Puerto de San Felipe. 1997. Municipal decree on the Actam Chuleb Marine Reserve.

Nigh, R. 2001. Maya pasts, Maya futures: The reflexive consumption of nature and culture in Laguna Miramar, Chiapas. Paper presented at the Symposium on Marketing Culture and Nature: Tourism in the Maya World and Beyond, 61st Annual Meeting of the Society for Applied Anthropology, Merida, Yucatan, Mexico, 2001.

Nowlis, J.S., and C.M. Roberts. 1999. Fisheries benefits and optimal design of marine reserves. *Fisheries Bulletin* 97: 604–16.

Ortiz, E., E. Ortiz y J. Hirose. 1998. Grupo de trabajo de la Reserva Marina de Actam Chuleb Plan de Manejo del Refugio Marítimo "Actam Chuleb". Documento en revisión.

Pérez-Gil, R. 1993. Completing Mexico's protected forests system. In *Parks and Progress*, ed. V. Barzetti, 119–31. Washington, DC: IUCN-IDB.

Rist, G. 1996. *Le développement. Histoire d'une croyance occidentale*. Paris: Presses de la Fondation Nationale des Sciences Politiques.

Roberts, C., Bohnsack, J., Gell, F., Hawkins, J., Goodridge, R. 2001. Effects of marine

reserves on adjacent fisheries. *Science* 294: 1920-1923.

Russ, G., and A. Alcala. 1994. Sumillon Island Reserve: 20 years of hopes and frustrations. *NAGA, The ICLARM Quarterly.* 8–12.

SEMARNAP. 1997. Programa de manejo de reserva de la Biosfera Ria Lagartos, México. México: Instituto Nacional de Ecología.

Suman, D., Shivlani, M., Milon, W. 1999. Perceptions and attitudes regarding marine reserves: a comparison of stakeholder groups in the Florida Keys National Marine Sanctuary. *Coastal and Ocean Management* 42: 1019–40.

Tejeda, J. 1995. Evaluación de la pesquería de lambí (L.) *Strombus gigas* en el Parque Nacional Jaragua, 1992–1993, República Dominicana. Masters thesis.

Tenenbaum, A.; Jeréz, M.; Pilar, A.; Portilla, M. y Cruz, L. 1998. *Estrategia de desarrollo sostenible, comunidad de Cocodrilo. Delegación Territorial del Ministerio de Ciencias.* Tecnologías y Medio Ambiente. Isla de la Juventud.

UNEP. 1996. *Common guidelines and criteria for protected areas in the Wider Caribbean region: Identification, selection, establishment, and management.* CEP Technical Report No. 37. Kingston, Jamaica: UNEP Caribbean Environment Programme.

———. *Guidelines for integrated planning and management of coastal and marine areas in the wider Caribbean region.* Kingston, Jamaica: UNEP Caribbean Environment Programme.

5

Community Mobilisation and Education in Contaminated Coastal Ecosystems

Liliana M. Gómez, L. Ciro Marcano, Zulay Poggy, Maria Elena Castellanos Gonzalez, and Clara E. Miranda Vera

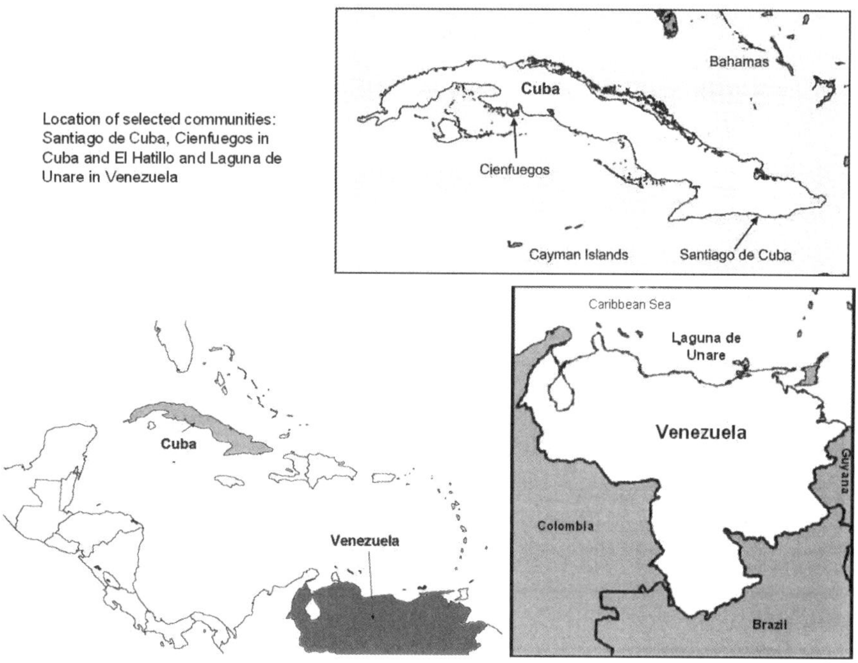

Figure 10
Location of selected communities

This chapter compares case studies of three Caribbean communities located within polluted coastal ecosystems—two bays in Cuba and a coastal lagoon in Venezuela—where environmental education programmes have been introduced. These have rallied community support in different ways, with particular focus on working with children and youth. In each case we conducted our studies using participatory research to strengthen local management. The chapter summarises the lessons learned from working with these three projects.

Bays and lagoons are among the most important coastal ecosystems because of the services they offer and because of their vulnerability. They are often regarded as estuarine systems, which, according to the most widely accepted definition, are coastal water bodies where communication with the open sea is limited and periodic. Population growth and economic expansion are placing increased pressure on these ecosystems. Activities such as fishing, trade, shipping, industrial development, and tourism, the establishment of new settlements, and the development of megacities have a direct impact on these zones, threatening swift and severe degradation along with loss of their natural resources. Large areas of lagoons and estuaries are being reclaimed, dredged, or filled for the creation of ports, town sites, and cultivable lands, in blatant disregard of the principles of sound management and a non-sectoral approach to coastal planning. This inevitably entails long-term economic losses. Indeed, such losses can make themselves felt in the very short term, as resources and ecosystems collapse.

These closed and semi-closed systems are especially vulnerable because of their limited surface area and shallow waters, the long hydraulic replenishment times involved, and the sizable population that derives its livelihood from their resources. They are subject to pressure from human activities and from natural processes and phenomena alike. Therefore, pollution is a recurring problem which is becoming more acute as human activities encroach on the system's threshold. It must be recognised, however, that coastal bays and lagoons differ in terms of their functionality. While bays are used as ports because of their geomorphological and operational characteristics, lagoons have great potential for aquaculture, fishing, and tourism. In addition, they are more affected by upstream activities in their tributary watershed. In most cases, the greatest contribution of pollutants comes from improper farming practices and urban and industrial development, as well as mining and port activities resulting from disorderly planning and unsuccessful management. If we want to bring positive change to the daily lives of the people involved and offer them comprehensive solutions, we must develop an understanding of the ecological functioning of these ecosystems. Also, we need to fully comprehend the economic activities that are taking place, including their particular social and political features.

This chapter presents a comparative study of efforts at community education and mobilisation for the purpose of restoring the quality of services from three polluted ecosystems in the Caribbean. The communities operate within very different political contexts: two bays located on the south coast of the island of Cuba, in the cities of Cienfuegos and Santiago; and the Laguna Unare in Venezuela. The study looks at the approach taken in each of the projects, the way the projects worked with and involved the community, the role of government institutions and industry, and the political context. There is single-party socialism in the Cuban case, and a highly polarised political climate within a capitalistic system in the case of Venezuela.

Contrasting Policy Approaches in Cuba and Venezuela

Legal arrangements and government policies

The effectiveness of any legal and institutional system will be influenced to a greater or lesser degree by the specific historical circumstances that prevail in the country. These refer to its political and socioeconomic regime; the political will to act decisively in environmental management and protection; the structure and organisation of government, legal, and regulatory provisions; and the traditions and customs ingrained in the society. Hence, proper environmental management necessarily requires administrative structures that can give reality to policies approved by government in this area, and to the commitments assumed vis-à-vis the international community. Given the need for integration identified above, special attention must be paid to a region's legal and institutional framework.

In the wake of coastal agreements and policies negotiated in the Caribbean, many countries have taken positive steps. Cuba and Venezuela are typical examples in terms of the impact that their economic activities have on coastal zones and their introduction of specific legislation to protect those zones. Our analysis starts from the basis that both countries exhibit great political diversity. Cuba has adopted a political system based on a unitary state and a single party, with a trend toward decentralisation in recent years, which is in line with the principle of public participation enshrined in the constitution. Venezuela has witnessed great political polarisation since 1998, and the current government is implementing new strategies in what amounts to a revolutionary plan involving a new concept of community participation in all public activities.

When it comes to environmental policies, Cuba issued an official document in 1997, entitled the National Environmental Strategy, which called for introduction of an Integrated Management System as the first step to preserving and restoring the coastal zone. With promulgation of the constitution on February 24, 1976, the environment became for the first time an official concern (article 27). In that same year, Law 1323, on Organisation of the Central Administration of the State, made the State Committee for Science and Technology responsible for establishing, directing, and overseeing the National System for Environmental Protection and the Rational Use of Natural Resources. A 1979 order of the Council of Ministers created the National Commission for Protection of the Environment and Conservation of Natural Resources, as the first step towards institutionalising the environmental sphere in the country. Decree-Law 147 of 1994, on Reorganisation of the Central Administration of the State, constituted a Ministry of Science, Technology and Environment (Centro de Estudios Ambientales de Cienfuegos, CITMA), transferring to it the powers and duties of the National Commission for Protection of the Environment and Rational Use of Natural Resources, which was thereby abolished. Subsequent amendments and regulations to Law 33 were issued, and in 1997 Law 81, the Environment Act, was approved establishing the Institutional Framework for the Cuban Environment (Article II). That law defines the powers of central government agencies as well as local agencies of the Poder Popular (Popular Councils), in an attempt to integrate the basic principles that must govern the design of an efficient and effective institutional system for the environment. It also defines the powers and functions of CITMA, making it the senior environmental agency and clarifying the structure of the system.

The great advantage is that CITMA is now represented in each province by provincial 'delegations', or centres, that can promote the required integrated approach to local management of coastal zones. Among the agencies and centres comprising that system are the ministries of fishing, tourism, agriculture, basic industry, interior, and transport, as well as the armed forces. Other government agencies involved include the Physical Planning Institute, the Environmental Information, Management and Education Centre, Environmental Control and Inspection Centre, National Centre for Protected Areas, and the National Centre for Scientific Research, among others. With this institutional and legal system in place, most of the environmental management instruments in Cuba now operate in accordance with article 18 (3) of the Environment Act. It stipulates that Cuban environmental policy must be implemented through sound management, using well-established instruments.

Venezuela possesses environmental legislation and regulations covering a broad range of aspects. However, environmental provisions are scattered and fragmentary. Attempts to apply them to the management of a specific geographic area have been frustrated by lack of consensus on the definition of management plans, or by lack of capacity to enforce them on the part of the responsible entities. The Ministry of Environment, created in 1976, is the government agency responsible for defining environmental protection policies and for administering certain laws and regulations. Like CITMA in Cuba, the ministry has offices in all states, which, in the most densely populated municipalities, deal with specific problems.

The guiding principles for environmental conservation, defence, and improvement as a means of raising living standards are contained in the 1976 Organic Law on the Environment. However, the definition of environmental crimes and their punishment are governed by the Environmental Crimes Law, promulgated in 1992. The environment law falls within the responsibility of the Ministry of Environment, and the criminal law falls to the judiciary, consisting of the Supreme Court of Justice and the country's other courts.

The biodiversity of all the country's ecosystems is protected by the Law on Biological Diversity of 2000, which sets out guiding principles for the conservation of biological diversity and its sustainable use in Venezuela. The municipalities have general responsibility for environmental protection, as well as for the related infrastructure and basic services, among which are sanitation, aqueducts, sewers, wastewater treatment, and electricity services. These activities are governed by the amendments to the 1989 Organic Law on Municipal Organisation. Despite this constitutional amendment, which gives the municipalities rights over the environment, and the changes to environmental regulations that occurred in Venezuela in 2000–01, most municipalities, including those located in coastal zones, have no municipal environmental bylaws (either general or specific) for giving effect to that change. Such bylaws are supposed to regulate activities that affect the environment, such as coastal fishing, construction, tourism, garbage disposal, and community participation. Thus, environmental management in Venezuela is not very effective, essentially because of factors such as duplication of functions, negligence on the part of public officials, lack of public awareness about the environment, little participation by the community in filing environmental complaints, the slowness of court proceedings in environmental cases, and the failure of the authorities to exert proper control.

Laws and regulations governing coastal ecosystems

In Cuba, Law 81 on the Environment was established as part of the institutionalisation process. It applies to environmental matters throughout the country, and has served as a point of departure for many regulations and decrees relating to the coastal zone and its resources, with a focus on integrated management. These include Decree Law 212 on Management and Protection of Coastal Zones, as well as others governing activities such as fishing, which is strictly regulated in the country. Coastal activities must be developed under the principles of sustainability, not only because this is in keeping with the demands of the international market but also because the country's legislation requires it. The legal foundation for the Integrated Management of Coastal Zones in Cuba empowers and requires all institutions, ministries, and government agencies to work in a coordinated and united manner to fulfill the legislation. This has undoubtedly contributed to the understanding and enforcement of coordinated policies, for which each ministry has specific rules. These provide legal support for any activity designed to raise living standards, as sustainable development itself demands. Nevertheless, this brings with it the risk of overlapping functions and responsibilities.

National laws and regulations are being put into effect in the bays of Cienfuegos and Santiago. One of the key agencies under this legal framework is the Office of Fisheries Inspection, through its provincial branches. Coordination among the sectors involved in management is of recent origin; as is the comprehensive treatment of disputes from a watershed focus, and problems of coordination among stakeholders still exist. These two ecosystems constitute an analytical priority for CITMA, the government, and for the national political leadership, and so concrete actions are underway at both the central and provincial levels. Nevertheless, fragmented and overlapping responsibilities for regulation, conservation, and resource management are common to both ecosystems.

Venezuela has a series of specific regulations governing aquatic spaces, overseen by the responsible state agencies. As in Cuba, there is inter-institutional coordination in defining policies and developing programmes. Yet instead of presidential decrees, Venezuela has a series of ordinary laws, decrees, and regulations for protecting coastal zones. The principal laws follow.

1. The 2001 Law on Coastal Zones governs the sustainable administration, use, and management of the zones.
2. The 2001 Fishing and Aquaculture Law defines general and specific policies for these economic activities and guarantees the right of people to fish and to participate effectively in government planning and policymaking in this area.
3. The 2001 General Law on Ports establishes guidelines for the system of ports and its infrastructure.
4. The 2001 Law on Aquatic and Insular Spaces asserts sovereignty and control over aquatic species in the country's rivers, seas, lagoons, bays, and lakes. It also covers sustainable planning and exploitation of water resources, and their biodiversity.

To enforce the new regulations on coastal zones, the Office for Coastal Management has been created within the Environmental Planning Directorate (although without adequate staffing or budget) to draw up a programme for coastal management, starting with a definition of the coastal zone. The National Fisheries Institute (INAPESCA), created in 2001, is responsible for orderly planning of the country's fishery and aquaculture resources, with a view to responsible and sustainable exploitation in accordance with the existing legal framework. It implements policies issued by the Ministry of Agriculture and Lands (INAPESCA 2004). The INAPESCA representative in the Laguna Unare also serves as the fisheries inspector for the area.

When it comes to environmental laws, there are some clear differences between the two countries. Venezuela is in the midst of a reorganisation and is only now taking initiatives for integrated management of coastal zones. In Cuba, the process is much more organised and has included new regulations and decrees that call for an integrated management approach for achieving sustainability. Yet the greatest difference between the two legal settings lies in the political structure, which, in Venezuela, is marked by a multiplicity of political players that has no doubt impeded progress towards sound policies. This is quite different from the situation in Cuba.

It should be noted, however, that the two countries have a similar paradigm concerning the state's relationship with the environment. Environmental management is seen as something that governments do on behalf of the citizens they claim to represent (Bryant and Wilson 1998). The state takes responsibility for the management of natural resources with a top-down focus that is based on the views of experts. The process is dominated by decisions based on scientific arguments and the implementation of technically viable solutions. Nevertheless, recent years have seen progress, both by the state and by the various social sectors, in terms of recognising the importance of traditional and local ecological knowledge. Efforts have been made to give power over local management to the communities that are the immediate users of ecosystems.

Heterogeneous Communities within Vulnerable Ecosystems

Ecosystems, resources, and economic activities

Cuba and Venezuela have an extraordinary wealth of natural resources, and there are complex interrelationships between natural and social systems in both countries. Fishery resources are among the most important associated with the bays and the lagoon falling under our study. As well, there is a significant interrelationship with major ecosystems in the region (mangrove swamps, pasturelands, coral reefs, and beaches) that support valuable commercial species such as mullet, bream, sea bass, red snapper, anchovy, lobster, conch, prawns, and turtles, and a diversity of coastal plants and wildlife with many endemic species. There are also valuable mineral resources, including iron, copper, nickel, manganese, chrome, salt, and calcium carbonate. All of this wealth exists side by side with the beauty of the landscape and the aesthetic enjoyment it produces. The main features of the communities are summarised in Table 6.

TABLE 6
MAIN FEATURES OF THE SELECTED COMMUNITIES

	O'Bourque	Cayo Granma	El Hatillo
Country	Cuba	Cuba	Venezuela
Location	Bahía de Cienfuegos	Bahía de Santiago de Cuba	State of Anzoategui, Central Venezuela
Population	1,300	748	1,564
Economy	Artisanal fishing, tourism, and public services	Artisanal and commercial fishing, tourism	Artisanal fishing and tourism
Other	Important industrial zone	Migration flows, important industrial zone	Negative economic impact of pollution

La Laguna de Unare (10.07°N–10.02°N and 65.14°W–65.02°W) is part of the Piritu-Unare coastal lagoon complex on Venezuela's western coastline, formed about 5,000 years ago (Roa 1991). It receives significant water inflow from the valley of the Unare River (22,450 km^2), as well as salt water from the Caribbean during periods when the mouths of the lagoon are open to the sea. Other rivers and streams of the Laguna Unare basin also provide water inflow. To a great extent, these hydraulic and marine dynamics determine the ecological conditions of the lagoon.

The lagoon completely dried up during the dry season (December–April) until the late 1970s. However, since 1980 the area has felt the effects from the construction of 14 dams upstream in the Unare Valley, which were built between 1964 and 1983. Now the lagoon has a more or less constant water surface (40–60 km^2) throughout the year. This hydraulic regularisation has had secondary effects such as gradual desalination of the lagoon, causing the invasion of freshwater species. These include cichlids, aleman or 'German' grass from upstream ranching country, and water hyacinth from the reservoirs; mosquitoes have also increased. The Laguna Unare is a reservoir for species that migrate between sea, river, and lagoon. Some of the most valuable commercial species are white shrimp (*Litopenaeus schmitti*), lebranche or Brazilian mullet (*Mugil lisa*), and white mullet (*Mugil curema*). The production of these has had a major economic impact, exceeding US$4 million annually (INIA 2003).

The lagoon fishery is artisanal: fishers use nets cast from small, low-powered outboard motorboats. The fishers manipulate the lagoon's hydraulics by opening the mouths of the Unare River and its two channels (the Mora and Nueva) through the isthmus which separates the lagoon from the sea. The ecosystem is also exploited by poachers who use illegal fishing equipment and methods, as well as by trawlers that frequently penetrate within the 9.75 km (6-mile) limit set for the artisanal fishery. Although their exact number is not known, it is estimated that there are some 500 fishers operating permanently in the lagoon, a figure that rises considerably during peak production times.

The Bay of Cienfuegos (or Jagua), is located in the south central portion of Cuba and is the most important local natural resource. The entire economic and social life of the region revolves around it, and it has influenced local traditions, customs, and legends since the nineteenth century. The shoreline and its attendant activities (such as fishing, beach activities, and scuba diving) are deeply rooted in Cienfuegos culture. The bay is nearly landlocked, being what is called a 'pocket bay', with a surface area of 88.46 km^2, a shoreline of 100 km, and a total volume of 1.84 km^3. It is 19 km long and 7.5 km at its widest point, with an average depth of roughly 9.5 m. Nature has divided it into two basins separated by a shoal (Las Cuevas) with an average depth of 1.5 m. This greatly influences water circulation within the ecosystem.

The access channel is narrow and tortuous, being 3.6 km long and between 30 and 50 m deep toward the middle. Its geography imposes limits on navigation because it forms a canyon containing coral reefs along with steeply eroded cliffs. Within the bay there are 50 promontories and 20 coves or inlets, three of which are used as shelter for small and mid-sized vessels during high winds. The most important coastal formations of the bay include rocky and sandy beaches, mangrove forests, marl deposits, sea grape groves, coastal scrubland (*manigua*), and dry bush. Vegetation is degraded in the eastern sector. The bay is dotted with 14 small islands or cays, the largest of which are Cayo Carenas, Cayo Ocampo, and Cayo Alcatraz (León et al. 2001).

This ecosystem exhibits estuarine characteristics and is strongly influenced by the seasonal flow of four rivers. During the rainy season (June to October) that flow dominates circulation and the bay becomes a highly stratified estuary. For the rest of the year, the influence of those rivers is minimal, and the waters of the bay reach oceanic degrees of salinity at around 30 to 32 per cent. The length of time water remains in the bay varies inversely with the flow of freshwater from the rivers and from precipitation. During the dry season, the flushing time is as long as 32 days, while in the rainy season it is reduced to seven, indicating that the bay has a high water-renewal capacity. Tide action is semidiurnal: there are two high tides and two low tides in 24 hours, with an average height of 25 cm. Winds are generally light, with an average speed of 2.5 m per second; the prevailing breeze is from the northeast in the morning and at night and from the south in the afternoon.

The third ecosystem—the bay of Santiago of Cuba—is located on the southern coast of the island's eastern region, in the central portion of the Basin (Cuenca) of Santiago de Cuba, at 19.97° N and 72.87° W. It was formed by subsidence along a north-running fault system that originated through tectonic erosion. It is a pocket bay with an extremely narrow mouth (225 m wide). The bay is 9 km long and 3 km at its greatest width. Its average depth is 8 m, and it is 21 m at its deepest point. The surface area is 11.9 km^2, its perimeter is 41.35 km, and the total volume of water is 90 million m^3. Its shoreline is highly irregular, marked by six inlets or coves, the largest of which is the Ensenada Miradero. There are two islands within the bay: Cayo Raton and the densely populated Cayo Granma. Tidal flow averages 3.5 million m^3 and the water is renewed only every 18 days, a rate that promotes pollution. This ecosystem receives inflow from five significantly polluted rivers: the volume of wastewater entering the ecosystem is approximately 3 million m^3 per day, while the volume of polluted rainwater is 110,000 m^3 per day (Gómez, Abrahantes, and Larduet 2001). In the middle of this setting stands Cayo Granma. Its physical context continues to be altered to accommodate living conditions along with facilities for agriculture, shipping, fishing, recreation, tourism, housing, energy resources, and other social needs. As a result, there are measurable and accelerating impacts upon Cayo Granma such as eutrophication, degradation, loss of habitat and species, and erosion of coastline and beaches.

The blue crab (*Callinectes sapidus*) is a valuable fishing resource that plays a great role in the community's identity. Its importance is symbolised by the community's trademark event: an annual crab-fishing contest called the *Carijai*, held every April. This event is widely covered by press and radio, and attracts children from the island and from nearby communities (Gómez et al. 2003).

The three ecosystems demonstrate the coexistence of different social and economic uses such as the preservation of nature, shipping and port activities, tourism and recreation, industrial development, urban areas, and fishing. Conflicts result in serious environmental problems such as pollution and sedimentation caused by the use of outdated and environmentally unfriendly technologies. There is little investment in environmental protection, and treatment plants are improperly used or defective, agricultural practices are inappropriate, and there is no integrated management of the watersheds that drain into the bays. These problems have been closely monitored and, in the case of Cienfuegos Bay, an integrated coastal resource management plan has been proposed to mitigate these conflicts. In Santiago, comprehensive efforts are being made to introduce proper management. However, it must be recognised that all of these conflicts stem from inadequately planned development that lacks a contextual and integrated vision. Sustainability is unachievable under these sorts of conditions.

Pollution and related problems

While there are some specific problems that affect each of the coastal zones we studied, it is pollution from various kinds of solid and liquid wastes that is the principal environmental issue common to the three ecosystems, and it is having multiple negative impacts on them. People must fully comprehend the environmental problem before actions can be started that will promote sustainable development. This means taking into account the existence and heterogeneity of coastal nations and cities, along with the characteristics of the industrial sector. It is one of the main sources of pollution in the coastal zone and has a sharp impact on natural resources and ecosystems of great ecological importance. Impacts include the conversion of mangrove swamps to agriculture and the attendant implications for the functioning of adjacent ecosystems. There are other environmental pressures, such as from tourism. There are also inherent risks in passenger and freight shipping, particularly the spilling of hydrocarbons and dumping of ballast, which introduce species of toxic phytoplankton. Other problems arise from erosion emanating from deforestation and improper management of farmlands, discharge of wastewater, wastes from domestic and industrial sources, and dumping of hazardous substances. Dumping is a particular concern because of the consequent increase in the concentration of heavy metals in the water column and sediments.

Heavy-metal pollution is an especially important aspect of the three ecosystems, particularly because its concentrations are increasing due to human activity. These substances are widely distributed, being used in a broad range of industrial and technical applications. Therefore, the problem is a consequence of industrial development.

Another major issue is population growth, which is generating a series of problems and conflicts of a socioenvironmental nature, including increased pollution and the depletion of resources. These exacerbate existing conflicts between various users and stakeholders, and introduce new conflicts. In the Caribbean region, the situation is particularly critical because coastal pollution problems are clearly associated with the lack of strategic development plans (Tran, Eúan-Ávila and Isla 2002) at the local, national, and regional levels, an issue that becomes even more complicated with the unequal distribution of resources and of economic opportunities for individuals. The communities we studied also exhibit some obvious social problems deriving from population growth. In many cases, these include cultural implications such as migration to suburban areas, which in turn generate conflicts between migrants and the local population. This phenomenon is clearly visible in Cayo Granma, where migration brings customs and habits more associated with rural farm life than with coastal living. During the course of several generations, conflicts over migration issues have evolved into conflicts of identity. Obviously, an analysis of pollution must start with industrial development and the accelerating process of urbanisation, with the consequent growth of cities and their demands.

In these three ecosystems there are problems such as the loss of biodiversity, imbalances, eutrophication and pollution of waters, introduction of exotic species, overfishing, degradation, loss of habitat, fallout from improper farming practices, and use of inappropriate fishing techniques. There is no evidence to show that communities established here are making sustainable use of natural resources, specifically coastal and marine resources, although there are some signs of a shift at the local level, where a few steps towards sensible practices are now underway. We may, however, refer to other specific problems that do not necessarily relate to pollution. For instance, Laguna Unare is a very rich ecosystem with great aesthetic value and available resources. Unfortunately it suffers from problems such as sedimentation, coastal erosion, disruption and loss of biodiversity, destruction of mangrove forests, and disruption of the hydraulic regime. In many cases, inadequate enforcement of environmental legislation does little to promote recovery or protection of the ecosystems. To this can be added poor planning of the fishery, overexploitation of resources, and problems in applying knowledge to natural resource management.

Although pollution is an important issue in all three ecosystems, the bays of Cienfuegos and Santiago are particularly exposed to nearby urban and suburban activities, and to continuing population growth because of migration sparked by the development of the provincial capital cities. In contrast, Laguna Unare is more influenced by inland activities in communities and areas remote from the ecosystem itself. The implication is that the limits of action must be carefully defined to achieve integrated management of the ecosystem. Strategies designed to enlist popular support through environmental education must take this situation into account.

Socioenvironmental diversity and community attitudes

Table 7 summarises the distinctive characteristics of the three ecosystems. There are some clear differences from the socioeconomic, cultural, political, and ecological viewpoints, and these have a defining impact on lifestyles, education approaches, and ways of doing things.

As noted earlier, when we were in Cuba we worked in two coastal communities located on major bays. Cayo Granma has 748 inhabitants and is particularly significant because its principal economic activity is not fishing. Instead, the people devote themselves to other activities, and many of them work outside the community. In all the studies we conducted, transportation proved to be a significant problem. This community stands in a setting greatly affected by industrial pollution, and it feels as though it is under siege and isolated because of its particular geographic features. O'Bourque is a somewhat larger community of 1,300 inhabitants located on the Bahia de Cienfuegos, which exhibits more of the features of an urban community.

In Laguna Unare, we worked with three communities. Ciudad Boca de Uchire (capital of the municipality of San Juan Capistrano) is a predominantly tourist community. In contrast, artisanal fishing is more important in the rural villages of La Cerca and El Hatillo, in the municipality of Peñalver. The population of the zone is predominantly Mestizo. Boca de Uchire, with 7,586 inhabitants (2001 INE Census), was founded in the sixteenth century and stands on the western shore of the lagoon beside the main highway that links Caracas with the eastern part of the country. El Hatillo and La Cerca are located to the east of the lagoon, on a portion of the Unare isthmus that separates the lagoon from the Caribbean Sea. El Hatillo was founded by migrants from the Isla de Margarita, who established small livestock farms in the area. El Hatillo has 1,564 inhabitants (INE 2001). La Cerca is a smaller settlement, devoted primarily to fishing. Its name derives from the netting or fence that fishers place in the channel linking the lagoon to the Unare River, which prevents fish and shrimp from escaping into the sea during the months of October through March. The seasonal nature of the fishery means that people must devote themselves to other activities during the rest of the year, and some of them emigrate temporarily. For the most part, the political groupings and the larger businesses in the Unare area have a negative impact on development of the communities—a situation that creates disunity. This problem is perpetuated through programmes such as scholarships and unproductive jobs which benefit only their supporters. Thus, the relationship between the different sectors of the community and the emigrants overshadows relationships among members of the community itself.

TABLE 7
BAHÍA DE CIENFUEGOS, BAHÍA DE SANTIAGO DE CUBA, AND LAGUNA DE UNARE: ECOLOGY AND ECONOMY

Ecosystems/ characteristics	Bahía de Cienfuegos	Bahía de Santiago de Cuba	Laguna Unare
Province or state	Cienfuegos	Santiago de Cuba	Anzoategui
Beneficiary population	156,372	439,669	50,000
Major settlements	O'Bourque, Punta Cotic, San Lázaro, Reina, Punta Gorda, Junco Sur, Aduana, Guanaroca, La Milpa, Cayo Carena, Castillo-CEN	Cayo Granma, Punta Gorda, Caracoles, Socapa, Cangrejitos, Ciudad de Santiago de Cuba	Boca de Uchire, Boca de Chavez, El Hatillo, La Cerca, Nuevo Unare
Principal fishing resources	Thread herring (*Opisthonema oglinum*), anchoveta (*Cetengraulis edentulus*), bonefish (*Albula culpes*), grunt (*Haemulom sciurus*), seabream (*Archosargus rhomboidalis*), crevalle jack (*Caranx hippos*)	Anchovy (*Anchoa* sp.), sea bass (*Centropomus undecimalis*), thread herring (*Opisthonema oglinum*), blue crab: (*Callinectes sapidus*)	White shrimp (*Litopenaeus schmitti*), lebranche mullet (*Mugil lisa*), white mullet (*Mugil curema*)
Important species for conservation or preservation	Pink shrimp (*Penaeus notialis*) and Caribbean flamingo (*Phoenicopterus ruber roseus*)	Manatee (*Trichecus manatus*)	Flamingo (*Phoenicopterus ruber)*
Principal sources of pollution	Oil refinery, fertiliser factory, thermal power station, sugar refinery, PESCACIEN (a fishing enterprise), sewage from the City of Cienfuegos	Cement factory, oil refinery, brewery and rum distillery, sewage from the City of Santiago de Cuba, copper mine	City of Zaraza, freezing plant, farming and livestock (Cuenca de Unare)
Communities studied	O'Bourque	Cayo Granma	El Hatillo
Population of the communities studied	1,300	748	1,564
Local government system	Popular councils	Popular councils	Municipal mayor and council

The two Cuban communities are located on the edges of large bays in areas that have a historically complex pattern of uses. A comprehensive comparative analysis allowed us to identify their principal socioeconomic and environmental problems, and that analysis remains valid, after systematisation, for Laguna Unare. Through the method of observation and participatory diagnosis, generally speaking we were able to detect problems we were able to categorise into seven groups:

1. Problems associated with water pollution (beaches and marine environment): from garbage, sewage, chemical pollutants, septic tank spills, and oil.
2. Alteration of coastal processes: increase in erosion and disruption of shore dynamics.
3. Low levels of instruction: environmental, educational, cultural, legislative.
4. Problems of infrastructure and community services: lack of permanent garbage dumps, transportation problems, mini-dumps, overflowing septic tanks, water distribution problems, poor state of roads, poor condition of recreation facilities, and lack of public spaces for culture, sports, and recreation.
5. Social problems: alcoholism, unemployment, family violence, lack of employment alternatives, lack of attention to the community, and poor housing.
6. Problems with the availability of natural resources: improper fishing methods, general pollution, over-exploitation of resources, degradation and loss of habitat, decline in biodiversity, and inadequate resource management.
7. Loss of aesthetic values: a decline in the attractiveness of the landscape caused by pollution, faulty resource management, and lack of finance.

A more detailed analysis suggests that pollution problems have the greatest impact on the coastal communities, followed by social problems, along with infrastructure and service shortages. This calls for an operational analysis for use in devising an action plan. From this approach, the problems can be classified according to their potential solutions.

1. Problems inherent in the community that the community itself must resolve.
2. Problems inherent in the community and nearby businesses, which they can resolve separately or through joint action plans.
3. Problems that affect the community that can be resolved only with the help of government or other institutions.

While 90 per cent of the 31 problems we identified have at least one component that cannot be resolved by the community, the community has had an impact on 93 per cent of them. This demonstrates the importance of community management. The community did have direct influence on only 55 per cent of pollution problems, while in 77 per cent of cases, the solution depends on assistance from government and other institutions. When it comes to other problems, such as those relating to infrastructure and services, the community alone can influence solutions for 60 per cent, while with help from government and other institutions, 100 per cent can be addressed. This analysis allows us to weight problems when evaluating a community's general situation and to assess the potential for local management. It also helps to understand the community's viewpoint on various issues, and to visualise the success of a given project by analysing its objectives.

However, it is important to consider the community's perceptions of the problems detected. Figure 11 explains how the problems identified in each of the communities are viewed, according to the systematisation performed. That process must be conditioned by variables such as level of education, individual livelihoods, length of residence within the community, and personal interests.

The most important problems in the perceptions framework were those relating to pollution and infrastructure, followed by the availability of natural resources. In fact, the community feels greatly affected by these issues and it is here that community participation can be most useful in seeking solutions. Yet, as shown in Figure 11, there are some significant differences among the persons surveyed regarding their perception of other issues relating to low education levels and social problems, alterations of coastal processes, and loss of aesthetic values. In Laguna Unare, however, the community viewpoint gives priority to problems associated with infrastructure and the lack of financial resources, despite the severe impact of pollution. This reveals the need to take account of local peculiarities when designing strategies for community mobilisation and environmental education.

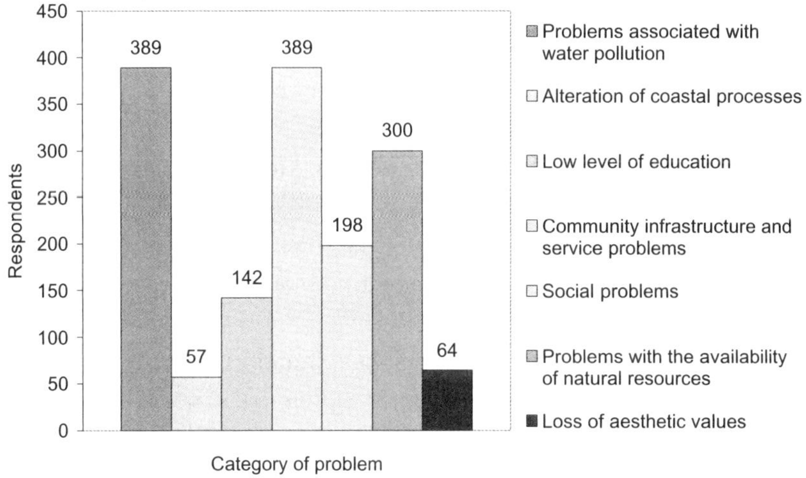

Figure 11
Problems identified at Cayo Granma

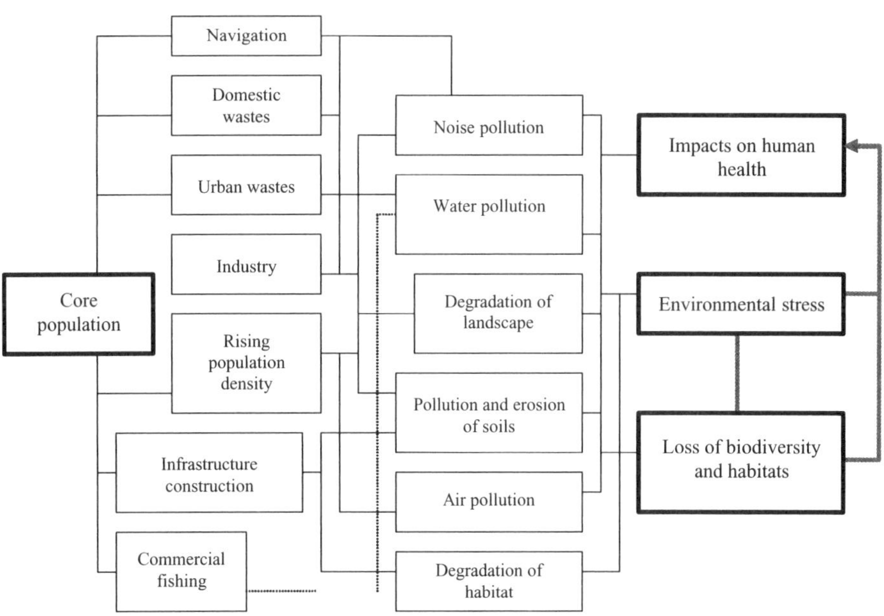

Figure 12
Impact interrelationships at Cayo Granma

Generally speaking, people see three broad groups of problems:

1. obvious problems that greatly affect the population;
2. problems recognised by the community that moderately affect the population; and
3. problems that are not recognised by the community very much.

By analysing the interrelation of impacts (Figure 12) we can pinpoint problems affecting habitat and health, the core community environmental issues. If we analyse the interrelationship between the three relevant aspects (impact on human health, environmental stress, and loss of biodiversity and habitat) it is clear that the focal point is the impact on health, which is conditioned by the other two aspects. This situation explains why health issues demand an immediate change of individual attitudes towards the environment—so that people will consciously minimise environmental stresses as well as biodiversity and habitat loss, key elements that have such a huge impact on improving people's living standards and health. Therefore, the overall education effort must include these three aspects. Notwithstanding this issue, integrating the community is the most important thing, regardless of the educational approach used.

Informing and Rallying Community Opinion

Environmental education: Goals and methods employed

We considered the following factors to develop environmental education activities in the three communities.

- Identifying community characteristics (cultural aspects, values, beliefs, and aspirations), socioeconomic conditions, infrastructure and services, livelihoods, and the environment. We conducted non-structured and semi-structured interviews for this purpose, and engaged in observation and conversation with stakeholders in various planned activities.
- Identifying the most important environmental problems in light of the activities pursued, through documentation, published studies, field visits, and workshops with fishers and community leaders.

- Identifying environmental factors that have an influence on the problem.
- Conducting successful experiments with international environmental education programmes.
- Identifying policies and regulations relating to the community and its problems.
- Emphasising principles of environmental education.
- Researching scientific and local folk knowledge about the problem.

Recognition of these elements allowed us to introduce environmental education programmes appropriate to the circumstances of each community. We also identified four steps that helped determine the success of each activity:

1. Reconciling the interests of all stakeholders involved in the issue.
2. Enlisting the active participation of government institutions and the overall community in developing policies. In the case of Venezuela, we used the local planning councils; in Cuba we used the popular councils.
3. Promoting the use of clean technologies in economic activities, using various means and incentives. Where people have access to infocentres, we encouraged their use.
4. Sensitising people to the need for sustainable development and emphasising their responsibility to help achieve it.

In Cuba, the national environment strategy treats environmental education as a key objective. As a result, in recent years, community work has increased and has become better organised. Within Cuban society there is a culture that implies strict adherence to highly standardised guidelines, where local peculiarities and interests may occasionally be overlooked. However, as a general rule, people are wholly or largely unaware of the legal framework in the different spheres of activity, and local management is weak. From a structural viewpoint, the popular councils represent popular government structures at the local level, formed and elected by the community itself. They offer exceptional possibilities for citizen participation, interaction, coordination, and integration of the various community stakeholders. Recent years have seen a trend to decentralisation, as ways are sought to empower local management in a macro-social context heavily influenced by a complex economic situation, and a micro-social context where some demands are conditioned by the macro environment. Other demands, which are no less important, are specific. Today, conflicts in national development strategies work their way into the local context. For example, tourism development is being pursued from a defined economic perspective, in terms of a compromise between economic development and integrated management of the coastal zone.

In the Cuban communities, the projects approached environmental education from different focuses and levels of priority. In Cayo Granma, instruction at the primary school level is being offered at the request of the community itself. The project's basic objective was to supplement efforts to monitor water for hazardous events and to involve the community in the sampling. Another goal of instruction was to sensitise people to the effects of polluted water on their health and to emphasize its connection with ecosystem pollution. A holistic focus was used, which entailed a thematic, conceptual, and methodological approach defined in advance, and incorporated actions for conservation and preservation of the ecosystem.

In O'Bourque, environmental education was a project objective from the outset: the goal was similar to that of the other projects, but was general rather than linked to a specific theme. The research group proposed this project to the community because an interdisciplinary workshop had selected it so as to compare environmental-education approaches in different contexts within the same ecosystem. The project goal was to enable this coastal community to achieve real and effective participation in resolving its own local environmental problems through a shift in environmental thinking.

In the case of Laguna Unare, the environmental education programme was designed to create public awareness of the most important problem in the lagoon: pollution. The focus was on aspects such as wildlife diversity—with particular emphasis on shrimp (the most important economic resource of the lagoon) and birds (because the zone is a major reservoir for local and migratory birds), and conservation of mangroves (which have been heavily impacted by human activity and treated as an unwanted plant). The most important aspects of the programme are based on sensitising people through various scientific, artistic, and environmental activities. These have been designed to encourage the community to think about its consumption patterns, its impact on the environment, and its shared responsibility.

Our working approach (as depicted in Figure 13) involved reaching out to the community in different ways. For example, with the Cuban projects, the methods for approaching the community differed from those used in Laguna Unare. In Cayo Granma the approach was made through the community leaders, who rallied key stakeholders. A community workshop contributed decisively to reformulating the objectives of the projects and, as a priority, identified the need to work with children through the school. In the end, it was the children who mobilised their families and, through them, the community.

Figure 13
Stakeholders and community outreach in Cuba

Involvement in designing a development project serves as a motivation for the community. For this reason it was important to select a strategic point or central focus for the project, such as habitat and health. The harmful algae which blooms around Cayo Granma was selected as the focal point in this instance. Any focal point must be neutral and must appeal to as many people as possible. Notwithstanding the methodological differences, all our working experience suggested that it would be best to select schools in every village for launching the project, and that they could represent a factor for success despite all the different contexts. Schools not only provide formal environmental education for students but also constitute a key point in the process of instruction and training for teachers, parents, and the community in general, through what we may call a multiplier effect. This does not mean that the entire environmental education programme has to start in the schools. Such a decision must be made after examining each community, as was done in the cases we discuss here. It is also important to consider the ability of the school principals to show leadership, and the degree of their personal involvement within the community, as well as the characteristics of each group of students and the willingness of teachers to participate in the programme.

In Laguna Unare we began by working directly with the school and the fishers in order to reach the broader community (Figure 14). The school was regarded as a neutral point for assembling all the children in the village. Thus, we were able to achieve a multiplier effect by providing training in environmental aspects for teachers, parents, and representatives. In all cases, the school proved the key to rallying the community. This was particularly true in the lagoon because of villagers' reluctance to discuss issues relating to it, and because the great number of research projects underway in the zone engendered a local mistrust of outsiders. In addition, the presence of groups led by people belonging to different political parties made it difficult to bring the whole community together. Nevertheless, we made contact with other stakeholders in the community and found there was a variety of public and private institutions and other groups conducting activities in the Unare area. These included political parties, non-governmental organisations (NGOs), universities, privately-financed foundations, government institutes, and municipal, regional, and national agencies. We designed a virtual network called the "Community of Knowledge of Unare" (http://unare.org) in an attempt to pool individual efforts and ensure access to information on the research work and documents prepared. A multiple-scale analysis of local to national stakeholders and interests was indispensable.

At that point, we proposed and encouraged joint activities with other stakeholders. Reaching the community involved understanding the bulk of interactions that take place in Unare or affect Unare and its people. The environmental education programme included multidisciplinary activities to foster thinking among participants as well as provide information, the primary purpose of which was to change public attitudes towards environmental problems. Activities ranged from formal events, such as a series of environmental chats and workshops for teachers, to informal ones, such as educational games designed around specific issues.

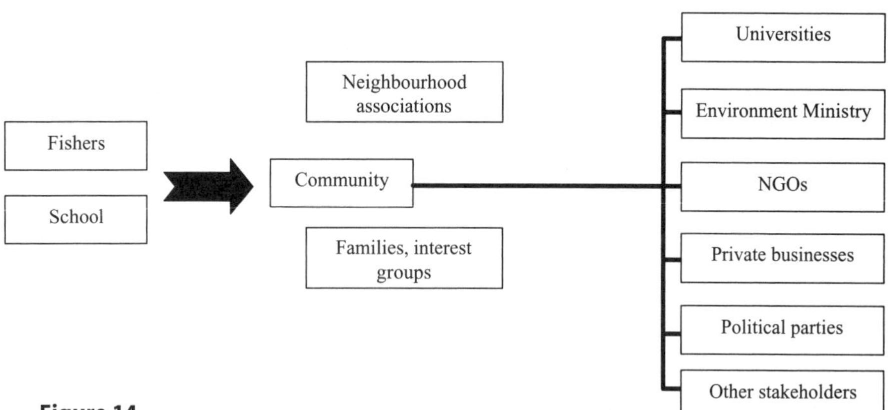

Figure 14
Stakeholders and community outreach in Venezuela

Working with key stakeholders

As the key stakeholder in this effort, the community must be involved in the entire educational process from the outset, and is the main player in the process. The dynamics of developing educational programmes in the various communities led us to understand that it is the community that must lead the process. Support is provided by scientific institutions, and researchers are involved as coaches or coordinators. In this way, these bodies can contribute to the sustainability of the education projects and to the transparency and acceptance of the strategies that are put forward.

Another important goal is sensitising the population. Our experience with these three projects shows the utility of integration activities. These included discussion sessions with professionals, as requested by the community and students, to ensure that the projects would have an impact on teaching. Environmental sessions were shown to permit successful outreach to the community and offered the opportunity to transmit specific messages on local issues, as well as the actions to be taken by each player. These activities were organised jointly with children, teachers, parents, and representatives. Other activities included the celebration of important dates, pageants in which people dressed up in masks of local animals, expert-led school discussions on reforestation to promote sound practices, and educational and recreational outings. These were accompanied by a series of chat sessions, ecological learning games, painting workshops on specific themes, role-playing games in conflict resolution, and diagnostic workshops for identifying children's viewpoints on community problems and the environment (something that proved very useful in the Bay of Santiago). There were also discussion sessions with scientists and university students from various fields, as well as with leaders of other projects. All recounted their experiences in a chat group, where children and other members of the community could also describe their own personal experiences. Some of the activities suggested by the children and other inhabitants proved very valuable: fishing days, beach clean-ups, and walks through the community to establish an environmental watchdog network were initiatives in which the community played a decisive role with the researchers. Using this approach, during visits with university students we made sure that the children and the community leaders could explain details about the community. They had to explain how it functioned and what its problems were, thereby paving the way for a transparent exchange of ideas with the scientists. All these practices contributed to creating an atmosphere between the community and work team that facilitated the participatory process. This strategy also encouraged the community to become involved in and respond to the challenges of a project that included environmental education among its objectives.

It is important to maintain a multidisciplinary view of the environment and a holistic approach at all times, regardless of the project's guiding theme. In communities where pollution problems are identified, as was the case with the villages studied, the focus of the environmental education programme must embrace all aspects of the problem: health, ecosystem balance, availability of resources and quality of services, nutrition, education, and recreation. In the end, we must offer a comprehensive, informal education that will contribute to the community's well-being. In all cases, there must be stress on functional integration of hydrographic basins with coastal zones. These aspects turned out to be crucial in the work conducted in the communities under study.

It is also essential to promote participation by civil society in the decision-making process, since in the final analysis it is the ordinary citizen who interacts with the environment, either through spontaneous individual action or through institutions. Therefore, it is essential that this action be increasingly conscious and responsible. Appreciating this participation depends on the cultural viewpoint or lens through which it is viewed. On this point, De Souza (2004) offers three visions of the world through which humanity has passed and that coexist today: the mechanical vision, the market-oriented vision, and the contextual vision.

De Souza's work raises the question of what we understand by community participation and how we assess it. There is no doubt that, within these visions, we must promote use of the cultural lens of contextuality to look at our surroundings and to project development with conscious, active, and effective participation, where responsibilities and ethical values are oriented towards a higher quality of life. Whether or not it is preceded by a process of instruction, community participation was of great value to our work on these three projects. In Cayo Granma we were able to establish a permanent system of participatory surveillance that allowed for systematic water analysis and for determining possible causes of unwanted phenomena. In Cienfuegos we were able to spark a beach clean-up campaign involving the systematic collection of solid wastes as part of community self-management.

Handling environmental information is a key issue in environmental education: this proved a weak point in the communities studied. The need to process information properly is clear from Ripoll's principle (2004): the better informed a community is about the impact of pollution, the less susceptible that society will be to sensationalism in the media, and the less the work of decision-makers will be held hostage to pressure from uninformed opinions.

Therefore, scientific knowledge must be socialised. If a community is to achieve its aspirations to participate in decision-making about the marine environment, that community must exercise 'informed participation'. Only in this way will the community's presence in government debate have practical meaning and be more than a mere formality; only in this way can the participatory process be efficient, effective, and, above all, authentically grassroots. In light of these considerations, we must note that this is a weak point in the communities studied. The outcome is sometimes conditioned not only by inadequate information processing but also by the world view and the understanding of science and technological innovation held by those involved in the process. This information must be processed so as to reach every level of the community.

Judging from our working experience in these three communities, inhabitants are moderately well informed about some aspects of interest to the ecosystem. But the sources of information are varied and need to be strengthened and channelled more effectively so as to involve all stakeholders. We noted that some sectors of the local population, such as the fishers, have a very rich scientific vocabulary for aspects of the ecosystem, thanks to their interaction with researchers and academics. This has been strengthened and diversified in recent years, leaving at least this as a positive outcome.

Just as processing information is important, so is the flow of information between state agencies and the community. As a general rule it is inadequate. An example of this can be found in the garbage dump located on the outskirts of Laguna Unare, which was the source of serious problems for the community, as noted in the environmental analysis. None of the government institutions accepted any responsibility for resolving the problem. We produced a report on the damage caused by the garbage dump, which was sent to the Ministry of Environment in Anzoategui and to the local state press. Subsequently, a series of meetings was held between the municipal government and the environment ministry to find solutions to the problem

(*Diario El Norte* 2003). The dump was finally closed and moved to another site. This example shows the influence that the news media can have in solving an environmental problem. In this case, the factor driving the decision was a newspaper report that unleashed a number of efforts to find solutions.

One positive experience can be cited in the case of Cayo Granma, where a framework for dialogue was established between the community and the companies that were dumping waste into the ecosystem. Under the leadership of the provincial government and CITMA, the results were excellent. In the case of O'Bourque, again, publicising project results via radio, TV, the press, and dialogue between researchers and government constituted a way of rallying a community that felt 'forgotten and neglected', and strengthening the commitment to improve the community's relationship with its surroundings. Now that this work is known, other projects are beginning to turn to the community for basic information, and they are supplementing the environmental education work under way in the community.

If an environmental education programme is to succeed there must be mechanisms for the flow and dissemination of information. In many coastal communities the traditional means of communication is by word of mouth, and there are no local print media except for district, regional, and national newspapers, whose distribution can be affected by transportation problems. For this reason, coastal dwellers tend to listen to the radio. The oral tradition means that information becomes distorted by the time it reaches its final destination; therefore, we recommend further work to improve channels of communication. The news media have an important role to play as disseminators of information and as catalysts and mediators in dispute settlement. The radio, press, and local TV must all be enlisted. In the case of Cuba, the government has made great efforts to maintain educational and informational programmes that have contributed to better work with the communities. There are also significant local efforts in radio.

Our working experience with the three projects also highlighted the importance of traditional knowledge. In the coastal communities studied, we found that children and women have valuable knowledge of aspects relating to fishing, plants, wildlife, ecosystem dynamics, the impact of the climate on sea-related economic activities, the impact of fishing, the use of different fishing methods, and the ecological and population dynamics of the principal fishery resources. Women are also greatly involved in planning the economic activities of the family. However, the greatest source of knowledge is the men who go to sea. Excluding them would be a great mistake, and that is why there was an initiative to appoint an environmental 'reporter' in Cayo Granma who keeps an environmental diary for the community. The community selected the oldest active fisherman for this duty, and both the children and community leaders have been helping him in his work. This initiative has been of great practical and documentary value.

Our analysis confirms that it is impossible to decontextualise each practice in the different communities. Therefore, it is important to consider the ecological context as well. Taking into account the environmental problems of the communities studied, as well as the laws for making people aware of them, is crucial. Only in this way can we define environmental principles that truly encourage community involvement—and that will serve to design strategies for the care and protection of a community's environment. We identified key strategies that we included for all three communities studied:

- use of natural resources within the limits of their regeneration capacity;
- conscious use and management of wastes;
- conservation of natural resources: species, habitat, and landscape (coastal and submarine);
- conscious and careful use of essential natural resources (water);
- conservation and improvement of the local environment;
- environmental information, training, and education; and
- sustained communication and coordination among stakeholders.

With respect to environmental information, training, and education, it must be recognised that, however much information we may have, it will be of no use as a working tool unless it is communicated. This fact emphasises the need to integrate the social and natural sciences.

Science is in the process of integration because society is demanding integrated solutions. Environmental education and instruction can start from essential situations related to health as a function of habitat improvement, or it can start from habitat, which in the final analysis conditions health (Figure 15). Thus, environmental education can contribute to improving both and, provided the core aspects are addressed, the focus of the process can be directed at one problem in particular or else address all the problems. Figure 15 represents key elements in the framework for environmental education.

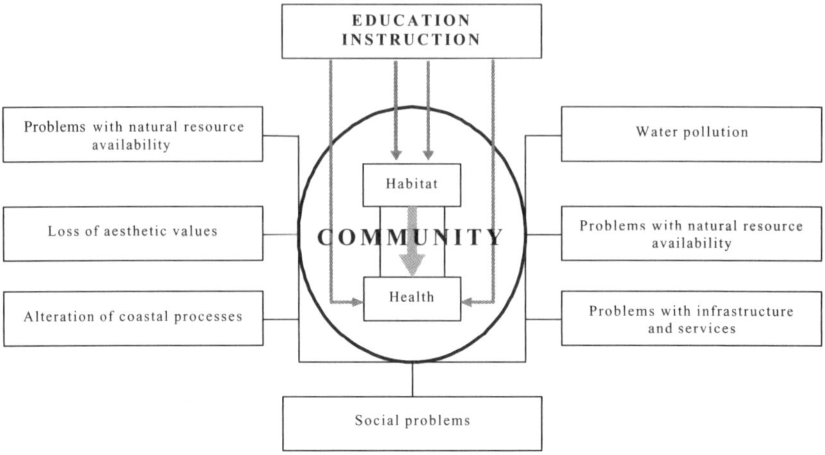

Figure 15
Community settings: key elements for environmental education

Environmental education, information, and instruction will work to the extent that people are aware of their problems and are motivated to find solutions, without necessarily having an action plan that calls for formal, classroom-type information sessions. This is especially true for children and youth, who were identified as important social players in both communities and who are the community leaders of tomorrow.

It must be emphasised that solving the problems of tomorrow will depend on educating the children and youth of today. Training human resources at an early age is crucial so that in the future they can take decisions about coastal resources. Developing a new mentality that incorporates the environmental dimension into the vision of development is sure to guarantee sustainability in the future. The concept of environmental education includes fostering environmental literacy, understanding, and awareness. Environmental literacy means having a basic understanding of worldwide ecological phenomena, including the greenhouse effect, the thinning of the ozone layer, and endangered species. Environmental understanding means recognising that issues such as water pollution and species extinction pose moral dilemmas that go beyond technological solutions, whether imposed or chosen. Environmental awareness means accepting that environmental issues raise political problems that must be resolved politically.

Lessons learned and factors for success

We derived several valuable lessons from our experience in the three communities.

1. Social and political dimension condition interaction with the community. Both the macro- and the micro-settings have an influence.
2. If projects are to be sustainable over time, the community should be encouraged to put forward its own initiatives, because it is difficult for a community to accept decisions or initiatives imposed from outside. On the other hand, when a community proposes a task, it must be committed to it. In most cases the community's decisions will be sound because they reflect multiple interests.
3. The community must be involved in the project from the outset. This is a key factor for success, because it commits the community up front, through its leaders or key personalities. It fosters transparent dialogue, allows potential risks to the project to be identified, encourages the pursuit of home-grown initiatives, and ensures that proposed tasks will not conflict with the community's own dynamics.
4. The community must document its environmental memory. The preparation of trend scenarios during an environmental project can sustain a community's environmental memory. Systematic sampling must evaluate environmental changes or natural and man-made variables that can affect the interpretation of given results. The presence in Cayo Granma of an environmental reporter united the community because, with the community's help, he documented daily happenings related to the environment, its uses, and its principal resources. This reporting function also strengthened environmental awareness, and based on documentation it enabled an assessment of such issues as high-risk months for oil spills, causes of coloration changes in the water, zones most at risk from improper fishing methods, and conflicting uses.
5. Sensitising or training community leaders is a factor for success.
6. The environmental issue, specifically the problem of pollution, constitutes an entry point into the community. It is important to recognise that pollution problems relating to human health and

environmental stresses (along with their general consequences and loss of habitat or biodiversity) are perceptible. Therefore, they represent a concern for the community.

7. Participation by the working team in training programmes on topics such as integrated coastal zone management can promote interdisciplinary research and prepare the team for interdisciplinary work. A team's capacity for this type of work is a key factor for success.
8. Traditional ecological knowledge and the community's recommendations for environmental solutions must be respected and taken into account.
9. Communities are demanding links to businesses. Because they are the link integrating key stakeholders in the management of coastal resources, the role of the researcher is crucial (Figure 16). Academia also plays an important role in reconciling and reinforcing links between the community and local industry or businesses. The academic role in the Cuban projects was important for strengthening links with industry, government, and the community. This helped to bring about a rapprochement between government and community, between community and industry, and between government and industry, not only in terms of production levels, profitability, and efficiency but also on issues relating to the environment, sustainability, and coastal resource management. In Figure 16, Model A represents the Cuban case. It is supported by academia, although the researcher and the project itself are important as the organisational and operational key for intersectoral articulation. However, in Model B, the Venezuelan case, NGOs are involved: the project has an articulating and reconciling element because it is designed as a collaborative effort among the different sectors.

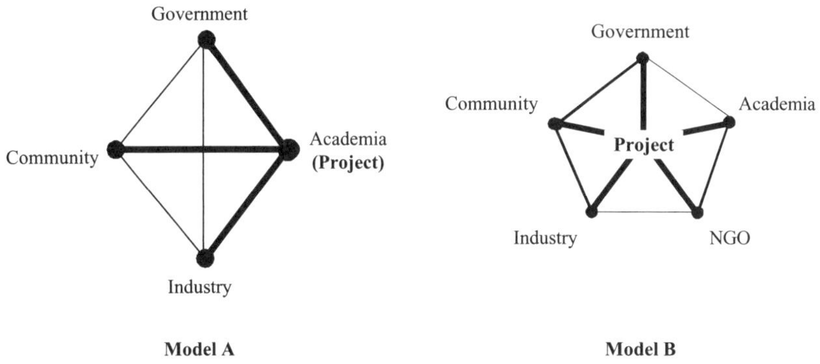

Figure 16
Models of environmental education in Cuba and Venezuela

10. Environmental education of children is a key factor for success. Work with children is less susceptible to political conflicts: the school is a neutral setting and a centre of power from the viewpoint of training and instruction. Children can help to rally the community through the family. Working with children is attractive, and there are compelling interests that facilitate paying attention to them. In the communities we studied, children played a clear mobilising role.
11. It is critical to disseminate results. In communities that feel isolated or neglected, disseminating the results of their joint efforts with other sectors in resolving specific problems is motivating.
12. Women have the potential to maintain community interest, to raise awareness, and to mobilise. It is important to recognise their importance not only in the community, but also in terms of their participation in the project team, and as decision-makers in government, industry, and academia.
13. The commitment of the institutions supporting the project will condition the model for action. In the communities we studied, institutions supporting the projects in Cuba are the universities, while in Venezuela there is an alliance of NGOs with close ties to the academic world.
14. Reconciling interests with other institutions or projects operating in the community or its surroundings is a key factor for success.

Conclusions

In the communities and ecosystems studied, pollution has its greatest effect on fishery resources, the population, and the local economy. The most severe impacts on these factors come from dumping liquid and solid waste and from commercial fishing. These may be the reason for the recent appearance of harmful algal blooms (HABs) at Cayo Granma, for instance, where the local population is completely unaware of the phenomenon as well as its implications.

Similarly, through the project, people became more aware of the presence of heavy metals as an important consequence of industrial activity, recognising for the first time their impact on human health. Pollution is a priority in the perceptual framework of coastal communities, but even if the causes are similar it is crucial to tailor educational efforts to the interests of each key stakeholder, and to analyse specific local aspects. In this respect, it is good to involve children through the schools as a way to rally the community through the family.

There are specific contextual situations at the economic and social level to consider while conducting citizen-participation processes in each community that are designed to strengthen local management. Researchers must bear in mind that communities are heterogeneous, even if they are part of similar sociopolitical or geo-environmental contexts.

We hope that this chapter, with its emphasis on interdisciplinary collaboration, has re-enforced the idea that environmental education can provide useful support for a CBCRM approach in the Caribbean.

References

Bryant, R., and G. Wilson. 1998. Rethinking environmental management. *Progress in Human Geography* 23(3): 321–43.

De Souza, J. 2004. El cambio de época y las relaciones cambiantes ciencia-tecnología-sociedad-innovación. Master's thesis, Universidad de Cienfuegos, Cuba.

Diario El Norte. 2003. In Un botadero de basura en expansión atenta aún más contra la Laguna de Unare, Regional News Section, 20 January, p. 3.

Gómez, L., N. Abrahantes, and Y Larduet. 2001. Contaminación y biodiversidad en ecosistemas acuáticos. El fitoplancton de la Bahía de Santiago de Cuba. *Revista de Investigaciones Marinas* 22(3).

Gómez, L., F. Ocaña, Y. Licea, A. Fernández, M. Díaz, N. Rodríguez, and M.E. Espronceda. 2003. proceedings of the CaricostasInternational Conference for Research Report, University of Orient, Santiago de Cuba.

INAPESCA. 2004. Web site: www.inapesca.gov.ve/. Accessed September 2004.

INE. 2001. National Institute of Statistics 2001 Census. Caracas.

INIA. 2003. Estudio para el establecimiento ecológico en las lagunas de Píritu y Unare, Estado Anzoátegui, Etapa B, Producto 2, Caracas, September. Technical Report for the Ministry of Environment and Natural Resources, Environmental Management Programme, Venezuela.

León, A., M. Araujo, M. Castellanos, C. Serra, I. Figueroa, A. Muñoz, and M. Caraballo. 2001. Final project report: Manejo integrado de la Bahía de Cienfuegos. Programmea Territorial Científico-Técnico de Medio Ambiente [Integrated Management of the Bahia de Cienfuegos. Territorial Environmental Science Programme]. Province of Cienfuegos. CEAC-UMA Cienfuegos. 95.

Ripoll, R. 2004. Nuevos enfoques para la educación ambiental en materia de contaminación marina generada por la industria naviera. Proceedings of the Comunidad y Mar (COMAR) international meeting. CITMA (Ministerio de Ciencia, Tecnología y Medio Ambiente), Havana, Cuba.

Roa, P. 1991. Sediments and Quaternary study of the coastal lagoon of Unare (Venezuela). In Proceedings of the Seventh Symposium on Coastal and Ocean Management, Long Beach, California, July 8–12, 2271–83.

Tran, K., J. Eúan-Ávila, and M. Isla. 2002. Public perception of development issues: Impact of water pollution on a small coastal community. *Ocean and Coastal Management* (45):405–20.

6

Seaweed and Mangroves: Improving Environmental Practices in Coastal Communities to Secure Sustainable Livelihoods

Daniel Robledo Ramirez and Winsome Townsend

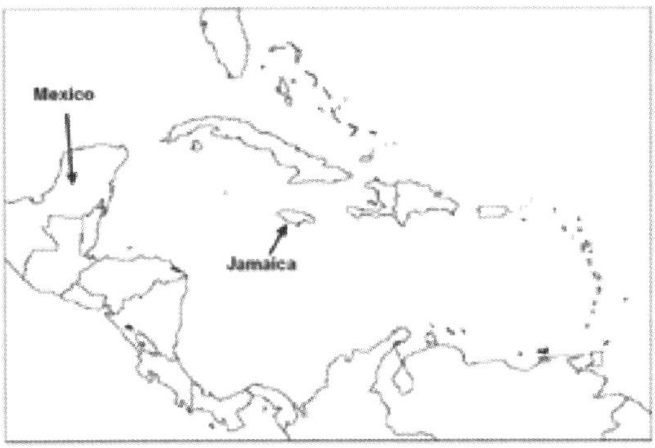

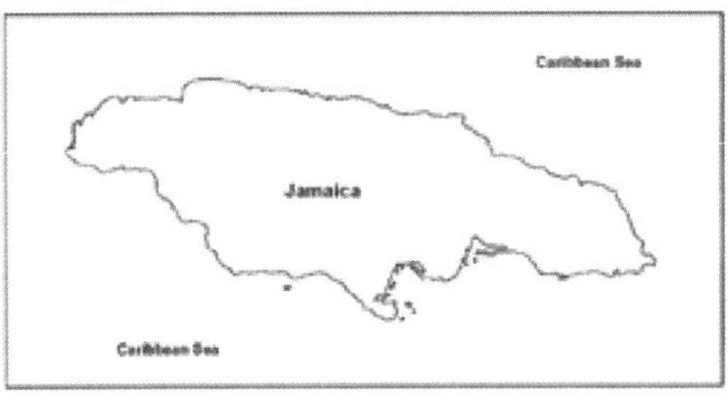

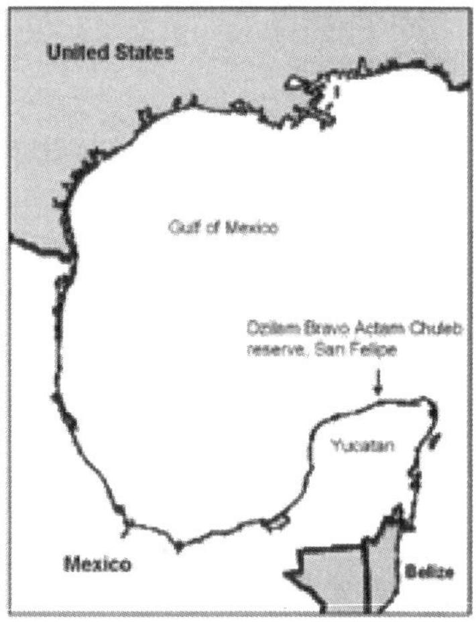

Mangroves and pastures in Dzilam Bravo in Mexico and Rae Town in Jamaica

Figure 17
Location of selected communities

The Caribbean Sea hosts an immense diversity of flora and fauna that is critical to the region's biogeochemical cycles and serves as an important source of food, and possibly pharmaceuticals. The diversity of marine life, however, is being dramatically altered by the rapid, increasing, and irreversible effects of human activities. The most critical stresses are eutrophication, overfishing, physical habitat alteration, and destruction associated with land-based development. These stresses result in serious and widespread social, economic, and biological impacts, including

- changes in the composition and abundance of ecologically important plants and animals;
- changes in the rates of primary production and the stability of populations;
- loss of plant species with important potential for biomedical products;
- altered aesthetic and recreational values of many coastal habitats; and
- dramatic reductions in many of the preferred edible species.

A better understanding of the diversity and proper use of marine plant life is urgently needed to prevent irreversible damage to these living resources. In this regard, and within the community-based coastal resource management (CBCRM) programme framework, two projects, in Mexico and Jamaica, were financed by the Canadian International Development Research Centre (IDRC). These projects demonstrate how issues surrounding a natural resource (seaweed in Mexico and mangroves in Jamaica) can be used to increase environmental awareness while examining the importance of the resource to the livelihood options of the communities. This chapter documents the approaches and experiences of both projects in the context of the similarities and differences between the two communities.

Target communities

TABLE 8
MAIN FEATURES OF SELECTED COMMUNITIES

	Dzilam Bravo	Rae Town
Country	Mexico	Jamaica
Location	Northeast coast of Yucatan	Kingston Harbour Island
Population	2,292	3,300
Economy	Artisanal and commercial fishing, tourism	Fishing, craft manufacturing, services
Other	Part of a state reserve	Local committee formed for mangrove replanting

Dzilam Bravo is a rural community located on the northwest coast of the Yucatan Peninsula. It lies 150 km from Mérida (21.38° N, 88.88° W), the capital of the state of Yucatan (see Map on page 172). The community has 2,292 people, of which 51 per cent are male and 49 per cent are female. Most inhabitants were born in Dzilam (79 per cent); the other 21 per cent are immigrants from nearby states or villages. Dzilam is a medium-sized fishing community with seasonal use of coastal resources. Nevertheless, because of declining catches owing to increasing pressure on resources, Dzilam's fisheries rank third in the state. This is a result of overfishing and of an increase in the number of fishers during the last 10 years. Roughly 858 people (45.5 per cent) are directly involved with fisheries, and 90 per cent of the community depends on this activity. Main exploited species are octopus (*Octopus maya*), lobster (*Panulirus argus*), and several species of fishes called *escama*. Other economic sectors are represented by *permisionarios*, industrialists who control the fishery market, primarily for export, and by restaurant owners. There are other livelihoods, mostly in agriculture, cattle rearing, shop and market selling, and trading. According to income data for the year 2000, the average salary for the majority of the employed population was between US$78 and US$162 per month; a minority received between US$162 and US$405 per month.

Rae Town is an urban community of 1.5 square miles, situated in central Kingston along the northeastern side of Kingston Harbour. It has a population of 3,300—49.7 per cent male and 50.3 female. There are diversified livelihoods here, with only 9.28 per cent of the labour force involved in fisheries. Other occupations are craft worker, shop/market seller, plant and machine operator, and technician. Rae Town is a comparatively large village that has declining fish stocks, increasing pollution from sewage, industrial effluents, and solid waste, and a deteriorating mangrove forest.

Natural resource focus of the projects and their benefits

Both seaweed and mangroves are marine plants that play important roles, not only from the ecological perspective but also economically, as they provide valuable services to the coastal marine ecosystem.

TABLE 9
ECOLOGICAL AND ECONOMIC IMPORTANCE OF SEAWEED TAXA

- Primary producers in aquatic ecosystems
  - Food for many invertebrates and vertebrates
  - Food for detritivores and decomposers
- Structuring of aquatic ecosystems
  - Kelp beds and forest
  - Intertidal algal belts
  - Coralline algal reefs
  - Algal turfs and meadows
- Economic importance
  - Food (sea-moss, nori, kombu, wakame, other sea vegetables)
  - Fooder (direct food and feed supplements)
  - Fertiliser and maerl
  - Phycocolloids (agar, carrageenan, alginate)
  - Specialty biochemicals (agarose, kainic acid, iodine)

Seaweed

The Caribbean has received much attention from phycologists, although most studies have been taxonomic. The first attempt to document seaweed use in the Caribbean was made by Richardson (1958), who compiled data from questionnaires. Despite a general lack of resource assessment available for the region at the time, Diaz-Piferrer (1969) noted 20 species in six genera of Chlorophyta, which were useful for nutritional flours; 20 species in seven genera of Phaeophyta, which were useful as sources of alginates; and about 28 species in 12 genera of Rhodophyta, which were useful as sources of agar or carrageenan.

The global review of algal resources by Michanek (1975) included some examples of agarophytes and carrageenophytes that were harvested as raw material for industrial processing. Species of *Gracilaria* received the most attention—for instance, *Gracilaria cornea* was exported to the United States for agar extraction. *Eucheuma isiforme* is the only Atlantic species in the genus, being one of several carrageenophytes in the Caribbean that produce iota carrageenan. The species has been harvested commercially in Belize, which exported approximately 800 kg (dry weight) annually to the United States for health-food applications. Robledo (1998) reported the commercial exploitation of *Eucheuma isiforme* in the Campeche Banks of Mexico during the 1970s, when there was a shortage of raw material from Asian countries. In all cases, commercial exploitation has been discontinued as a result of severe overharvesting.

The most widespread use of seaweed in the Caribbean at present is the harvest of a limited number of red algae for the preparation of traditional drinks and puddings (Smith 1992). There is no documented history of traditional use of seaweed concentrates and beverages, but according to some authors the practice dates back at least to the first half of the nineteenth century. This tradition is found primarily in the English-speaking islands, but also in a few Central American locations, including southeast Mexico, Honduras, and Panama (Espinosa-Avalos 1994), where the habit was probably introduced by West Indian migrants. In most islands, these algal species as well as the drinks are known as sea-moss; in Jamaica they are called Irish moss, and in Belize, simply seaweed. Clean, dry, and bleached sea-moss species (*Gracilaria cornea*, *G. crassissima*, G. *dominguensis*, and *Eucheuma isiforme*) fetch high prices, commonly retailing for around US$8 per kg. Despite the richness of the Caribbean seaweed flora and the region's proximity to industrial processing facilities in North America and Europe, far less attention has been paid to seaweed as raw material for the phycocolloid industries. Prices range from US$250 to US$1,000 per dry ton, depending on species and quality.

Mangroves

The mangrove community of the Gulf/Caribbean region (Mexico, the Antilles, Central America, northern South America) consists of four principal components: *Avicennia germinans* L. (black mangrove), *Laguncularia racemosa* L. (white mangrove), *Rhizophora mangle* L. (red mangrove, plus other species and hybrids), and *Pelliceria rhizophorae* Planchon and Triana (palo de sal). The first three are widespread; the last grows along the Pacific side of Costa Rica and Panama, along the eastern side of Panama and Nicaragua, and on the Pacific and Atlantic coasts of Colombia. *Conocarpus erectus* L. (buttonwood) is also commonly found in coastal brackish-water environments, even though it lacks many of the morphological specialisations typical of mangroves (aerial roots, vivipary).

Several beneficial effects of mangroves in Kingston Harbour have been identified. These trees form the basis of a complex and highly productive marine food chain that recycles nutrients and assures continued productivity of the coastal waters. They encourage a high biological diversity by being a nursery and feeding, roosting, and nesting ground for a wide variety of fauna, including seabirds, a small population of rare birds, and commercially important mammals and fish including the bottlenose dolphin, crustaceans, and mollusks.

The mangroves provide a filtering field for land-based pollutants that find their way in via the water flowing into the harbour. Mangroves, thereby, play an important role in improving water quality. Another important function is stabilisation of the harbour shoreline. The Palisadoes tombolo is a good example of this; it is an area of considerable economic significance, forming the land bridge between Kingston and Port Royal. The mangrove forests around Kingston Harbour also provide a safe haven for small boats during storms.

Purpose of the projects

Seaweed cultivation

A recent analysis of the marine fisheries in the Gulf of Mexico and Caribbean Sea showed that of a total of 29 exploited species, two were over-exploited, 26 were fully exploited, and only one fishery had the potential to increase its harvest (Hernández and Kempton 2003). Economic opportunities such as timber extraction, agriculture, shipping, and tourism are alternative industries for coastal communities. However, conflicts and competition for limited coastal resources plus escalating environmental deterioration constitute a significant development challenge. In this regard, it has been pointed out that small-scale aquaculture and habitat restoration represent environmentally-friendly or low-impact alternatives for coastal communities' economies (Newkirk 1994). But very few efforts in this direction have been attempted in the Yucatan peninsula.

Other marine resources in the area, such as seaweed, have been poorly surveyed or face the same situation. Diaz-Piferrer (1969) noted that uncontrolled exploitation of seaweed in the Caribbean would exterminate many valuable species in a relatively short time, and recommended both the regulation of wild harvest and the development of methods for cultivating commercial species. At present, even harvesting for traditional sources within the region has led to a decline in stocks wherever they are exploited. Nowadays, the region's largest processor of seaweed drinks, Jamaica, relies entirely on imported carrageenophytes from the Philippines to meet the demand. Given the shortage of raw material for processed products in the region, there is potential for expansion of mariculture to meet the demand.

The rationale for this CBCRM project in Mexico was to promote seaweed cultivation in Dzilam de Bravo and evaluate the community's interest in this activity as a viable economic alternative to fishing.

Mangrove replanting

Several studies of Kingston Harbour document a decline in fish stocks. This harbour is known to have been the site of a flourishing fishery that supported more than 10 fishing villages, including one of the largest in the island, Rae Town. The fishing community used to be enriched by mangrove habitat. The mangrove forests have deteriorated owing to reclamation of land, waterfront development, and mounting pollution related to these and other activities. The deterioration has resulted in significant decline in fish stocks and an ensuing decline in the economic and social status of the villages on the harbour. Fishers are leaving the area because catches from the shallow waters are decreasing. Despite the obvious environmental deterioration that people saw in their daily lives, they did not take action to save the mangrove forests, partly because of disinterest and lack of knowledge.

The purpose of this CBCRM mangrove replanting project was to replant 2 km of shoreline with mangrove. The goal was to improve the community's environmental awareness of the importance of natural resources to their own sustainable livelihoods. This awareness is crucial for an island state such as Jamaica.

Framework for environmental management

Dzilam Bravo

In Mexico, the exploitation of coastal and marine resources had been done on a sector-by-sector basis, without any attempt to integrate the governance and management of the coastal zone and its resources (Pérez-Sánchez and Muir 2003). Nonetheless, government efforts provided multiple policies and regulations for the control of resource exploitation. In the case of fisheries, such policies and regulations applied to fishing licenses, quotas, length of fishing seasons, and fishing bans. Because these policies and regulations do not offer ways to rebuild stocks, however, thousands of people whose main activity is fishing are looking for alternative labour options. In the face of increasing population, declining fisheries production, and decreasing financial resources, particular attention must be paid to attaining an appropriate balance between the roles of institutions and communities in resource management.

Dzilam Bravo is one of two communities sharing a state reserve (the State Reserve of Dzilam Bravo) created in 1989, which comprises 61,706 ha. Its purpose is to preserve natural resources from all the area's representative ecosystems—marine, coastal, and terrestrial. Since 1995, the management of the coastal zone has been part of the National Development Plan for integrated coastal management; however, these programmes are not yet extended to fisheries and aquaculture.

Under this plan, several institutions form the framework for environmental management in the area. The most relevant federal institutions are the Ministry of Agriculture, Livestock Farming, Rural Development, Fisheries and Feeding (SAGARPA); the Ministry of Environment and Natural Resources (SEMARNAP); and, to a lesser extent, the National Institute of Fisheries (INP). In the Yucatan, other institutions such as the Secretariat of Ecology (SECOL) and the Rural Development Plan of the State of Yucatan play an important role. Academic institutions are represented by the Advanced Study and Research Centre of the National Polytechnic Institute (CINVESTAV) and the Regional Centre for Fisheries Research (CRIP). Both deal with environmental management and fisheries issues.

In general, Mexico's national and state governments recognise that economic development depends on effective management of natural resources and the maintenance of sustainable yields from ecosystems, with the participation of local communities. However, marine resources and the environmental and cultural constraints upon their use vary greatly from community to community.

Dzilam Bravo stakeholders

In the Dzilam de Bravo community we identified 162 organised fishers belonging to one of six cooperatives; 1,173 non-organised local and foreign fishers (*pescadores libres*); local and foreign traders (44 fish vendors, 14 of whom are the most important based on their capital); and indirect users (six restaurant owners). The organisational level of fishers is low because only 10 per cent of them belong to cooperatives. Nearly half of the non-organised fishers are not from the community, a situation that may cause conflicts over the use of the coastal resources.

Rae Town

Rae Town has several active civic organisations including the Rae Town Citizens Association, Rae Town Community Club, Rae Town Police Youth Club, and the Rae Town Fishermen's Cooperative. Their local authority is the Kingston and St Andrew Corporation (KSAC), which is responsible for local governance including approval of building plans, cleaning of minor drains and gullies, and other municipal issues. The other relevant governmental organisations, including the Fisheries Division, the National Solid Waste Management Authority, and the National Environment and Planning Agency (NEPA), are all central agencies. NEPA's role is regulatory, particularly with regard to environmental licences and permits. In addition, NEPA has community outreach programmes that bring the community environmental awareness and education, as well as mitigation programmes for restoring the natural resources, such as the mangroves which are the focus of this project.

Major project strategies

Seaweed cultivation

The Dzilam Bravo community became involved in the seaweed cultivation project in late 2002. Before that, during 1999, a group of 38 fishers from the community participated in experimental cultivation of seaweed as a temporary employment programme operated by SEMARNAP with technical support from CINVESTAV. After this experience, a series of problems were identified:

- Lack of markets for small quantities of seaweed: although fishers were able to export their first harvest, volumes above 18 dry tons were required by processing industries.
- Non-organised fishers had to develop their own cultivation strategy. The 38 fishers initially involved in the project were organised mainly by family bonds: all were male and some of them were full-time fishers. Therefore, the time devoted to the activity was not constant.
- Lack of fast-growing cultivars. The cultivar used in the first experience (*Gracilaria cornea*) was a slow-growing species with a restricted and competitive market (agar).
- The season when the cultivation was performed was inappropriate because prevailing environmental conditions precluded high levels of production.
- Given the identified problems, our major strategies under the CBCRM programme were focused on:
- Identifying species with high demand and international markets. We accomplished this by contacting industries that required seaweed for processing agar or carrageenan, and asking them for letters indicating an interest in purchasing seaweed cultivated on farms in Dzilam.
- Scaling up from an experimental farm of 120 m^2 to a pilot farm of 2,800 m^2. Such an increase would allow a harvestable biomass to reach the quantities that are required by processing companies.
- Organising fishers who were already involved in seaweed cultivation, and other interested parties, to join the project. We encouraged female participation, but male fishers were reluctant to include women. We distributed questionnaires and socioeconomic surveys to evaluate the fishers' interest in the activity, assess their income range, and measure the time and effort they spent in their normal and main occupation.
- Obtaining information from other community members and stakeholders who might be interested in the programme, through community workshops and seaweed-cultivation courses.
- Selecting, in the laboratory, a fast-growing strain of *Gracilaria cornea* and introducing a highly in-demand species, *Kappaphycus alvarezii*, (commercially known as 'cottonii') a kappa-carrageenan producer. Another species was evaluated: *Eucheuma isiforme*, a native iota-carragenan producer species that was exploited in Mexico several years ago.

- Extending the cultivation period to include both dry and rainy seasons. This was important because the best environmental conditions for growth were found during these seasons according to the selected species, and also because of the closed season for main fishery species.

Mangrove replanting

The community of Rae Town became involved in a mangrove replanting project in June 2002. The communities around the Kingston Harbour do not derive direct benefit from mangroves. For example, there is no evidence that there is any widespread use of the mangroves either for timber or for charcoal burning, and only 9.28 per cent of the employed workforce is engaged in fishery-related activities. Therefore, when emphasising the importance of mangroves, it was important to offer environmental education that linked the ecological benefits of mangroves to the livelihood of the communities.

The main goal of our project was to educate the community about the importance of mangroves to the marine ecosystem, to the livelihood of fishing, and to the general aesthetics of the area. The objective of the training was twofold: to increase knowledge levels regarding the environment, and to train a cadre of community members as community animators. In this way, those who were trained would be able to impart the information to others in Rae Town and its environs. We did the training with a view to changing attitudes and practices, especially as they relate to mangroves and to increasing community support for the project. The key community members who were trained in community animation techniques helped spread the environmental message and helped prepare the community for the mangrove replanting exercise.

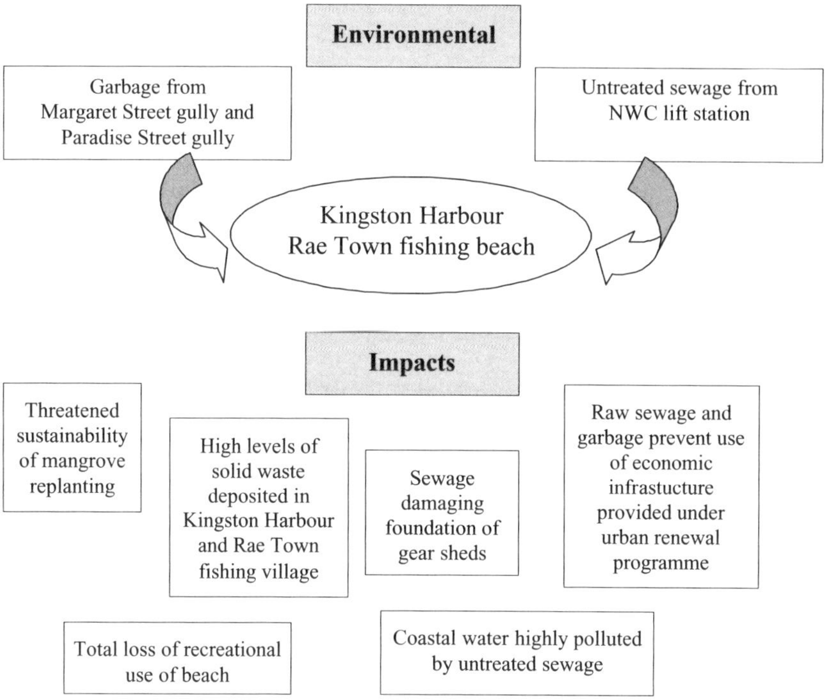

Figure 18
Community analysis of issues threatening Kingston Harbour/Rae Town fishing beach

We recognised that replanting the mangroves would not have an immediate and direct benefit for the community. However, the community members were encouraged to use their enhanced environmental awareness to advocate on other environmental issues that continue to affect them. Therefore, our project was used as a launching pad for environmental animation, as well as for initiating collaboration between the community and the various government agencies responsible for providing services.

Another important strategy was the use of community labour whenever possible. For example, community members were employed to provide snacks for meetings and to do videotaping and photography.

Community participation

Dzilam Bravo

During the project, 38 fishers were involved in year-round cultivation at the 2,800 m^2 seaweed farm. They worked on the scaling-up of the experimental farm, and on the seeding, maintenance, and harvest of cultured species (*Gracilaria*, *Eucheuma*, and *Kappaphycus*). Current techniques such as bottom cultivation were applied, but modification and development of local cultivation methods, such as net lines, were also tested. Other community work included distributing questionnaires to 92 fishers to evaluate socioeconomic information and alternative activities that were developed during different seasons, and a workshop that included 40 participants. In addition, 26 people attended a community-based course on seaweed cultivation, during which all the participants took an attitudinal test.

Rae Town

Various methods were used to ensure community participation in the Kingston Harbour Mangrove Rehabilitation Project. These included community meetings, focus-group discussions, environmental awareness training, tours of the harbour, and a high-profile project launch.

Representatives from the community selected a team of three women who were trained as community animators. The women used their newly acquired community animation skills to act as change agents and mobilisers in the church and the citizens' association; they also acted as community health educators teaching hygiene habits. Their activities included:

- leading discussions on issues raised;
- performing skits to emphasise targeted messages;
- engaging small focus groups in community yards situated along the gullies and the fishers' beach;
- administering questionnaires to obtain a sample response on garbage-disposal practices and related issues to help develop the education programme;
- preparing plans for engaging schools in the environmental initiatives;

- conducting initial meetings with school principals to inform them about the project and to facilitate entry into the schools;
- assisting in the organisation of the local steering committee meetings; and
- helping to make the proceedings of meetings more professional.

With regard to the technical aspects of the project, community members were trained in the theory and techniques of selecting and planting mangrove seedlings. Using the Riley Encased Methodology for mangrove propagation, they planted 1,000 mangrove propagules.

Project outcomes and sustainability

Seaweed cultivation

The community perception regarding seaweed cultivation gave rise to the question: Is the income from seaweed cultivation higher than or comparable with the income from our primary occupation (or other income-producing work)? In Asian and African countries where cultivation has been successful, seaweed provides a better income for the people involved than other occupations. Although in some parts of Latin America beach dwellers can earn a better income from tourism and fishing for shrimp and lobsters, seaweed cultivation may represent a welcome additional source of income. In Dzilam Bravo, 67 per cent of the community knew about the seaweed cultivation project and its results, but only 18 per cent of the fishers involved wanted to develop it more.

This led us to a second question: Is there a need in the Caribbean region for a programme to cope with sociocultural barriers against changing from subsistence fishing to seaweed farming? Fishers may prefer to be hired and receive periodic payment for their labour, and may feel insecure about becoming owners and managers of their own small farm. People who have a subsistence lifestyle may not want to adapt to the regular, routine work required for seaweed farming. Frequently, experimental farming trials and wild-crop surveys appear promising, but lack of experience in the commercialisation of seaweed production is a problem that needs addressing.

In Dzilam Bravo, we identified socioeconomic and ecological indicators to develop seaweed farming as an alternative livelihood, together with technical solutions for its year-round cultivation. Analysis of the most successful and sustainable seaweed industries in other countries over the past 30 years showed that most were initiated by international buyers and processors from developed countries (Ask and Azanza 2002). These developments have been market-driven and, although they were supported by aid agencies and research institutions, the catalyst and the driving force was the international commercial sector. We surveyed the market for seaweed production in the region and identified at least three interested companies. We noted that non-organised fishers (*pescadores libres*) in Dzilam Bravo represent an important work force that could develop seaweed cultivation because they have insufficient income and capital to develop other alternative occupations.

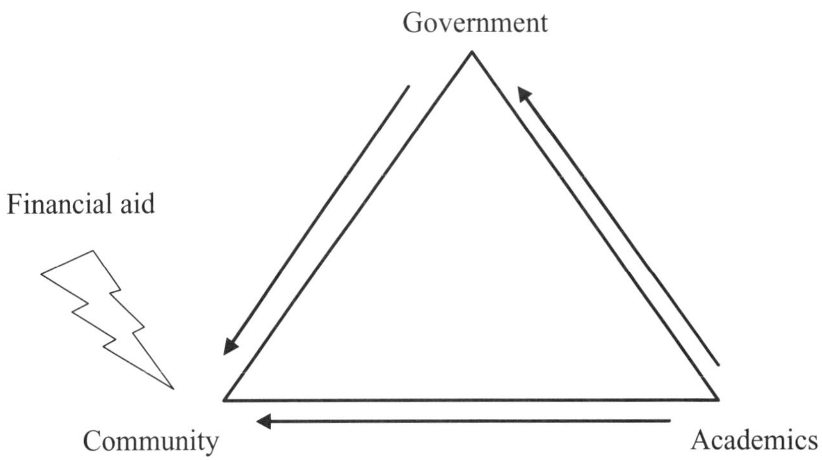

Figure 19
Mode of action to secure sustainable projects within coastal communities in the Caribbean region

To ensure the development of sustainable seaweed cultivation in Caribbean countries, the following factors should be considered.

- Labour costs necessary to make seaweed cultivation viable are low.
- Capital outlays are usually small and will depend on the scale of operation.
- Less capital is required for vegetative propagation with selected cultivars than for other cultivation methods.

- More productive cultivation techniques must be developed, particularly those that require less labour.
- More exhaustive surveys are needed to identify native carrageenan-containing seaweed species.
- Seaweed consumption by coastal communities in the Caribbean should be encouraged to secure a market for farmed seaweed.
- Production requirements for pilot cultivation should be set to at least 200 dry tonnes per year.

Mangrove replanting

During the Jamaica project, on its own initiative the community formed a large, multi-agency 'Local Steering Committee of the Kingston Harbour Mangrove Replanting Project', which continues to be chaired by a community member. This testifies to the success of the project and the sustainability of the replanted mangroves, which represents the project's output. In addition, the project animated the community to such an extent that they have, under the Local Steering Committee, developed another proposal: Kingston Harbour Restoration: A Low-Cost Waste Management Solution. The goal of this project is to reduce the solid waste entering the Kingston Harbour via the Rae Town Gully. The committee is actively seeking funding for implementation.

Expected outcomes from this offshoot initiative are:

- cessation of the discharge of raw sewage in and around the Rae Town fishing complex in Kingston Harbour;
- reduction of solid waste deposits on the Rae Town fishing beach in Kingston Harbour;
- a face-lift for the Rae Town fishing complex, which would to fit the vision for diversification because it would include entertainment and recreation; and
- establishment of a seafood restaurant, which represents alternative employment.

Lessons learnt

Seaweed cultivation

In terms of seaweed farming, Caribbean countries are best suited to processing seaweed for their own local markets, which are often the people who traditionally have consumed seaweed. Success will be achieved only if long-term programmes (of more than three to five years) are supported, with less emphasis on short-term contracts. For cultivation to be commercially viable, production levels in any area must reach 1,000 dry weight tonnes per year (about four shipping containers per month). This volume covers operating costs. The goal should be to achieve at least 2,000 tonnes per year when fully established. The time frame for development should be roughly four years, to allow for setbacks—for instance, from hurricanes or epidemics. In addition, there should be a qualified project manager in charge, and qualified field technicians should be in the villages training and making sure everyone is moving in the right direction. At a beach price of US$200 per dry tonne and an output of 2,000 tonnes, US$400,000 per year could go directly into the villages (Muñoz, Robledo, and Freile-Pelegrín 2004). The fishers would be much more interested in growing seaweed if they could be assured of a secure export market.

With all new projects, initial surveys and feasibility studies should be done to ensure that there is a viable market; that political, social, and economic factors are favourable; that logistics and infrastructure are sufficient; and that government support will be forthcoming. A three-way commitment is ideal, whereby academics provide scientific and technical information to the government agencies involved (and other expertise and opinions directly to the community) and the agencies give technical and financial support to the community involved in the development project. Financial aid from governments, international agencies, or private companies must go directly to the community to secure the establishment of the programme. (Figure 1).

Mangrove replanting

In communities where the predominant occupations are not related to the sea, the importance of mangroves can be used as an entry point for explaining other environmental concerns that affect the health and well-being of the people. These factors can be proposed as discussion points:

1. Community-animation techniques are an excellent method of getting the community interested in environmental issues.
2. Women are pivotal in order to maintain community interest.
3. It is important to link environmental issues with livelihood issues.
4. A multidisciplinary, multi-stakeholder project team is important in order to link the interests of the community, government, and academia.

Many Caribbean coastal communities include a significant number of artisanal fishers, who must develop strategies that target multiple fish species according to their seasonal variations. However, many fishers live in a flexible occupational structure that includes part-time work in agriculture, charcoal production, wood cutting, or craft work, and sometimes occasional work in various wage labour works. In other words, livelihood issues in coastal communities do not evolve only around fishing activities but depend on the use of many other natural resources. In light of the generalised depletion of fish stocks and increased water-contamination problems in the Caribbean, new productive strategies and conservation of other natural resources should be promoted to ensure the communities' future. Our research project emphasised the relevance of this approach.

Our project proved that interdisciplinary research is required at the local level to better understand the producers' resistance to (or acceptance of) innovation, and to deepen the governance mechanisms that enable a given community to mobilise for resource preservation or enhancement.

References

Ask, E., and V. Azanza. 2002. Advances in cultivation of commercial eucheumatoid species: A review with suggestions for future research. *Aquaculture* 206: 257–77.

Díaz-Piferrer, M. 1969. Distribution of the marine benthic flora in the Caribbean Sea. *Caribbean Journal of Science* 9(3–4): 151–78.

Espinosa-Avalos, J. 1994. Seaweed as food in the Caribbean. *Applied Phycology Forum* 11(3): 13.

Hernández, A., and W. Kempton. 2003. Changes in fisheries management in Mexico: Effect of increasing scientific input and public participation. *Ocean and Coastal Management* 46: 507–26.

Michanek, G. 1975. *Seaweed resources of the ocean.* Rome: FAO Fisheries Technical Paper No. 138.

Muñoz, J.S., D. Robledo, and Y. Freile-Pelegrín. 2004. Mariculture of *Kappaphycus alvarezii* (Rhodophyta, Solieraceae) color strains in tropical waters of Yucatán, Mexico. *Aquaculture* 239: 161–77.

Newkirk, G. 1994. Transforming stressed waters: Moving ahead with an ecosystem view of coastal aquaculture. Internal report, Biology Department, Dalhousie University, Halifax, Canada.

Pérez-Sánchez, E., and J.F. Muir. 2003. Fishermen perception on resources management and aquaculture development in the Mecoacan estuary, Tabasco, Mexico. *Ocean and Coastal Management* 46: 681–700.

Richardson, W.D. 1958. Preliminary investigations on the utilization of marine algae in the Caribbean. *Abstracts from the International Seaweed Symposium* 3: 49–50.

Robledo, D. 1998. The seaweed resources of México. In *Seaweed resources of the world,* ed. A.T. Critchley and M. Ohno, 331–42. Japan: JICA.

Smith, A.H. 1992. Seaweed cultivation in the West Indies. In *Sustainable seaweed resource development in sub-Saharan Africa,* ed. K. Mishigeni, J. Bolton, A. Critchley, and G. Kiangi, 337–51. Windhoek: University of Namibia.

7

Political Organisation and Socioeconomics of Fishing Communities of Trinidad and Tobago, Belize, and Grenada

Rosemarie Kishore, Marisa Clarke-Marshall, Hema Ramsundar, Gregory de Souza, Herbert Haylock, and James Finlay

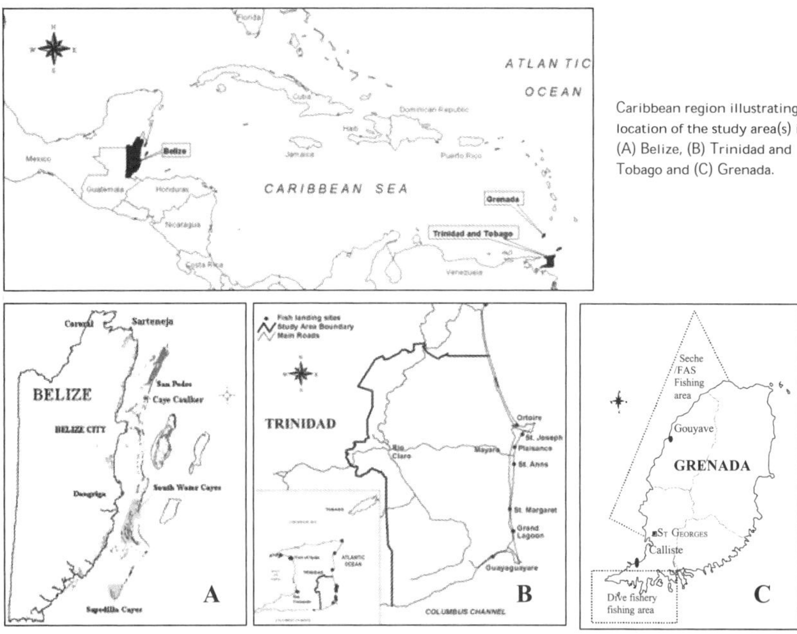

Caribbean region illustrating the location of the study area(s) in (A) Belize, (B) Trinidad and Tobago and (C) Grenada.

Figure 20
Location of selected communities

Caribbean fisheries are threatened by the same factors that are affecting global fisheries, including collapsing fish stocks from overfishing and environmental degradation as a result of pollution and habitat loss. Capture fisheries production in 2001 for the western-central Atlantic region was 1.7 million metric tonnes, minor compared with the global production figure of 92.4 million metric tonnes (FAO 2000a). However, in small-scale artisanal fisheries of the Caribbean countries, the problem of collapsing fish stocks is further complicated by the relative dependence on fishing of the respective national economies and, in particular, the livelihoods of coastal communities. Fishing in the Caribbean also occurs alongside industrial development, tourism, conservation, and recreational and other traditional uses, all of which compete for access to the coastal area. This often leads to user conflicts.

Traditional fishery management strategies have often been implemented through interventions such as gear restrictions and catch quotas. This old perspective focuses on sustaining fish harvests based on the sustainable-yield concept (Charles 2001). A new perspective based on the sustainability concept redefines the fishery to include the fish resources and the fishery's ecosystem as interacting with the human system towards a balance of resource conservation and human concerns (Charles 2001). Inherent in this new approach is the requirement of incorporating the human system into the management regime. The World Bank (1992) noted that fish biology studies represent the focus of fishery research in developing countries, while other disciplines generally have been neglected. Other studies include stock assessment, capture and post-harvest technology, and aquaculture. However, little attention has been paid to fishery resource users, despite the fact that socioeconomic problems confronting users are the main factor leading to resource over-exploitation and, ultimately, to the success or failure of management and development of the fishing industry.

The involvement of users in the decision-making process has been a recent initiative. Chuenpagdee, Fraga Berdugo, and Euán-Ávila (2004) attribute this partly to the Rio Declaration in 1992. Specifically, its Agenda 21 marks one of the first global initiatives to recognise the importance of involving people in addressing environmental and developmental issues (UN 1994). The essential idea of fishery co-management is the sharing of decision-making and management functions between government and stakeholders in the fishery. More formally, it can be defined as the creation and implementation of suitable management arrangements through which a set of agreed stakeholders (fishers and their organisations) work jointly with government to develop and enforce fishery regulations and management measures (Charles 2001).

Community-based co-management is another derivative of co-management, with special emphasis on communities. Community-based management is a major force in reshaping resource management in developing countries (Charles 2001). There are varying definitions of community-based coastal resource management (CBCRM). Charles (2001) described this arrangement of co-management on a geographic basis, whereas Berkes et al. (2001) suggested that while there are many similarities between co-management and community-based management, the focus differs. These differences centre on the level and timing of government participation in the process. CBCRM is people-centred and community-focused, while co-management focuses on these issues plus a partnership arrangement between government, the local community, and resource users. The process of CBCRM is organised differently too, co-management having a broader scope and scale than CBCRM. The government may play a minor role in CBCRM; on the other hand, by definition, co-management includes a major and active government role (ibid.). Berkes et al. (2001) also noted the involvement of other external agents, such as non-governmental organisations (NGOs) and academic and research institutions, as well as other coastal resource stakeholders, as part of this partnership. Thus, co-management covers various partnership arrangements and degrees of power sharing, as well as the integration of local (informal, traditional, and customary) and centralised government management systems.

This focus on specific areas or communities affords a unique opportunity to examine how the socioeconomic and cultural environments, indigenous local knowledge, political organisations of communities, and the fishing operation itself can all play a role and perhaps point towards developing new fishery management strategies.

This chapter presents three case studies from Trinidad and Tobago, Grenada, and Belize, and examines the approaches taken on their journey towards co-management of their community-based fisheries. Despite their different scenarios, they share many features in their use of common fishing areas, targeting of multiple species, and using multiple gear. These conditions reflect the Caribbean's open-access fisheries. When dealing with human systems, the projects identified not only the organisational arrangements of the fishing communities but also their social structure, customs and traditions, and existing indigenous management systems, which are critical in this co-management approach.

In Trinidad and Tobago, the study area is located on the southeast coast of Trinidad, comprising several residential fishing communities that operate from seven fish landing sites. The sites target coastal pelagic and demersal fish species in addition to lobsters, where multiple gear is used (Table 10). In Grenada, two fishery systems are examined; one comprising several residential fishing communities (with emphasis on Gouyave) which target pelagic fish aggregating sites (FAS) utilising hand-lines. The second community, Callistes, targets shellfish and collection of sea moss by both free-diving and scuba-diving. In Belize, a single fishing community was studied, Sarteneja. Its fishery targets lobsters using traps, shades and hook sticks, while conch are harvested by free diving on the reefs. Our study included examining fishing activities on Belize's barrier reef system.

The relative importance of fisheries to the national economy is highly variable among Trinidad and Tobago, Grenada, and Belize (Table 10). This is probably a significant indicator to determining the resources allocated to the development of the respective fishery sector in each country. In Trinidad and Tobago, there was a move away from the plantation-type economy to a petroleum-based economy, whereas in Belize the movement is from logwood and mahogany exportation to agriculture and tourism. In Grenada, economies are shifting from agriculture to tourism. The fishery is considered a sub-sector of agriculture, and contributed 0.19 per cent of gross domestic product (GDP), or 8.9 per cent of the agricultural contribution to the GDP of Trinidad and Tobago in 1998 (Fisheries Division 2000). The relative contribution of the fisheries sector to both the agricultural sector and to GDP at large has been on the decline since 1994 (Ibid.). A similar decline in the agricultural sector has also been observed in Grenada, where it declined from 13 per cent in 1990 to 8.2 per cent in 2000 (Commonwealth Business Council 2004). At present, the fisheries sub-sector contributes 1.5 to 2.0 per cent towards the national GDP and is a major source of foreign-exchange earnings. Since unemployment has always been high (exceeding 20 per cent), the fishing industry is a major source of employment and income generation (www.fao.org, January 2000b). In contrast, in Belize the agricultural sector exceeded 35 per cent of the country's GDP, with primary agriculture, fisheries and forestry contributing more than 21 per cent of GDP. From 1990 to 2000, the contribution by agriculture increased by 5 per cent: this is largely attributed to the increases in the fisheries sub-sector, which reports a rise from 2 per cent to 5 per cent of GDP. In 2002, the fisheries sub-sector in Belize ranked third behind tourism in foreign exchange earnings and contributed 7.2 per cent to the GDP (Government of Belize 2002).

TABLE 10
DESCRIPTORS OF FISHING COMMUNITIES FROM TRINIDAD AND TOBAGO, BELIZE, AND GRENADA.

Descriptors	Trinidad &Tobago	Belize	Grenada
Communities	Eight residential communities (approx 10,500 people)	One community — Sarteneja (1,600)	Seche/FAS fishery— several communities (focus on Gouyave); dive fishery—Calliste
No. of fishers	Roughly 350	Roughly 300	82 (Gouyave, 38; Calliste, 44)
Local economy	Oil and gas, fishing, tourism, agriculture	Fishing, agriculture	Fishing, agriculture, tourism
Fishing areas	East and south coast of Trinidad up to 40 km offshore	Entire north-south coast of Belize, the barrier reef, and beyond to 48.75 km offshore	Seche/FAS fishery— seches on west coast of Grenada; dive fishery—south coast of Grenada
Gear types	Gill nets, fish pots, hand lines, long lines, lobster nets, shark nets, beach seines	Traps, shades, hook sticks, free diving	Seche/FAS fishery— hand lines; dive fishery —free diving, SCUBA
Target species	Mackerels, carangids, snappers, lobsters	Lobster, conch, some finfish	Seche/FAS fishery— pelagics, demersals; dive fishery—conch, sea-moss
Fish habitats	Continental oceanic waters; estuarine inshore waters, rocky and muddy substrates	Continental oceanic waters, coral reefs	Continental oceanic waters, coral reefs
Fishing operations	Trips conducted mainly over one day/night. Spatial migration of boats across the seven fish landing sites. Migration seasonal depending on target species.	Seasonal migration. Several weeks at Caye Caulker and then to Belize City/Sarteneja.	Trips are conducted on a daily basis. Boats fish over the seches on west coast.
Markets	Wholesale vendors collect fish at landing site, ice and distribute them to processors outside the communities for sale to local supermarkets, restaurants, and regional markets	Mainly fishing cooperatives for lobster and conch sales to exports and restaurants; some limited retailing of finfish.	Seche fishery —target the low- to medium-scale local market; dive fishery —target upscale and export markets

TABLE 11
COUNTRY PROFILES OF TRINIDAD AND TOBAGO, BELIZE, AND GRENADA

Descriptors	Trinidad and Tobago	Belize	Grenada
Country size	5,128 km^2 [b]	22,960 km^2 [b]	340 km^2 [b]
Population	1.2 million [2]	256,800 (2001) [c]	104,600 [b]
Fishing area	EEZ (58,722 km^2); archipelagic waters (7,158 km^2); territorial sea (9,337 km^2)[b]	EEZ (169,840 km^2); shelf (9,800 km^2) [b]	EEZ (7,700 km^2); shelf (1,300 km^2) [b]
Contribution of fisheries sub-sector to GDP	0.19% (1998) [a]	7.2% (2003) [c]	1.5–2.0% (2000) [d]
Main income earners	Oil, natural gas, petrochemicals	Tourism, agriculture	Tourism, agriculture
Number of fishers	4,900 (registered); 2,500 (estimated unregistered)[a]	2,700 (registered) [c]	2,200[b]

[a] Fisheries Division 2000. [b] www.caricom.fisheries.com/member.asp.
[c] Central Statistical Office 2002. [d] www.fao.org, Jan 2000.

Political Organisation

Both formal and informal institutional arrangements exist within the fisheries described in the three projects. Formal arrangements are more dominant, but vary among the three countries. Informal arrangements include local rules and traditions, which make up the indigenous management systems at the community level.

Institutional arrangements for fishery management

The institutional arrangements are very similar among the three countries, which is not surprising given their common colonial history. There is a linear organisational structure of the fisheries sector, which is centrally regulated by the government, as identified in Figure 21. There are varying levels of involvement from other government agencies, research institutions, and the fishing industry. The responsibility of the government is in formulation of fishery policies, administration of fishery regulations, and the provision of extension services. In Trinidad and Tobago the Fisheries Act (1916) is the main piece of legislation that regulates the size of mesh, form, and dimensions of nets or appliances for fishing.

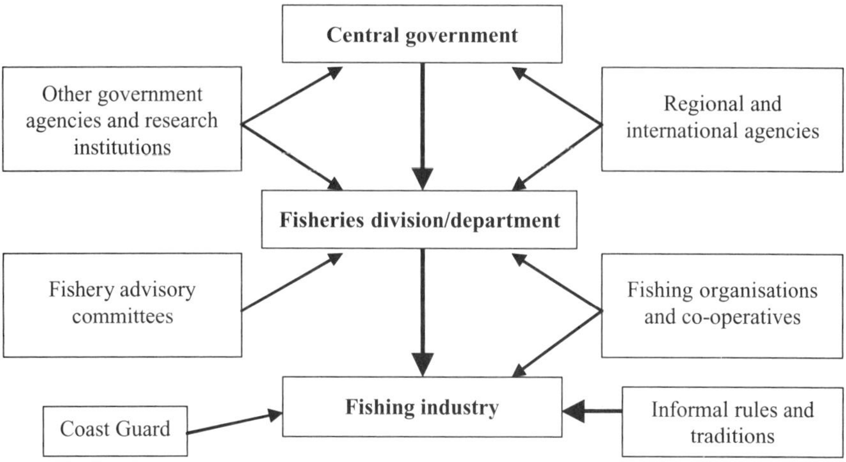

Figure 21
Schematic outline of institutional arrangements for the fisheries sector in Trinidad and Tobago, Belize, and Grenada

In conjunction with the Food and Agricultural Organisation (FAO) of the United Nations, in the 1990s the government proposed new policy guidelines for the marine fisheries sector (Fisheries Division 1996). These guidelines sought to address deficiencies in the existing legislative framework and management approaches to suit the changing needs of the sector, including the stakeholders' involvement in the management process. These guidelines have not been formalised, and the fishery is still regulated by the Fisheries Act (1916) with respect to the size of mesh, form, and dimensions of nets or appliances for fishing. Despite this, however, the political climate is not averse to stakeholder involvement. The Monitoring and Advisory Committee (MAC) of Trinidad and Tobago, which was established in 1997, is both a fishery advisory body and an industry initiative. It is composed of representatives from various fishing associations, NGOs, government agencies, and the University of the West Indies (UWI). Other state agencies and research institutions including the Institute of Marine Affairs (IMA), the Caribbean Fisheries Training and Development (CFTDI), and UWI also conducted research and provided training and support to guide the development and management of the fisheries sector.

Some of the current conflicts are external to the fisheries sector, and the current fisheries legislative framework cannot adequately address them. While there is no comprehensive legislative framework for coastal area management, the establishment of an Environmental Management Authority (EMA) along with the enactment of the Environmental Management Act in 2000 provided some means of consolidating and addressing issues from a fisheries perspective. Of particular importance is the passage in 2001 of the Certificate of Environmental Clearance Rules. They allow environmental impact assessments (EIA), which are now mandatory for certain types of development, including industrial development, especially energy-related projects. However, perusal of available EIAs reveals that the fishing activities are usually poorly characterised, and the fishing industry's contribution to the economy, at both the community and national levels, is weakly articulated (Kishore, Chin, and Ramsundar 2003).

The fishing industry under study in Trinidad was largely unorganized at the start of this project, and there were no formal fishing associations. Two fishing cooperatives had existed in the past in Mayaro, but had become dormant. The fishers noted several reasons for their demise, including lack of trust and accusations of larceny. At the start of the project, survey results for Trinidad indicated that only a small percentage (<10 per cent; N=83) of fishers or members of their households belong to community organisations or are associated with groups with special fishing interests. However, the fishers realised they needed to improve their livelihoods and obtain representation. They also were concerned about the increasing conflicts with the oil and gas sector in 2004. As a result, the fishers formed the Southeast Fishing Association (SFA). Another group that is a direct initiative of this project, the Women in Fishing Association (WIFA), was also formed in 2004. It is important: WIFA is the first women's group involved in fishing to be formed in Trinidad and Tobago. Through the SFA, fishers have been able to access equipment and safety-at-sea training from British Petroleum of Trinidad and Tobago.

In Belize, the Ministry of Agriculture and Fisheries and Cooperatives (MAFC) is the government agency with the lead mandate as provided by the Fisheries Act (1980) to formulate, execute, monitor, and coordinate fisheries management policies. However, the Forest Department of the

Ministry of Natural Resources and the Environment (MNRE) and the Fisheries Department of MAFC are the primary government departments responsible for the establishment and management of marine protected areas (MPAs). To date, six co-management agreements have been signed between these two agencies and with local NGOs for the management and protection of theses areas.

In contrast to the Trinidad fishing community, all the Sarteneja fishers belong to one of the two largest cooperatives: the Northern Fishermen Cooperative or National Fishermen Cooperative, both operating out of Belize City. In Sarteneja, a political structure exists within the community, as shown by a village council. However, there has been little movement or progress through this council in past years. Community members reported that within this core structure, there is a separation between the older and younger members. While the older council members continue to think traditionally, the younger members want to engage in more modern practices and alternatives. A rift also exists within the membership of the cooperatives, where perceptions and alignments run along national political-party lines.

In Grenada, the Fisheries Act (1986) obligates the minister responsible for fisheries to take measures to promote the management and development of the fisheries sector. In facilitating coastal-zone initiatives, the Fisheries Division collaborates with such agencies as Land Development Control Authority/Physical Planning Unit, Ministry of Health, Grenada Board of Tourism, Grenada Coast Guard, and Grenada Ports Authority. A fishery advisory committee (FAC) is provided for in the Grenada Fisheries Act 1986 (Grenada Fisheries Regulations 1987). The FAC was operational from 1987 to 1990 and from 1991 to 1993. Since 1993 it has been difficult to recruit fishers to the committee. During this project, attempts to create a fishers' group in the diver community of Calliste have been identified.

Informal rules and traditions

To date, fishers' local rules and traditional rights have a role in the informal management practices of the fishery. The open-access nature of the fishery in Trinidad emphasises the powerful role of boat owners with respect to ownership of resources, participation in the fishery, and benefiting from the fishery. The number of boats owned determines a person's potential influence.

People who own more than one and up to four boats have an elevated status. Most boat owners captain their own vessels, but in the case of the absentee boat owner, the captain has a greater role in determining who participates. In Trinidad, the 'rules of the sea' are recognised and observed with respect to the sea code, navigational aids, and marker lights for gill nets and fishing vessels at night. Safety at sea is a priority, so most vessels are equipped with life vests and carry excess water and food in case of emergency. However, there is limited formal training in safety at sea; most of the fishers who are trained work in the oil and gas industry.

An informal code of ethics exists among fishers. There is some level of trust regarding theft of gear and equipment, and a rule of vigilance whereby everyone looks out for strange boats at sea as well as strangers within their communities. This mutual dependence also applies to helping to haul boats ashore during bad weather, and giving assistance at sea to boats in distress. With respect to anchorage, home-port vessels are given preference over visiting vessels for safer or more accessible berthing spaces.

In Trinidad, all participants appreciate the traditional system of shares that dictates how people benefit from the catch. Costs for fuel, ice, and bait for each trip are accounted for before shares are distributed. For fishing trips using hook and line, fish pot, or nets, the distribution is relatively similar, with one share each to boat and engine gear/equipment, and one share for each crew member. In this way, a boat owner can receive three to four of the six available shares per boat. The beach seine fishery is different because of the nature of its operations and the large crew that is required. The money from each catch is first divided into two. The first half goes to the owner, which includes 10 per cent to each of the two captains. The other half is distributed to the crew: this includes two groups, the boat crew and the shore crew, and ranges from 10 to 20 fishers. The shares for the boat crew are divided according to the specialised nature of the jobs—for example, corkman, leadman, oarsman, engineman. Shares for specialised participatory roles (net menders, engine repairs man, scale man) consist of fish, cash, or a combination. There are also subtle variations in these arrangements, depending on the owner. The role of the captain is important in the beach seine fishery, as he decides who participates and how the share is paid out.

There is a common understanding that preference should be given to vendors who bring fuel, bait, and ice for fishers, which saves them the time and inconvenience associated with procuring these necessities. In Trinidad traditionally, women were not allowed to participate in the 'man business' of fishing at sea because of ill omen, nor were they allowed to hold higher-paying jobs within the beach seine fishery. However, women are taking on increasingly significant roles in all aspects of the fishery (as discussed in a later section).

In Belize, fishers are very careful to protect fishing grounds and will not divulge secrets to other fishers. In the central and northern areas of Belize, where use of traps is prevalent, there are fears that poachers might remove catch in traps laid down for lobster. In the south, fishers tend to rely more heavily on diving with hooks and using shades. Most of the fishers in Sarteneja work on or belong to one boat. Boat owners traditionally go out with their boats, supported by members of their immediate and extended family. Income generated from the sale of the catch to either cooperatives or private establishments is shared among the owner and boat crew, with the owner taking a larger share. The pre-season preparations are done with help from immediate and extended family. The cost of repairing and painting engines and boats and mending sails is covered by the owner, while the labour cost is absorbed by the fishers working on a free voluntary basis on that particular boat.

In Sarteneja, as well as in the Calliste dive fishery in Grenada, rules regarding closed seasons and catch limits of target species are recognised. The motivation for compliance may be a desire for sustainability of the target resource or fear of punitive action against transgressors. In contrast, in Trinidad and Grenada's Seche/FAS fisheries there are no rules regarding closed seasons, and the driving force for diverting fishing efforts over time and space is strictly economic—that is, whether fish 'is catching', along with the market price of the fish.

Co-management initiatives

In Trinidad, the fisheries legislative framework does not provide for the participation of industry stakeholders in managing the fisheries. Nevertheless, there are some mechanisms through which such participation has occurred. Government interventions have been mainly through institutional strengthening and capacity-building mechanisms. Interventions by the industry stakeholders are more directly as a consequence of user conflicts.

One of the major initiatives arising from a meeting between fishers and the government was one which sought to promote the sustainable management and optimal utilisation of the inshore fisheries resources on all coasts of Trinidad and Tobago. This agreement established new zoning for trawlers, gear restrictions, and no-fishing zones as well as a mechanism for self-regulation (Fisheries Division 1997). The fishery advisory committee, MAC, comprising representatives of government and non-governmental agencies, research institutions, and fishing organisations, was established to monitor this agreement. It also represents the first initiative of co-management at a national level. However, there is no representation on the MAC by the area under study because of the absence of any fishing organisation. It is against this backdrop that the project in Trinidad sought to develop a community-based co-management framework for the fisheries, involving the eight communities from Ortoire to Guayaguayare on the east coast of Trinidad.

In Belize, the Fisheries Department of the MAFC and the Forest Department of MNRE are the principal government agencies overseeing the establishment and management of MPAs in Belize. Both departments established co-management agreements for six MPAs, four of which fall within the Belize Barrier Reef World Heritage Site. A number of NGOs, including the Belize Audubon Society (BAS), the Toledo Institute for Development and the Environment (TIDE), and Friends of Nature (FON), have signed co-management agreements for the Half Moon Cay Natural Monument and Blue Hole Natural Monument, Port Honduras Marine Reserve, and Laughing Bird Cay National Park, respectively. Evidence shows that, where vested, the NGOs are more efficient than government agencies in exercising management responsibilities, and resources are more effectively protected. Accordingly, the government has adopted a strategy of engaging in these co-management arrangements with NGOs and CBOs. Under the aegis of a Global Environmental Facility (GEF/UNDP) project, the Coastal Zone Management Authority and Institute (CZMAI) has earmarked funds to support the Fisheries Department and MAFC in matters related to the management and use of the MPAs.

The co-management approach is proving successful in the case of the Blue Hole and Half Moon Cay Natural Monuments, which are being operated and managed by the Belize Audubon Society. Through the appointment of advisory committees, the MAFC has given stakeholders an opportunity to participate in managing these areas.

In a limited way, co-management in Grenada is anticipated in Part II Section 5 (1 and 2) of the Fisheries Act of 1986; however, this arrangement is only now slowly gaining momentum. In Grenada, building co-management relationships is very difficult in small-scale, multi-species, seasonal, multi-gear, multi-occupational fishing communities. Fishery managers have the task of recognising divergence and fostering and promoting both cohesion and consensus. The communities of Gouyave and Calliste possess similar political and socioeconomic conditions and demonstrate a distinct willingness to collaborate with relevant stakeholders for the purpose of building co-management relationships. As a result of this project, Calliste fishers decided to organise a fishers' cooperative to build such relationships.

Socioeconomic Aspects of Fisheries

Fishing operations and evolution of fishing communities

The diverse nature of Caribbean communities is a result of sociocultural, economic, political, historical, and physical factors. As discussed in chapter 1, fishing communities within the Caribbean often reflect this prevailing diversity, and can consist of a wide array of various social and sometimes physical units. An added dimension of the fishing community, besides being a place where a group of people are tied together by residence, identity, and history, is the idea of fishers who function as a group or unit, and who exploit a shared resource or common fishing areas, using similar gear. Such differences are explored by Jentoft, McKay, and Wilson (1998), who draw a contrast between a functional community and a local community. In addition, it is becoming increasingly difficult to describe Caribbean communities, particularly those that support coastal fisheries, as being predominantly rural or urban. This is because degrees of urbanisation and development vary, and also because of external sociocultural influences.

The fluid concept of the fishing community, which can alternate between the local community and the functional community, is also exemplified in the three case studies of Trinidad and Tobago, Belize, and Grenada. All three fisheries are typical of Caribbean artisanal fisheries, which are best described as relatively open-access, multi-species, multi-gear fisheries. Although the size of the study areas and the number of fishing communities involved vary among the countries, the manner in which the fishers operate strongly influences their interactions both with the targeted fish resources and among themselves. The sharing of common fishing areas with no regulatory zoning allows for the free movement of boats and access to shared resources. This boat mobility gives rise to the functional concept of community, whereby fishers using similar gear types can be grouped according to their fishing methods or target species. In the case of Trinidad and Tobago, this results in the gill net fishery, fish pot fishery, beach seine fishery, and line fishery; in Grenada, the line fishery and dive fishery; and in Belize, the trap fishery.

Boat mobility has added dimensions. The resultant functional community can create a sense of belonging based on fishing method. Or, issues may arise that are specific to a particular fishing method and thus unite the fishers for a common purpose. In Grenada, the fishers collectively exploit the seches along the west coast of Grenada, giving them the opportunity to come together to share information on the development and deployment of a fish aggregation device (FAD) in the Seche/FAS fishery.

In Trinidad, boat mobility is predominant among the gill net boats (boats that use gill nets as their primary fishing gear). This type of mobility has both spatial and temporal elements, as fishers exploit the *carite* (Spanish mackerel, *Scomberomorus brasiliensis*) from January to May and, to a lesser extent, the *ancho* (bluefish, *Pomatomus saltatrix*) from October to December. Although in the Trinidad study, the boats (mainly gill net boats) were moored at one site (home port), they could use any of the landing sites (Table 10) to offload their catch. Especially during the *carite* season, there is a migration of boats from several landing sites to Guayaguayare, which acts as a home port.

Simultaneous to the mobility of boats is the mobility of the fishers. In the case of Trinidad and the Seche/FAS fishery in Grenada, landing catches at different landing sites allows the fishers to mingle, share information, and develop social networks which are not necessarily restricted to their immediate communities. In Trinidad, this practice has led to the whole-community concept of 'Ortoire is Mayaro is Guayaguayare'. It also offers the vendors the advantage of being able to follow the catch and the boat owners, thus obtaining better prices because of the auctioning system. The fish pot fishers in Trinidad, although their fishing areas are just as extensive as the other fishers', have less of this sort of mobility and consequently are more separated from the other fishers.

The mobility of the Sarteneja fishers differs vastly from that of Trinidad and Grenada. Their high mobility is a result of the fishing grounds being located far enough from their community that they must relocate during the fishing season. The fishing grounds of the Sarteneja fishers are located on the entire north and south coasts, as far as 48 km offshore. A fishing trip in Belize can last up to several weeks at a time, and, as a result, fishers relocate to the community of Caye Caulker, an offshore community, for the duration of the fishing trip. Belize City also plays a significant role in the migration of fishers. By virtue of its harbour, it functions as a main sheltering port and supply depot for boats. A seasonal relocation does not occur in Grenada or in Trinidad and Tobago because the distances to fishing areas are much shorter. Although the distance travelled by fishers in Trinidad can exceed 40 km, outboard motors ensure that trips are usually completed within one day.

Mobility of fishers and their activities affect the functioning of the community. Observations in Belize indicate higher levels of activity when fishers are located at their home base during down time, with shops and businesses benefiting from their spending. The same increased social and economic activity is observed at the Guayaguayare landing site in Trinidad. Boat and fisher mobility also affects the local organisational structure of the fishing community as well as relationships both among fishers and within the fishers' households. These aspects are explored in later sections.

The varied habitats on the north and east coasts of Trinidad allow fishers to target many different species using multiple gear. Although the fishers can be grouped based on their primary fishing methods, almost all boats (excluding the land seine) use at least three methods, and some up to five. Fishers thereby take advantage of the seasonal nature of the fisheries resources and the habitats that allow such diversity. The fishers gain an intimate knowledge of the local conditions, which improves their ability to fish; however, the boat owners also invest an increasing amount in equipment. The use of multiple gear serves to diversify fishing techniques and maximise returns on investment, after years of declining catches. These fishing alternatives are not so easily available to the fishers of Belize and Grenada, partly because of the homogeneity of the fish habitats compared with those of Trinidad.

Heterogeneity of fishing communities

The Sarteneja community in Belize is a traditional fishing community of approximately 1,600 people, heavily dependent on fisheries as their main source of income. Geographically isolated from Belize City, the community has only basic household amenities and physical infrastructure, and external economic influences are minimal. The east coast fishing community in Trinidad is actually several contiguous villages containing a total of about 10,500 people linked by sociocultural, historical, and economic ties. These villages display an interesting blend of rural and urban characteristics, have a high level of access to social amenities and infrastructure, and are heavily affected by external influences, especially increasing investment by the oil and gas and related sectors. Most recently, there has been a resurgence of the tourism industry on the east coast. In Grenada, the Seche/FAS fishing community comprises several villages, including Gouyave, that exploit the same fishing grounds. The other community of Calliste is more physically cohesive. These two communities represent approximately 8 per cent of Grenada fishers.

The heterogeneity of Caribbean communities extends to the fishers themselves. Caribbean fishers are not homogeneous and may be categorised as full-time or part-time, career or transient (Espeut 1992). Research has distinguished the category of transient fisher or 'jumpers' in Grenada and Trinidad. They not only engage in fishing on a part-time basis but often remain unattached to a particular boat crew. Fishing is generally linked to the short-term need to secure immediate income. The experience is different in Sarteneja, mainly because fishing is family-oriented, with the boat crew consisting only of family members. Career or economic fishers have been identified in the fishing community of east-coast Trinidad and in the dive community of Calliste in Grenada. In the case of Trinidad, the investment for the career or economic fisher is significant. Such a fisher may own three or four boats and employ several fishers, yet will operate mainly with a fixed crew. The fisher regularly maintains his boats and equipment through active trade within the local fishing community and in adjacent communities outside of the study area. Including all landing sites, the combined asset value reported for the east coast fishery is approximately US$812,115 (US$1=TT$6.29). In Grenada, the fishing investment of the Calliste diver community is at a commercial level, whereas for the Gouyave (Seche/FAS) community it is at semi-commercial and subsistence levels.

Sociocultural and economic characteristics

There is a close link between the way people use resources and their sociocultural and economic background. An understanding of the socioeconomic attributes of fishers is vital for advancing alternatives for managing fisheries. In order to find an appropriate equilibrium between conserving fisheries resources and economic benefit to the fishers, it is critical to establish the socioeconomic status of the people that use and affect the fisheries, their use patterns, and their perceptions of the ecosystem. Additionally, the physical condition of ecosystems and the health of fish populations directly affect the viability of fishing economies. Moreover, the economic imperatives of fishing directly affect the health of fish populations because they dictate the activities of fishers and fishing communities (Hanna 2000). This association implies that in order to ensure healthy ecosystems, as well as viable fisheries and economies for the future, it is necessary to maintain the sustainability of both natural and human systems.

Research indicates that attempts to limit access to the fishery in order to control the fishing effort are more likely to be successful where employment opportunities are available in other sectors. For example, in the case of east-coast Trinidad, employment is available in the energy and related sectors and may account for 43 per cent of the part-time fishers interviewed. In Belize, however, the Sarteneja community has based its survival on the fishing industry, with 57 per cent of the working population being directly employed in fishing and agriculture. Few livelihood opportunities exist outside of the fishing industry. In Grenada, in the dive community of Calliste, people are involved in different aspects of the fishing industry as divers, traders, suppliers, providers, and processors, but in the more isolated community of Gouyave, the fishing industry consists mainly of fishers. Variations in sociocultural characteristics among the three study areas and within each study area appear to be linked to the cultural evolution of the communities and the impact that external influences have upon them. How the resource is exploited will also affect the community.

In assessing social linkages within the communities, it is interesting to observe the role of family within the fishing experience. For Sarteneja, fishing has traditionally been and remains a male-dominated and family-oriented activity. The male members of a family constitute the boat owners and crew, and male children are expected to follow in their elders' footsteps. In Sarteneja, there is a strong tradition that as soon as boys finish primary school, they are recruited into the fishery, in more or less an initiation into the primary role of men in this fishing society.

In contrast, and although there are some fisher families in the Trinidad study area, the family group does not dominate the fishery. There, boat crews and owners are primarily unrelated. Fishers' relatives, especially the women, usually help manage the fishing if the fisher is temporarily absent for any reason. In the Trinidad and Tobago study, 30 per cent of fishers indicated that they were related to another fisher, either at the home port or at another fish landing site within the study area. Although not fully explored, several sets of brothers who are fishers have also been identified within the Trinidad study area.

The Calliste community in Grenada closely resembles Belize, but the Gouyave community does not necessarily. The Calliste community exhibits strong kinship within the fishing community, with good organisation and cooperation among the fishers. Here, the industry has structured itself to address its needs, from exploitation to marketing. It has also established initiatives to deal with the occupational hazard of developing the 'bends' from scuba diving.

Alternative livelihoods

Small-scale fishing communities are sustained by fishing livelihoods, which require community members' constant access to fisheries. McGoodwin (2001) identified important types of fisheries capital as:

- natural capital: marine ecosystems and the living species they support;
- physical capital: fishing vessels, gear, landing sites, and processing and marketing facilities;
- financial capital: for sustaining operations, providing various items of physical capital, and supporting other social and economic activities, as well as, sometimes, for sustaining or enhancing natural capital; and
- human social and cultural capital: human skills and information utilised in fisheries activities, as well as broader accumulated knowledge containing guidance on how to go about living in general.

McGoodwin (2001) suggests that in most small-scale fishing communities, there are usually alternative livelihoods. These are supported by the sorts of capital that are particular to them, which are likewise integrated into the community's social and cultural fabric. Usually a community's alternative livelihoods support and complement one another, with community members collectively having more security by virtue of more alternatives available to them. However, it is also possible that some of the alternative livelihoods may compete for the various sorts of capital that support fishing livelihoods. Other demands for water resources (such as those prompted by developing agriculture, tourism, and mariculture) may create hardships for members of a fishing community.

East-coast fishers in Trinidad tend to seek alternative livelihood options available in the community to deal with the uncertainties of fishing as an occupation. Most fishers interviewed had been involved in fishing for over 20 years, and for 43 per cent of them, fishing was their main occupation. Forty-two per cent of fishers indicated that they fished on a part-time basis, otherwise working as lifeguards, mechanics, offshore oil workers, and estate managers. Three boat owners who own seven boats among them also own companies that service the oil and gas industry.

As mentioned previously, fishing is the main source of livelihood in Sarteneja, Belize, and few alternative livelihood options exist within the community. The younger generation, whether fishers or not, have chosen to venture outside the boundaries of the community to seek alternatives. Yet we saw during the community discussions that they are eager to create other livelihood options within Sarteneja. For Sarteneja, finding alternative sources of income was critical because this fishing-dependent community has been faced with rapidly declining catches over the last five years. The focus of our project was to build capacity within the fishing community, which can lead to the development of feasible alternative livelihoods and, in so doing, decrease the impact of fishing on the Belize Barrier Reef System.

Role of gender in fisheries

Normative trends of social organisation, social behaviour, and social and gender roles significantly influence fishery and other activities in small-scale fishing communities. Normally there is a division of labour along gender, age, and class lines, with correspondingly different social-role expectations for men, women, children, adults, and the elderly (Kailola 1996).

Gender differentiation in fishing activities is observed among the fishing communities of Sarteneja, Belize, east-coast Trinidad, and Calliste and Gouyave in Grenada, and may be linked to boat and fisher mobility to a degree. It is clear that the women of Sarteneja play no active role in the actual fishing activity. That community's high degree of fisher mobility may account for this phenomenon. Indeed, the length of time between fishers' visits to their home community and the short closed season may also contribute to a division of roles along gender lines, with men as primary producers and women managing all aspects of the household. Sarteneja women, who represent approximately 82 per cent of those outside the workforce, manage the family and home affairs during the active fishing season. The women, however, have demonstrated a very real desire to become involved in the development of the community. It was clear that they had a thorough knowledge of economic alternatives and what could be done to pursue some of them.

The situation is different in Trinidad and Grenada. In Trinidad, the early presence of pioneering women in the fishing industry and the fishers' daily interaction with women may account for the active role women play in all aspects of the east-coat fishery. Here, women are boat owners who actively fish and manage the fishing activity on behalf of their fisher husbands or sons. They are also involved in fishing groups and community organisations that promote fishers, as well as performing the more traditional roles of fish processors and vendors. Indeed, in 30 per cent of the households interviewed, women played an active role in fishing, selling of fish, and mending of nets for income-generating purposes. In Grenada, the role of women was limited to those who acted as vendors in the Gouyave community.

The extent to which women are aware of the fishing activities also varies among the studied communities. The younger women of Sarteneja are now seeking alternatives to the traditional livelihood options and are taking part, on an equal basis, with men in discussions pertaining to community development. Discussions with the women in east-coast Trinidad, specifically those who are boat owners or the relatives of boat owners, revealed a high level of awareness of fishing operations. These women were knowledgeable about almost every aspect of the fishing operations, including the methods used, the types of fish caught, pricing, and marketing. They had definite opinions on problems of the industry and solutions to these problems. The women felt they could contribute in a meaningful way to the organisation, management, and consequently the improvement of the fishing industry on the east coast. In fact, many of these women opined that their organisational and managerial skills were superior to those of the men in the industry. Therefore, during the life of the project they created WIFA.

Local knowledge

Local knowledge represents what fishers believe to be true about the resource, based on their interpretation of the evidence (Kaneko et al. 2001). Local knowledge, acquired by the fisher, is distinct from scientific and technical knowledge, and has been defined by Berkes (1999) as traditional ecological knowledge (TEK). It is experientially accumulated in the process of hunting, in competing with fellow fishers for share of fishing opportunity, and generally in coming to terms with the physical and human environments and other externalities. This local knowledge also includes the fishers' beliefs, which are the foundation for their particular positions on resource management.

Similar assessments of local knowledge in Trinidad and Grenada show that the fishers use landmarks to navigate. They are aware of the tides, moon phases, and currents affecting their fishing. However, because this knowledge is experiential, it is dependent on the type of fisher or fishing gear used, the nature of the stock (sedentary or not), and the geographic area. In Trinidad, many of the local names of fish reflect the country's colonial history of Spanish and French occupation and are not indigenous. Nonetheless, they form part of the wider body of knowledge on folk taxonomy.

Names of fishing areas share a similar fate, dominated by the French influence. Names of nearshore fishing areas are related to natural landmarks and are evidence of the fishers' use of landmarks for navigation. Other names areas have evolved to match the names of oil rigs, light sources, and boat channels that are associated with the oil and gas industry. Many of the differences and similarities in fishers' local knowledge are related to their primary fishing method. Those who use mainly fish pots and bottom-set gill nets know the topography of the sea floor and the conditions of the bottom environment. The local knowledge of fishers who use fish pots, however, has a greater geographic spread. Fishers in Trinidad use a variety of methods to help them decide where to fish. These include the awareness of tides, moon phases, colour and smell of water, currents, and presence of food sources, birds, and vegetation. They are aware that the moon phase, tide, and amount of food are inextricably linked. Fish-pot fishers who use a global positioning system (GPS) are not entirely dependent on this body of local knowledge. In Sarteneja, most of the traps are placed by means of triangulation using the land and other markers.

In Grenada, the divers who deal with sedentary stock such as sea-moss and shellfish also apply knowledge of landmarks. More important, they have created named zones within the local fishing area. These are referenced as navigational points and areas, and fishers characterise them based on bathymetry, coastal currents, tidal movements, benthic features, fish stock growth, fish movement, and catchability, related to seasonal differences. In the Seche/FAS fishery, fishers apply their knowledge of landmarks both for navigating to the fishing grounds and for maintaining the boat's position while adrift at distinct limited-area sites. They assess feeding depths and movements of target stocks by using their sunken fishing lines. They also apply their knowledge of current movement and behaviours of particular species in order to track and capture the fish. Characteristically, they treat their repertoire of knowledge as property—as capital to be traded or reserved. Similarly, in Trinidad, the practice of not sharing information about unique fishing areas is common. The fishers are quick to say that there is a definite ploy to lead other fishers astray if a good fishing area is found. Fishers can identify spawning grounds, spawning periods, nursery areas, and migration patterns, as well as the riverine influence from South America on breeding and supply of food. The fishers examine the gonads of the *ancho* to determine the length of time the fish stay in any particular place. In turn, gonad analysis determines the migration of their boats.

In Trinidad, there was a general consensus among the fishers that the quality of the nearshore coastal area and associated bays, the water quality (both nearshore and offshore), and the quantity and quality of fish ranged from good to very good. Fishers are aware of the functional relationship between reefs, mangroves, sea grasses, and fish production, and noted the relatively poor condition of these three habitats.

In a study on fishing and management issues with emphasis on the village of Guayaguayare, fishers overwhelmingly saw their fishing industry as important to the economy of the community of the east coast and to the rest of the country. They identified Guayaguayare as an important fishing village, and acknowledged that the oil and gas industry contributed greatly to its economy. They suggested, however, that the major decline in their catches was directly related to pollution from the oil and gas industry, as well as to overfishing. They also felt that increased oil and gas exploration would make fishing on the east coast more difficult. The fishers understood the need to protect the fish resources on the east coast to ensure future stocks, as well as the need to manage all aspects of the fishing industry—but few of them were aware of the existing fishing regulations. Nevertheless, besides identifying strategies such as monitoring of catches, gear, and boats, they expressed a need for increased dialogue with fishery managers, better representation from local politicians, need for a patrol by the local sea surveillance unit, and a reduction in the pollution. This suggests that what is needed is a more holistic approach to fisheries management.

Community-Based Coastal Resource Management

Much of the foregoing has attempted to set the context for a CBCRM strategy. As initiators of this approach, we relied on agents external to the central fishery regulatory mechanism. In Trinidad, the agent was a government-funded research institution, the Institute of Marine Affairs; in Belize, Programme for Belize (a national NGO) assumed the responsibility; in Grenada, we relied on a fisheries consultant, a past director of the fishery regulatory agency. Although the three projects had similarities in approach, owing to differences between the initiators and in the specific goals of each project, some strategies differed. Differences were also affected by the existing institutional co-management mechanisms within each country.

Building relationships

The overriding strategy of the CBCRM approach has been participatory in nature, with the goal of improving the livelihood of fishers in the communities. The three projects achieved this in varying ways, because of the specificity of each area and the issues and concerns therein, as well as the starting point of each project.

In Trinidad and Tobago, the starting point was to build relationships with the communities through meetings with fishers from the main fishing landing sites and with organisations involved in fishing. It was important to introduce the project in a visual format through the use of PowerPoint presentations. The IMA's previous work in the study area had been involved with EIAs for oil and gas companies. Researchers had noted the general decline of the fishing industry in the study area; however, contact with the fishers was limited. The IMA had been approached by a local community organisation on the issue of the fishing industry, but discussion with fishers revealed that the organisation was not widely accepted and its sub-committee on fishing was not operational. The IMA also had to market itself, as there was confusion between it and other government agencies.

Although many fishers were open to the goals of the project, there was a degree of reluctance and apathy because they were much more interested in obtaining physical infrastructure to assist them in their fishing. As a result, there were varying levels of acceptance of the IMA by the fishers, and the whole process took approximately a year. The IMA held one-to-one interactions through focus groups, workshops, personal interviews, and observations, and met the fishers at their convenience. Every day offers an opportunity to fish, with an average down time of one week during the year. The constant preoccupation with fishing was a factor in extending the time it took to build this relationship and to collect primary information from fishers. IMA's work with the fishers, both in developing the co-management framework for the industry and in establishing WIFA, contributed to the trust built between the institute and the community. IMA's provision to the fishers of maps of the fishing grounds to aid in navigation, and its representing of some of their immediate concerns at a national level, also helped in building relationships.

Roughly six months was required in Sarteneja, Belize, to build relationships that included mutual trust and respect. It was the first time that the NGO Programme for Belize had worked with a coastal community; their previous work had been with terrestrial communities. The only previous assessment of Sarteneja's fishing community had been conducted by Palacio (2002), despite the community's being the third highest contributor to the country's fisheries sector. During the initial period, numerous meetings were held with outside stakeholders and agencies involved directly or indirectly with the community. The community was met both in groups and on an individual basis with community leaders and people in key positions. This approach to participation was used to build the community's comfort level with the project.

Women and youth were engaged as well as the fishers. As in Trinidad, it was essential to understand the fishing operations. Discussions could be carried on only during the Easter holidays and during closed seasons for the lobster and conch fisheries. Prior sensitisation to the concept of overfishing by the fishing cooperative to which these fishers sold their catch increased the likelihood of collaboration. In meeting with some of the external stakeholders, one of the key foci was ensuring that the cooperatives gave their approval and, more importantly, their endorsement of the project's objectives and goals. Additional support came from the Belize Fishermen's Cooperative Association (BFCA). The BFCA was alarmed and concerned at recent trends and the forecasts being done for the fisheries sector, and was in the process of advising members and fishers of the immediate threats to the sustainability of the industry in the short and long term, given current pressures. Therefore, the cooperative welcomed the involvement of Programme for Belize and the project.

In the Grenadian fishing communities of Gouyave and Calliste, relationship-building also took some time. Both initial and sustained engagement with local communities was shown to require a legitimate point of entry, backed up by credibility generated through the research intervention. The use of local knowledge fitted such purposes and proved highly useful to both fishery managers and fishery biologists, along with the participation of the fishers in the research process. The process of gathering and validating local knowledge demonstrated the value of working with people from the community. Validated local knowledge also provided a new dimension for science-based participants, and the discussion of local knowledge in focused multi-stakeholder groups provided the opportunity for science-based and community-based stakeholders to engage face to face, which facilitated cross-fertilisation of ideas.

Focus group and multi-stakeholder group consultations were accomplished using field-based data collected by the community. This provided a legitimate and acceptable instrument for unifying the team of stakeholders who participated in the process. The research group consultations and engagements served to initiate relationships among the participating stakeholders for the longer term.

An advantage was the knowledge of the project leader (a previous director of the Fisheries Department) on the operations of the Seche/FAS and dive fisheries, in addition to that of the fishers themselves. The development of mutual respect and the exchange of information took place during these workshop sessions, which required all participants to work together, especially in the construction of an FAD and in workshops facilitated by the project leader.

The participatory approach was extended to data collection by community members and was part of all the projects. In both Trinidad and Belize, community members collected socioeconomic data about the fishers' households. In Grenada, both fishers and scientists participated in an assessment of sea-urchin stock for the dive fishery. In all the projects, much of the discussion about management of the resources took place in workshops and focus group meetings.

Community-based management strategies

The overall purpose of the management strategies was the improvement of the livelihood of fishers. Fishers in Trinidad wanted an improvement in the infrastructure of the fishing facilities, reduction of the conflicts between fishers and the energy sector and among themselves, and training so they could improve their capacity. Additional concerns were the improvement of the quality of the nearshore environment and compliance by fishers with the regulated mesh size for gill nets. (Approximately 72 per cent of fishers use non-conforming nets.) In the Sarteneja community, the management strategy has been towards developing alternatives to fishing, given the drastic decline in fishers' earning capacity and the overexploited status of the target species. In the Seche/FAS fishery in Grenada, the issue of paramount importance is sea-space conflict. It leads to territoriality, sea lords, navigational responsibilities of fishers, rules for sharing of sea space, negotiation of rules of conduct among fishers, ownership and control of artificial fishing devices along with conditions arising from their deployment, and the safety of fishers at FAS.

In contrast to the start of the project in Trinidad, when fishers were wary of forming any kind of fishing association because of previous failures, during 2004 two fishing associations were formed. One was the SFA, which represented fishers from Ortoire to Guayaguayare; the other was WIFA. These organisations sprang up not only as a result of conflicts with the oil and gas industry within the preceding two years, but also as a result of the awareness created by this project. To date, the SFA has successfully negotiated for radar reflectors and life jackets for their boats and sea training, including the use of GPS. The SFA has also been instrumental in obtaining redress for damage to fishing equipment by the energy sector. The developmental plans of both associations have sought to address many concerns and issues through engaging and working with both the government and the energy sector.

One of the main objectives of the work in Sarteneja was to establish a set of strategic development plans for and generated by the community. These provided several potential alternative occupational options that the community could pursue, such as a variety of tourism initiatives including guiding, fly-fishing, and scuba diving. Small-scale aquaculture was also identified as an option that could build on skills the fishers already possessed.

In Grenada, fishers recognised that addressing sea-space management was beyond their own control and that it was crucial to collaborate with the fishery regulatory agency. During the life of the project in the dive fishery based at Calliste, a fund was established to assist divers who contract the bends.

Much of the process used to engage the fishers has been participatory, an approach that is characteristic of co-management strategies. Community-based resource management, however, incorporates both advantage and opportunity. Because of its focus on the community, it deals with management issues that directly affect communities. This results in immediate changes, which, if positive, can create greater acceptance and buy-in and lead, in turn, to greater success.

The CBCRM approach is very inclusive and allows much participation and representation at the community level. Fishing operations have a direct impact on the participation of the resource users, as exemplified in these three cases studies. In Trinidad, the daily operation of the fishery is a constraint to political organisation and participation because boat owners, particularly those who go out to sea and those who are involved in other jobs, usually cannot spare the time.

Therefore, women in Trinidad can play an important role in organising these fishing communities. They possess excellent working knowledge about the fishery and its operations. In addition, they are boat owners, managers, and caretakers of the family, and their enthusiasm and motivation are indicated by their willingness to form a fishing association. Women's involvement in community committees can also foster stronger links between the fishing industry and other sectors at the community level. In contrast, women in Belize have no active role in fishing. However, because of their role as caretakers, they have been equal participants in workshops to explore alternatives to fishing as a livelihood option. In Grenada, women also have a limited role: there they are only processors and vendors. Perhaps through the CBCRM approach, the stigma associated with women in the fishing industry can be examined.

The lack of representation on the MAC by the area under study in Trinidad has meant that the fishers' only link with the central government is through its extension officer. The resulting isolation has been a detriment to the fishing industry in the area because the end result is a reduced political visibility at the national level. Nonetheless, the fishing community has rallied to obtain redress from the oil and gas industry, which has led to the formation of the SFA. Such communities demonstrate that they are already using their own indigenous management arrangements to effect change. The fact that it is a geographically focused area with common fishing issues (including conflict with another sector and lack of fishing facilities) allowed fishers to come together despite being from heterogeneous fishing communities. This ability to deal with fishery issues by themselves to some extent has created greater social empowerment and cohesion of the communities.

The CBCRM approach in managing fishery issues in the fishing communities from Ortoire to Guayaguayare can be used as a role model for other communities. One of the objectives of this community-based resource management approach has been to encourage representation of this area on the MAC, which provides a direct link between the CBCRM approach and the existing co-management arrangement in Trinidad. Such a proposition has been made to the MAC by the IMA on behalf of the SFA. This link is essential in order to increase the political visibility of the fishing communities and legitimise the CBCRM approach in Trinidad and Tobago.

Conclusions

As outlined in this chapter, the heterogeneity exhibited by coastal Caribbean communities extends to communities associated with fishing. The fishing industry provides a livelihood for many residents, who are, in some instances, dependent entirely upon the fishery. The varied nature of the habitats, target species, and fishing methods and the distance travelled to the common fishing grounds directly affect the daily life of the fishers and their families and therefore the community. The differences in the composition of the fishing units (either family-only or community members), the demographics of the fishers, the degree of importance of fishing at a community level, and the social networks all add to the complexity and diversity that characterise the fishing communities. The management of exploited fish resources is highly dependent on the social structure of the communities.

The CBCRM approach is a natural process because it builds upon indigenous management systems that use local knowledge of the fishery, key leaders, and social networks. It also affords an opportunity for coastal communities to increase their visibility at both the community and national level. This is particularly true in countries with no legal framework to accommodate co-management. The geographic specificity of the CBCRM approach must be appreciated, and the design of any interventions must take it into consideration.

Lessons learnt

- Participation is fundamental to the CBCRM approach. The participation of the community must be incorporated from the start to the end of the project. Wherever possible, the participatory approach includes consultation, feedback, and participation in data collection. It is important to obtain buy-in by the communities, and the goals and objectives must be properly communicated to the communities. Any expectations on the part of the community that are not addressed in the project must be discussed.
- The project must have a degree of flexibility built in to accommodate developments during its life.
- There must be a sense of empowerment among the community to achieve tangible success through participation. Players must respect one another's views, particularly regarding conflict. This forms the environment for dialogue, negotiation, compromise, and, ultimately, resolution. The process must be seen to be fair to all involved, and there should be no bias towards any one group.
- Some goals should be implementable in the short term and future successes built upon them.

- The heterogeneity of the community extends to different interests, some of which may be complimentary, others not. There must be the expectation of a degree of competition among the stakeholders.
- Key leaders and knowledgeable people are not necessarily the most visible or vocal. Care and time must be spent in properly identifying them.

Acknowledgements

The authors of this chapter are extremely grateful to the people of the communities of Ortoire, Plaisance, St Joseph, St Ann's, Grand Lagoon, St Margaret's, Guayaguayare, Sarteneja, Gouyave, and Calliste for accommodating us for the past two years. We thank you for opening your lives and your homes to us. We appreciate your participation in the project in data collection, workshops, and meetings and for unselfishly giving of your time. Without your participation this project would not be possible. Thanks also to Sandra Grant for her useful comments on the draft version of this chapter.

We would also like to thank the following for their assistance and participation: Fisheries Division, Ministry of Agriculture, Land and Marine Resources; British Petroleum of Trinidad and Tobago; Coastal Zone Management Authority and Institute; the Fisheries Department, Ministry of Agriculture, Lands and Forestry and Fisheries; United Nations Development Programme; and Global Environmental Fund.

We are especially grateful to the following agencies and institutions for financial and technical support: International Development Research Centre, CARICOM Fisheries Unit, IOI-Costa Rica, and Laval University, Québec, Canada.

References

Berkes, F. 1999. *Sacred ecology. Traditional ecological knowledge and resource management.* Philadelphia and London: Taylor and Francis.

Berkes, F., R. Mahon, P. McConney, R. Pollnac, and R. Pomeroy. 2001. *Managing small-scale fisheries. Alternative directions and methods.* Ottawa: IDRC.

Charles, A. 2001. *Sustainable fishery systems.* Fish and Aquatic Resources Series 5. London: Blackwell Science Ltd.

Chuenpagdee, R., J. Fraga Berdugo, and J. I. Euán-Ávila. 2004. Progressing towards co-management through participatory research. *Society and Natural Resources* 17: 147–61.

Commonwealth Business Council. 2004. Country report. November 1. www.cbcglobelink.org/cbcglobelink/country/Grenada/cr.htm.

Espeut, P. 1992. Social and economic considerations for fisheries management planning in the Caribbean. Paper delivered to the Fisheries Management Planning Sub-project Specification Workshop of the CARICOM Fisheries Resource Assessment and Management Programme (CFRAMP), Kingston, Jamaica, Dec 14–17.

Fisheries Act. 1916. Laws of Trinidad and Tobago. Chapter 67: 51.

Fisheries Act. 1980. Laws of Belize. Chapter 210.

Fisheries Division 1996. Policy directions for marine fisheries of Trinidad and Tobago in the 1990s (draft). St Clair, Port of Spain: Fisheries Division, Ministry of Agriculture, Land and Marine Resources.

Fisheries Division. 1997. Report of the committee appointed by the Honourable Minister of Agriculture, Land and Marine Resources Dr. Reeza Mohammed. Trinidad: Ministry of Agriculture, Land and Marine Resources.

Fisheries Division. 2000. 1998/1999 Annual report. Trinidad and Tobago: Ministry of Agriculture, Land and Marine Resources.

Food and Agriculture Organisation of the United Nations. 2000a. Summary table A-1 Fish, crustaceans, molluscs, etc. World capture production [168K]. June 11. ftp://ftp.fao.org/fi/stat/summary/a1a.pdf, accessed September 27, 2004.

Food and Agriculture Organisation of the United Nations. 2000b. Fishery country profile. January. www.fao.org/fi/fcp/en/GRD/profile.htm, November 1, 2004.

Government of Belize. 2002. Medium-term economic strategy 2003–2005. Belize: Ministry of Economic Development.

Grenada Fisheries Act. 1986. Act No. 15 of 1986. pp. 111–41.

Grenada Fisheries Regulations. 1987. Grenada statutory rules and orders No. 9 of 1987. pp. A53–A80.

Hanna, S. 2000. Change and resilience in New England and Pacific groundfish fisheries. In *Resilience and change in fisheries: Experiences from New England and the Pacific,* ed. S. Hanna and M. Hall-Arber, Chapter 1. Corvallis: Oregon State University.

Jentoft, S., B.J. McKay, and D.C. Wilson. 1998. Social theory and fisheries co-management. *Marine Policy* 22: 423–36.

Kailola, P. 1996. An assessment of the role of women in fisheries in Vanuatu. FAO Technical Report No. 3. Technical Cooperation Programme.

Kaneko, J., P. Bartram, M. Miller, and J. Marks. 2001. Local fisheries knowledge. The application of cultural consensus analysis to the management and development of small-scale pelagic fisheries. Project final report. Hawaii:

Pelagic Fisheries Research Program, National Oceanographic and Atmospheric Administration, and University of Hawaii.

Kishore, R, X. Chin, and H. Ramsundar. 2003. Potential impacts of industrial development on coastal fisheries in the Gulf of Paria, Trinidad. In Proceedings of the 54th Annual Gulf and Caribbean Fisheries Institute, 13–27. Port of Spain: Institute of Marine Affairs.

McGoodwin, J.R. 2001. *Understanding the cultures of fishing communities: A key to fisheries management and food security.* FAO Fisheries Technical Paper (401). Rome: FAO.

Palacio, J. 2002. Community management of protected areas conservation project (COMPACT). Belize City: Programme for Belize.

United Nations. 1994. *Agenda 21: Program of action for sustainable development. Rio Declaration on Environment and Development.* New York: United Nations Publications.

World Bank, United Nations Development Programme, Commission of European Communities, and Food and Agriculture Organisation of the United Nations. 1992. *A study of international fisheries research.* Washington, DC: World Bank.

8

Analytical Insights, Lessons Learnt, and Recommendations

Yvan Breton and Brian Davy

This volume's introduction strongly emphasised the need for a flexible management approach. The Caribbean represents a highly diversified and fragmented context, both at the ecological and cultural levels, and it is not characterised by a long tradition of community-based management. Deeply influenced by the processes that took place during the colonisation period, Caribbean societies are now fully engaged in the processes of globalisation, and both phenomena continue to have strong impacts on heterogeneity. While these phenomena are not particular to the Caribbean, through time they have acquired some specificity that constitutes an important independent variable for any researcher interested in the identification of relevant issues on coastal management in the region. However, this task is not easy: there is a complexity of resilient forms arising from the colonial past which has resulted in a mix of cultures and institutions, as well as various groups of stakeholders. All have recently been influenced by simultaneous globalisation and decentralisation trends.

This concluding chapter attempts to build on the previous comparative case studies pinpointing how a local-community approach to management still remains critically important, in spite of the precedence and resurgence of protectionist approaches for conservation. Eco-regional planning, ecosystem-based management, and transboundary protected areas can be considered as possible paths to implementation. However, they must be considered within a series of approaches, among which community and participation remain central precepts for conservation (Brosius and Russel 2003). Given the expanding literature on these alternatives, partly explored in the introduction to this volume, we do not intend to fully enter into the debates and discussions that emerged from it. Instead, we rely on the ethnography that precedes (chapters 3 through 7), and we present concrete examples from which readers can draw their opinions and experiences.

We start with a discussion of analytical issues, paying attention to various forms of resilience that might influence collective action. However, we emphasise that, despite sharing similarities at the analytical level, these forms entail diverse research strategies and mobilisation efforts. This is particularly true in a context where a strong tradition in CBCRM does not exist. The relationship between communities' diversity and the larger institutions into which they are embedded in a governance perspective follows, with an emphasis on a flexible and cross-scale approach to management.

This section ends with some remarks on the lack of critical analysis of epistemology linked to coastal management. We then proceed to an examination of a series of variables stemming from the comparison of previous case studies, pinpointing some lessons that have been learnt during Phases I and II of the IDRC-CBCRM Caribbean programme. Finally, we draw a series of recommendations aimed at researchers and decision makers involved in the management of coastal areas, hoping to influence their future management interventions in this region.

Rethinking Analytical and Methodological Issues

One challenge that we better understood during the course of our analyses was the lack of a typology or integrated research framework within which to frame these analyses. We initially thought that the existing literature offered enough insights into these questions to allow us to develop such a framework. However, we now realise that at best there exists a mixture of papers on resilience theory, and others on participation and interdisciplinarity. Few make the linkages to each other and to coastal management—and almost none do so in the Caribbean. Therefore, we had to work from a very mixed bag of theory that made it extremely challenging to have an overall, agreed-upon framework for all projects. We believe that more cross-analysis of the various interconnecting schools of thought is needed so as to develop a more broadly based framework that can guide future research in the Caribbean.

Resilience factors in Caribbean coastal management

There has recently been a surge of interest in the importance of resilience—that is, the ability of systems to buffer change. Heterogeneity (in both cultural and ecological systems) is seen by many as one of the most important factors in promoting this. An improved understanding of the concept and how it played out in the Caribbean context was a central factor guiding much of our research. Resilience exists in many forms, and this work has clearly only scratched the surface in looking at these details.

In studying cultural systems that interact with ecological systems, a better understanding of individual-, household- and community-level issues is needed. Such issues are complex. They include how fishers organise their time, not only around different types of fishing (which may vary by season, species sought, or gear used) but also by integration with other livelihoods; according to seasonal migration, following the movement of selected fish stocks; by involvement of different members of the family or extended family; and according to historical knowledge and roles. Clearly, we do not understand the various forms of organisation and the choices individuals and groups make on the use of their time. Building on past and present knowledge systems is crucial. Indigenous knowledge and values, as well as other forms of traditional knowledge, continue to exist and play a role. In the cases examined during this research, Belize, Guatemala, and Panama provide particularly good examples of this reality.

The absence of a significant CBCRM tradition in the Caribbean is a phenomenon often mentioned in the previous chapters of this volume. However, its absence does not mean that CBCRM cannot be consolidated in the future. Despite colonisation's strong negative impact on native communities, contrary to what has been assumed by several authors, indigenous cultural features and institutions were not entirely eliminated. Chapter 3 makes this point very clearly. Some indigenous communities, such as the Kuna and Garifuna, have lost some of their pristine elements. However, they have been able to adjust to new contexts while maintaining some form of cultural continuity, either at the techno-economic, linguistic, and/or religious level. In general, the loss of key heterogeneity factors takes place in centralised management contexts (Berkes and Folke 2002). This represents a challenge in developing a more community-based approach. Unfortunately, our research was unable to probe this set of issues adequately.

We were unable to provide further clarity on what might be in danger of being lost when local management is supplanted by more central management.

Similar remarks can be made for other ethnic groups who migrated to the area, even though the colonisation processes undermined and destabilised their previous socioeconomic organisation. In other words, if these long-term interactions have generated a significant cultural hybridisation and weakened previous mechanisms of community-based organisation, they also allowed the experimentation and consolidation of new organisational devices at the economic and institutional levels. Resilience factors, in which heterogeneity is a salient characteristic, are an inherent component of Caribbean peoples' use of their coastal areas, and they should represent key markers in the research and intervention efforts here. The important point, at the analytical level, is that different forms of resilience must be taken into account. That is the why the implementation of a CBCRM approach in the Caribbean is a difficult process.

These case studies illustrate this point very clearly. Without making an exhaustive review of current management problems in the region, the chapters in this volume nevertheless emphasise that the same problem can be dealt with in various ways according to the local context. The importance we give to this level of explanation (with its ecological and social components) is not rooted in an absolute faith in CBCRM approaches. Instead, in several cases, it stresses that prior knowledge of local institutional constraints and users' behaviour is a critical requirement for management problems to be solved.

Resilience, however, can also refer to the notion of "epistemic communities" (Jones 2004) whose membership largely bypasses a given socio-spatial unit. Around a particular management issue, individuals with diverse backgrounds and status can develop a shared focus leading to a gradual understanding of their different perceptions and values. Local actors are often obliged to deal with individuals who belong to research centres, non-governmental organisations (NGOs), or government agencies. These intermediate and cross-scale levels of interaction, in which the bureaucracy plays a central role, are often characterised by different types of resilience. If we define the latter as the people's capacity to maintain some form of continuity within a previously changing situation, we must admit that in general, both science and bureaucracy (which is management by the state) are characterised by less 'flexible responses'. In general, their practices and orientations are conditioned by stochastic and formalist models; within institutional contexts these are more oriented towards the future than the past. If we add to this their reliance on different forms of knowledge for grasping reality, given their inclusion of several specialists, many perceptual differences can arise that affect the identification of adequate initiatives for solving management problems. Very often, local people have a more practical vision of their problems, given their constant interactions with their ecosystem.

Finally, it is useful to make a distinction between individual and collective forms of resilience. The first refers to one's behaviour and perception in a given situation; the second, to having a more elastic and abstract content, which consists of basic value-orientations that a group acquires through time in a more or less visible way. To pay attention to these two levels of resilience presupposes various research strategies, going from short, direct observation in the field to longer-term involvement in the group's history and evolution. Attention must be paid not only to the physical aspects of ecosystems but to the people's diverse perception mechanisms. Conceived through various ecological and social scales, resilience and heterogeneity are not incompatible concepts but rather integral parts of a same phenomenon: a changing continuity. The case studies clearly show that several management initiatives in the Caribbean could benefit from greater methodological care at the intervention level. Indeed, if more attention had been paid to local variations at the outset, there would have been less need for retroactive and rectification efforts. Now these are necessary. The range of problems encountered in the numerous marine protected areas (MPAs: see chapter 4) in the region provides an instructive set of examples.

Local disparities and sub-regional governance channels

Striking elements that emerge after studying Caribbean coastal management issues are the diverse forms of communities' boundaries, the variety of their economic activities, and the diversity of political and institutional contexts in which they are embedded. However, as one moves from the community to the national or regional level, this diversity has to be reduced to a more generalised form at a methodological level and captured in more structural terms. As stated by Olsen (2001, 10), one option is

> to build systems of planning and decision-making that operate across a range of spatial scales and to develop governance systems as nested systems in which the goals/actions taken at one scale do not contradict those at higher and lower levels.

In other words, the establishment of management policies must rely on research approaches that balance the respective weights of local and national/ regional features.

Our work begins the process of better understanding what is happening at these levels in coastal areas. We list below a number of sub-issues that are emerging from our work to date. These issues are overlapping and represent initial 'first cuts' at what is a complex situation that is evolving without much of a defined theoretical framework. Nonetheless, these issues should be useful for enriching our comparative efforts; hopefully they will lead to the examination of policy changes with some operational value.

Spatially and temporally fluid boundaries

These are examples based on cases of resources, fishers' and harvesters' movements, and tourism expansion. The preceding chapters examined great variations in the communities' spatial extension. These communities' situations are influenced not only by their population size, but also by the nature of their economic activities, the availability (migratory nature and/or seasonal variations) of their target resources, and the need to be mobile in order to harvest these resources.

In Grenada and Trinidad, for instance, the fishers' mobility entails recurrent seasonal moves in given coastal areas, with a return to inland locations during periods of inactivity. A similar situation prevails in the Jaragua Park of Dominican Republic. In Sartaneja, Belize, fishers undertake weekly migrations with extended stays in secondary locations. In spite of their differentiated capital assets and technical specialisation, over time these producers and their families have developed a sense of sociological belonging to the notion of place. They have an understanding of 'their' coastal area, which has evolved into more than merely the area in which they live. This type of spatial/temporal flux or movement, combined with a deep understanding of their environment, must not be neglected in management plans that seek to promote more sustainable livelihood options. The transformations taking place in artisanal fisheries are characterised by the pressure to search for more distant and more productive fishing sites and the expansion of pelagic fisheries and aquaculture. These issues represent good examples of the necessity to pay attention to the evolving contexts in which the fishers live and work at both local and regional levels.

The Yucatan coast of Mexico offers a different example, because incomes from fisheries has improved. A variety of non-traditional fishers seasonally migrated to the coast and took up fishing as an income (or perceived income) source. Therefore, income was greater in the fishery sector than in other occupations in inland regions. Other examples of this phenomenon are plentiful in our limited examination of this set of issues. Therefore, management approaches that seek to promote a fixed-in-one-place, full-time, one-fish-stock-focused approach would seem to run counter to the traditional situations found in most of our research cases. In them, a more heterogeneous approach based on fishers' movement/migration was a critical element of resilience in the communities studied.

On the other hand, these fluid boundaries at a local level are embedded in larger economic-political contexts that also are evolving. For instance, the importance of the fisheries at national-regional levels, relative to local levels, is often inadequately understood with reference to the management implications of such boundaries. In countries where fisheries represent a minimal portion of the gross domestic product (GDP), as is the case in oil-rich Trinidad and Tobago (T&T), where fisheries make a contribution of only 0.19 per cent (see chapter 7), fishers have low economic and political power. This makes their negotiations with and recognition by the authorities more difficult. By comparison, in Belize, where fisheries represent more than 7.2 per cent of GDP, fishers have successfully developed strong social coalitions that are often referred to as models throughout the Caribbean.

So here again, local contexts have to be examined within a changing, larger spatial and political framework if one aims to better understand their specificity. For instance, despite their differences, fishing communities in Belize share a number of positive features, compared with those in T&T, in the sense that they belong to an economic sector which is of vital importance and in which they have some political weight. By contrast, in T&T fishing has a much lower priority both economically and politically. This affects fishing communities in several ways, particularly in terms of their ability to influence policies and related activities above the local level.

Finally, in the midst of these larger management issues concerning economic activities at the local level, the Caribbean communities are more and more faced with an increased expansion of tourism, ranging from beach mass tourism to scuba diving and sport fishing. At the governance level, this economic sector implies the presence of differentiated social actors, many of them possessing more political power than the local inhabitants. The expansion of tourism can promote greater conservation efforts and help local communities to develop new activities around ecotourism and related projects, thus offering a variety of new livelihood opportunities, but also generating many conflicts in relation to the access to and ownership of coastal land and marine areas, as well as associated resources. This is especially true when those who initiate the projects belong to outside institutions. The Isla de la Juventud case in Cuba is a good illustration of this, with the almost complete eviction of local fishers from a 'protected area' now reserved for international tourism. Given the economic importance of tourism in the Caribbean, it remains a key structural variable for grasping management problems that interfere with communities' specific management options.

Understanding the barriers to decentralisation

We have assumed that the lack of successful CBCRM experiences in the Caribbean, combined with a history of top-down interventions of many state bureaucracies, is the major factor in the limited decentralisation to date. Development of successful cases of community-based management will help to test this assumption. This barrier to decentralisation is also partially explained by the political-territorial fragmentation in the region. This phenomenon likely did not support the establishment of common and robust decentralisation policies in which communities could have acquired greater decisional autonomy. Colonisation was a process in which the political leaders, who often relied on authoritarian measures, were external to the region. This situation established a distance from the local populations. For a long period, productive incentives were oriented mainly towards the needs of external economies. This plantation-economy approach has prevailed until recent years. Now, greater economic diversification is increasingly recognised as a more useful policy orientation. Even in socialist Cuba, the plantation-economy orientation was at work until recently (Doyon 2003).

Continuing the search for improved understanding of the diversity, we have observed that the Caribbean Sea has diversified marine ecosystems (see Map 1 on page 191 and Table 10 in this chapter for more information on this heterogeneity). These represent a strong set of ecological drivers that operate in the more than 30 Caribbean countries. These processes have led to various management traditions and institutions whose integration is still in considerable flux. We also need to emphasise how these political and economic structures are evolving, particularly in recent decades. During this period, some regional institutions (such as ACS, CARICOM, and CRFM; see Haughton et al. 2004) are now seeking to rationalise their management efforts within a wider set of policy drivers. However, it is evident that important gaps still remain in the promotion of effective collaboration between many of the key countries. These gaps negatively influence regional collaboration and generate disparate impacts on local communities.

Improved understanding of institutional capacities

Important sub-regional differences are found in the countries' research-organisation capacities. This must be taken into account in the promotion of CBCRM approaches in the Caribbean. There is no doubt that Mexico, Cuba, and Dominican Republic—and to a lesser extent Jamaica, Barbados, Costa Rica, and T&T—possess relatively strong capacities, with known institutions in marine affairs that are actively involved in coastal zone management initiatives. But we should be aware that, in spite of their advantages, these countries have been strongly influenced by the top-down approaches of international agencies before and after the 1992 conference in Rio de Janeiro. Indeed, they have created numerous marine parks and reserves in which the consolidation of CBCRM was not a priority.

As mentioned by Begossi and Brown (2003, 136), 'participatory' consultations often took place when decisions had already been made behind closed doors, thus relegating various management concepts to the realm of 'rhetoric'. As was illustrated by the initiatives that took place in several coastal areas covered in that book, the criteria put forward by international agencies and applied by national agencies and bureaucracies often prevailed over local perceptions and uses of the resources. Chapter 4 explains well how the population of San Felipe, Yucatan, Mexico, wanted to create its own marine reserve in the mid-1990s. Nevertheless, the community had to engage in several retroactive skirmishes with the authorities to regain more autonomy and decision-making capacity. To date, considerable resources have been put into building local capacity to pursue these objectives, but the battle is not over yet. Further implications of this issue of improved understanding of institutional capacity and what is needed to promote change are taken up again under the section on lessons learnt.

Common regional and sub-regional issues and meso levels of governance

Recent approaches to CBCRM (Kearney 2004) suggest that all stakeholders must pay more attention to 'meso-levels' of management instead of putting too much emphasis on generic images of both state and communities. These meso levels presuppose that in the interactions between the state and the communities, various agencies or individuals (state agencies, NGOs, private-sector groups) seek to intervene, with different mandates, interests, and responsibilities. Legal bases for community-based natural resource management (CBNRM) derive from particular contexts, both ecological and institutional. Therefore, we believe that another barrier is a lack of understanding of the relations that communities develop with such institutions or their representatives. At the level of the communities themselves, there is a need to better understand the heterogeneity at this bureaucratic level when examining the decision-making process (horizontal and vertical) linked to a particular management problem.

In summary, the major difficulty lies in the fact that the central government has almost absolute power in most Caribbean countries. The presence of political delegations or subdivisions, whether federal, provincial, or municipal, often generates a nominal decentralisation in which local populations possess limited autonomy. The presence of a new institutional mechanism, such as a ministry representing a federation of local communities (or the like), could be an important idea to explore in selected countries in the promotion of a community-based coastal resource management (CBCRM) approach.

CBCRM and paradigmatic shifts in management issues

As is often the case in the consolidation of a new paradigm, the initial assumptions that surrounded the consolidation of CBCRM and related management concepts a few decades ago relied on what was possibly a lack of clarity between their explanatory power and their apparent novelty (Brosius, Tsing, and Lowenhaupt 1998). A new paradigm generally emerges when, in a given context, the existing devices are progressively losing their previous usefulness in the face of a changing reality. Without entering here into the differences between paradigmatic shifts in natural and social sciences, new ideas about management have been rooted in the prevalence of natural resources (natural-science approaches) over human beings (social science). The latter have been progressively taken into account with the consolidation of bio-economic science and debates about common-pool resources.

However, the 'tragedy of the commons' paradigm sets aside many social and cultural factors that should be inherent components of any management effort. Promoted by international and national agencies as well as academic institutions, management paradigms have suffered from the beginning from a lack of internal critique. The result is that they were often thought of as universal devices applicable to a variety of contexts within a top-down framework. Therefore, it is not surprising to see that the consolidation of CBCRM approaches has been strongly promoted by NGOs, in recent decades, to counterbalance the power of the state. At first, this led to a generalised model, which was thought to be applicable in several contexts within a relatively mechanical framework.

However, after a few decades of experimentation, these paradigms have led to new sub-paradigms in which there is a greater recognition of the complexity of the real world and the interconnectedness between humans and ecosystems. The numerous continuing discussions about co-management are very illustrative of this situation and draw attention to the unfinished state of the debates (Wilson et al. 2003; Pomeroy et al. 1997; Jentoft and McCay 2003). Overall, and in spite of sub-paradigmatic shifts, mainstream narratives on management continue to lead to attempts to cope with a large number of empirical cases without sufficiently taking into account their specificity, and remain influenced by state and global capital investment (Nichols 1999). The epistemology linked to coastal management is a good example of the emergence and consolidation of paradigms in a context in which political and economic factors prevailed over more scientific criteria. As well, the resilient logic of bureaucracy always tended to standardise rather than differentiate social groups within which it interacts. This is what we call the homogenising approach, which runs counter to the need to recognise and conserve the key group components, or the heterogeneity factor.

In summary, several gaps can be identified between the existing theories and practices that are linked to management initiatives in many countries. Despite recent and positive reorientation efforts, in which both co-management and community-based management are the object of analytical refinements, most of the epistemological basis supporting their central concepts is still rooted in a westernised culture that has a tendency to expand its own logic at the expense of other cultural premises.

This volume seeks to focus attention on the limited operational value of several management concepts in the Caribbean. This body of work rejects the nominal use of the notion of 'community' in its traditional sociological sense. Instead, it places emphasis on the importance of traditional ecological knowledge (TEK) in the establishment of protective measures in fishing communities. In addition, it shows that local people's resilience capacity can lead to initiatives that contradict the state's formal plans, and emphasizes the importance of cognitive or local people's mapping for critical issues such as the definition of boundaries of a given management area. Rooted in the promotion of interdisciplinary frameworks coupled with a focus on the communities' heterogeneity, this volume seeks to question the often too-mechanical approach that still prevails in several management institutions. It aims to underline the importance of continuous interactions with community members at the research level as a crucial methodological approach to better understanding of the heterogeneity factors.

Lessons Learnt in the CBCRM Caribbean Programme

This section consists of a brief review of the methodological orientations that prevailed during the two phases of the above programme, which took place between January 2000 and February 2005. We examine both its positive outcomes and its shortcomings. In addition, this section provides some guidance for future programmes of a similar nature.

Looking back over the admittedly broad original project objectives that led to our initial project design, we feel that, generally speaking, our plan to undertake applied research in and around communities and their links to coastal management in the Caribbean was a good idea. However, hindsight tells us that our thinking shifted, early in the programme, towards developing research teams and building an appropriate interdisciplinary capacity for conducting research. This shift was unforeseen in the initial design, and we look at it as part of our adaptive learning process. Overall, it was probably one of the significant lessons learnt. This realisation conditions the remarks that follow, where we aim to enrich readers' views of the Caribbean context for research initiatives on management issues.

Advantages and limitations of a small-grant approach

The IDRC Caribbean programme was developed after the International Workshop on Capacity Building for Coasts and Oceans Management in the Wider Caribbean, held in Havana in July 1998. Having had the opportunity to exchange extensively with various donor agencies and researchers involved in the area, IDRC representatives decided to establish a specific component on the coastal Caribbean, within its larger MINGA programme in Latin America (*minga* is a Quechua word meaning communal work or cooperation). After examining a variety of project methodologies, the small-grant approach (SGA) was deemed a relevant strategy in this initial step, with awards ranging from US$20,000 to $30,000 per project. Given the general lack of CBCRM initiatives in the area, this funding limit was based on what seemed a reasonable start-up grant, when combined with our objective of reaching a reasonable number of research teams. At the same time, we wanted to allow for a comparative examination of the diversity of problem sets and specific issues, all involving interdisciplinary research in CBCRM. A pan-Caribbean framework was considered an important part of this work, one in which a better equilibrium could be reached initially between Spanish- and English-speaking countries, without neglecting the presence of other languages. Two regional institutions, International Ocean Institute (IOI) in Costa Rica and the Caribbean Fisheries Research and Management Programme CFRAMP (now CRFM) in Belize, agreed to act as the regional partners. They were responsible for the administration and monitoring of the projects, in collaboration with Laval University in Canada, on the social-science methodology. Representatives from each institution formed the scientific and administrative committees of the programme.

Altogether, 32 projects were selected and funded, starting with 17 in the first phase. In total, more than 120 proposals were received despite limited publicity efforts, especially at the beginning of the second phase. The proposals came from 12 different countries in Phase I and from more than 20 countries in Phase II. During the second phase, the most populous countries—Mexico, Cuba, and the Dominican Republic—submitted the highest number of proposals. In retrospect, the SGA appeared to be a wise choice as well as a functional one, revealing that there is surprisingly widespread interest among individual researchers and regional institutions. As explained in the introduction, the objectives were relatively broad and allowed the programme a certain visibility and continuity in the area. In terms of subject matter, the SGA also allowed the identification of a highly diversified set of coastal management issues, ranging from fish stock depletion to drinking water contamination, from the establishment of marine reserves to gender and stakeholder analysis, and so on (see Table 12 for a summary).

TABLE 12
HUMAN USES OF COASTAL AREAS IN PHASE II OF THE CARIBBEAN PROJECTS

Marine ecosystems					
Bays	**Lagoons**	**Coastal zones**	**Mangroves**	**Intertidal zones**	**Coral reefs**
Cuba	Venezuela	Grenada	Panama	Mexico	Belize
Cuba		Trinidad	Mexico	Jamaica	Guatemala
		Cuba	Jamaica	Dominican Republic	

Economic activities				
Artisanal fisheries	**Mariculture**	**Tourism**	**Forestry**	**Agriculture**
All the countries	Mexico	Trinidad	Jamaica	Panama
		Cuba	Panama	Trinidad and Tobago
		Belize	Mexico	
		Mexico		
		Dominican Republic		

Note: Internal and external wage labour is a widespread phenomenon in several communities.

Such diversified project topics led to a variety of challenges in the establishment of a rigorous monitoring process. They also led to various operational constraints, including travel (mainly monitoring but also team exchanges) and communication problems (mainly with e-mail). More important, the research teams presented strong internal differences that did not make it easy to develop a systematic research framework. But probably the most salient shortcoming of the SGA was the high transaction costs that led to major time management problems, both at the level of the individual research teams and at the higher management levels (for instance, scientific and administrative committees).

As the programme evolved, we became very aware of a major miscalculation of time. One important lesson involved examining time far more carefully in the future. We must be more specific in our up-front calculations and criteria, so that time expectations will be more defined and spelled out at the outset. For most of the people involved in the programme, whether on the research or administration side, the work had to be done on a part-time basis. This project represented one portion of their larger responsibilities. In many cases this problem was not recognised adequately, either at the outset or later on, during the various implementation stages. As a result, some field visits had to be postponed, causing discrepancies in the follow-up of the projects, and the plans for disseminating results had to be constantly readjusted. This project has involved a major learning-by-doing process in which the outcomes have to be balanced within a series of constraints (more details are available in some of the programme reviews; see, for example, Den Heyer and Savard 2002). A reduced number of projects certainly would have facilitated the monitoring efforts but would have impinged negatively on the programme's pan-Caribbean orientation.

Many of the projects in the second phase built on the experience of Phase I. In addition to selecting projects based on a better disciplinary equilibrium in the research teams, the selection criteria strongly insisted on the notion of community as the main locus for activities. Greater attention was also paid to women as local stakeholders. In addition, early on during Phase II, all project leaders collaborated in designing the content of this final publication, including a process where each team was engaged in collective writing through what became chapter sub-groups. At the beginning, this generated cohesion that afterwards facilitated group exchanges and communication between the projects, in spite of the reliance upon a mixture of Spanish and English languages.

Note, however, that our desire to strike a regional balance probably gave rise to the selection of too many projects. In addition to linguistic criteria, the selection sought to include the insular and continental location of the projects, particularly with regard to communities located in small as well as large countries. In one case, a project was terminated because of poor performance in terms of interdisciplinarity, as well as undue delays in initial planning. In other teams, the intrinsic diversity of the Caribbean communities represented a challenge that even a well-planned SGA approach could not entirely overcome. Thus, to some extent, this created a complexity misdiagnosis. Overall progress was nevertheless made between Phases I and II on processes for the selection and monitoring of the selected projects.

Difficult implementation of interdisciplinarity

Convinced that true CBCRM projects could not be conducted without a strong emphasis on interdisciplinary efforts, the organisers clearly promoted this orientation from the beginning of the programme. It gave rise, at the end of Phase I, to a collective publication dealing mainly with that orientation (IOI-CFU-LAVAL-IDRC 2002). In this volume, chapter 2 re-examines this issue, discussing the collaboration mechanisms between researchers involved in two Yucatan communities.

In the Caribbean, as in other regions, the precedence of marine sciences in research and administrative institutions that are linked to coastal management partly explains the low number of social scientists involved in the field. The limited social-analysis skills in some research teams was also probably a function of historical research training paradigms; some of this capacity gap appears to be more specific to some countries. Nevertheless, we were surprised that there was such a limited ability to undertake this aspect of the work, and we spent a considerable amount of time trying to understand and remedy the problem. For instance, it became apparent later that in some proposals the social-science contribution was inserted nominally, and did not reflect true interdisciplinary approaches.

Overall, in the approved proposals, only about 15 per cent of the project leaders came from a social science background. Among the 15 projects of Phase I, 11 reapplied but only three were selected, the rest being eliminated mainly because they did not show sufficient progress in this regard. Through the selection process of Phase II, however, coupled with a stronger emphasis on the community as a unit of observation and the search for a better gender equilibrium among the project leaders, we were able to reach an improved balance between the disciplines and get closer to the initial objectives of the programme.

However, this improved context probably led us to assume too rapidly that all the existing staff was capable of undertaking initial, basic or elementary level interdisciplinary research. We also assumed they would engage in a variety of tasks despite conflicting responsibilities in their own organisations. For example, they had to obtain the necessary support from their supervisors and spend adequate amounts of time doing field research. This was particularly true in the initial stages of research programme design, so as to build adequate links with the communities. Finally, they needed to develop a research team and not just rely on individuals to execute the research programme.

Similar remarks can be applied to the experiences and capacities of the scientific steering committee. The process of developing the research objectives, choosing the appropriate regional partners, setting up the programme governance mechanisms, defining the process of soliciting the applications, and then choosing the grants to be funded, refining the research design, developing a monitoring and evaluation process, and preparing a dissemination phase implied coordination efforts in which the members' experience was far from being homogeneous.

In addition to complexity linked to responsibility-sharing between the actors involved in this CBCRM Caribbean programme, all were somewhat influenced by and formed part of the existing larger and widespread disequilibrium between the number of natural and social science researchers in coastal management. On both sides, various epistemological frameworks remained characterised by an institutional resilience. But it valorises specialisation at the expense of interdisciplinary collaboration. On the one hand, biologists are familiar with referring to models that successively stem from one individual's efforts, with a tendency to verify quantitatively the explanatory potential and limits. Such analysis is greatly enhanced with computers.

On the other hand, although some individuals might have a more salient contribution in the consolidation of a given paradigm, social scientists refer to 'schools of thought'. In these, dominant paradigms are the object of constant internal critique, within an overwhelming qualitative approach that seeks to explain a changing reality. This basic difference partly explains why natural scientists pretended, over a long period, to reach a higher-quality scientific level than their social sciences colleagues, given their apparently more stable operational models. But there have been numerous problems and failures in fisheries management during the last decades. The progressive promotion of precautionary and responsible approaches within national and international agencies, combined with a stronger interest among scientists in multiple species–oriented research (the former 'scientific image' of marine sciences) has produced a less formal and predictive content.

This opened new paths of collaboration with social scientists. At the same time, however, the latter were influenced by post-modernist trends that were oriented towards questioning their former normative models. These elements are visible in many of the projects of this CBCRM programme. As the programme evolved, we noticed slight but constant changes in the attitudes of the researchers towards a better recognition of the value of interdisciplinary exchanges. We never reached the level of collaboration that we so ideally sought at the beginning. Considering the aforementioned constraints, we are convinced that one of the main outcomes of this programme lies in the progressive, changing attitudes regarding the necessity for more collective research efforts among the researchers and institutions involved. In all probability, we should have sought to capture these changes in more specific ways. However, as a further example, these changes were also shown by hiring practices, such as the occasional hiring of social scientists by local research teams, or in the direct financial support or facilities provided by research centres for programme activities. Discussion with the senior management of many of these institutions clearly showed their desire to improve this orientation in the future, where institutional policies permitted.

This CBCRM research programme offers first research on marine ecosystems and communities. Therefore, although it appeals to biologists and social anthropologists, it is important not to limit the interdisciplinary approach solely to these disciplines. Any CBCRM programme that looks for good results cannot neglect the impact of new management measures on the people's livelihoods, nor on their future relations with the regional or central political authorities. In this regard, the quality of many Caribbean projects could have been enhanced through the insertion of micro-economists, political scientists, and environmental lawyers, who could have better studied these various dimensions linked to the suggested changes in the selected communities.

Overall, building the hoped-for research teams is more complicated than we originally thought. We need to spend more effort on capacity building, but capacity building alone will not be adequate. We also believe that more effort should be put into building interdisciplinary teams. Clarity of purpose, goodwill and cooperation, and information sharing and trust are some of the important factors (Marshall and Lowther 1997). We do not sufficiently understand the impediments to interdisciplinarity, and undoubtedly we must examine this aspect more critically. Also, we now know that a more detailed examination of fundamental capacity-building approaches in which most of the staff have been trained should be a part of any future pre-project analysis.

Diversity of institutional affiliations

In the proposals received in the two phases of the CBCRM programme, there was considerable diversity in the institutional affiliations of the applicants. Given our desire at the very beginning to promote a pan-Caribbean framework, we were aware that research facilities would vary to some extent from one country to the other. In this regard, the selection criteria emphasised more the diversity and the quality of the research topics than the strength of the institutions to which the proponents belonged. Early in the process, we decided against preliminary local site visits and evaluative investigations by the selection committee. Our decision may be worth revisiting, particularly if larger-size or longer-term projects are planned. We received proposals from researchers located at known research centres, university departments, state agencies, and NGOs. We were also contacted by graduate students engaged in PhD programmes in and outside the Caribbean.

With regard to the researchers' status and affiliations, however, various difficulties can be pointed out. The first one was that the majority of researchers were members of specialised sub-units. They rarely shared a meaningful background in terms of interdisciplinarity, in spite of their access to a wider mix of research facilities in their own institution or other nearby organisations. Whether they were from natural- or social-science departments, their previous practices were oriented towards collaboration with colleagues of the same discipline. We noticed that in some research teams, the inclusion of staff of different disciplines often led to an arduous working process within the project team and within the institution. This meant that support and stimulation from the regional and collaborating partners was often needed. As well, where they existed, interactions among team members were sometimes rather nominal, whereas we had hoped at the outset for a real collaborative approach. In some cases, the interdisciplinary partners terminated their collaboration in the initial phase of the research. In another project, the activities had to be cancelled after a few months because it was impossible to form an interdisciplinary team. In addition, many researchers from academia and government agencies were often obliged to negotiate and justify their additional workload with their immediate superiors. This situation created additional constraints for the planning of activities with the 'outside' researchers and added to the increased transaction costs. Needless to say, this diversity of institutional affiliations added specific constraints for the regional partners who were in charge of the administration of the projects. This was particularly true given the variations in fiscal year and in the internal administrative procedures in each institution.

Given their omnipresence in several institutions related to marine research, it was easy to find well-qualified biologists interested in CBCRM research. The same cannot be said for their social-sciences counterparts. In some countries, social sciences do not have high status and are often merged with related disciplines such as education, psychology, geography, and philosophy, in which stakeholder analysis within a community is not given priority at the methodological level. Nevertheless, we noticed that younger researchers, some of whom had recently trained in interdisciplinary work while at university, showed a greater appreciation and understanding of collaboration with colleagues from other disciplines. Perhaps we should focus our future efforts upon these researchers.

Finally, some projects stemmed from NGOs, most of which had worked for more than a decade in the region. Many of their researchers already had significant contacts with the community under study and had developed communication and relationship channels that facilitated their interactions. On the other hand, even though these research groups have been at the forefront of the debates for better recognition of the role of the community in management plans, they often gave priority to conservation objectives rather than true community participation. Their minimal familiarity with social-science methods often led them to confuse community workshops and environmental education with a larger and more systematic investigation of the community's social structure. The Rapid Rural Appraisal approach that had become popular in several programmes a decade ago did not help in promoting this orientation; in fact, often it had the opposite result, simplifying their vision of the on-the-ground reality.

In most of the research teams composed mainly of natural scientists, they gradually became sensitised to the complexity of social organisation. In particular, they are now more aware that specific research techniques are needed for understanding a social organisation's evolution and contradictions.

In summary, the great variations in the basic characteristics (both academic and institutional) of the research groups represented an important challenge for the promoters of this CBCRM programme in the Caribbean. Selecting and/or developing interdisciplinary research teams in target institutions in the region will be a critical next step in the facilitation of future work.

Monitoring, group exchanges, and the devolution principle

From the very beginning, the promotion of a pan-Caribbean framework entailed strategies aimed at reinforcing exchanges between the projects. Faced with the necessity of dealing with projects in English and Spanish, and because bilingual communication capacities were weaker on the English side, it was necessary to adopt a division of labour, taking into account the basic features of the projects and their variable time frames. The identification of two regional partner institutions, IOI and CRFM, each with bilingual and interdisciplinary staff who were in charge of the administration and monitoring of the projects, was an important step. It should also be recognised that, particularly in Phase I, most of the researchers were (and in many ways still are) in a learning-by-doing process. Their intervention strategies varied according to the projects, thus generating continual adjustment efforts for the programme's promoters. In addition, changes in personnel in some institutions during the second phase created additional constraints to building strong interdisciplinary teams

Monitoring and evaluation

Project monitoring was built into the programme as an important methodological support mechanism. Taking into account the number of projects, their internal diversity, and the travelling time and efforts required to interact with some of them, this operation certainly led to several positive outputs for the programme's development. But as mentioned earlier, we believe we learnt some lessons that should improve similar initiatives.

Two rounds of field visits were forecast for each phase of the programme. Each regional partner had relative autonomy in setting the specific schedule. Therefore, all partners did not adopt exactly the same guidelines, even though these had been previously discussed as part of the general framework for the overall programme. In addition, the forecasts of the projects' durations evolved within a variable time frame, ranging between nine and 24 months, according to the researchers' research programme and availability. This obviously made it difficult to adopt more systematic evaluation criteria, and above all it jeopardised the establishment of a more structured, collective follow-up of the projects. Finally, for administrative purposes, each project had to submit an annual financial report in which its expenses were justified. Since many of the field visits coincided with the same period of the year, confusion arose between these financial reports and the progress reports that normally should deal more with the content of the projects. In addition, along with the direct monitoring and evaluation visits, other interaction tools must be added. These include such things as literature, technical support tools, regional training sessions via workshops and exchange visits, collaborative partner mentoring, and evaluation questionnaires. To sum up, we probably incorporated too many implicit factors into our design without sufficiently checking on their status.

Networking and regional exchanges

During Phase I, there were limited exchanges planned between the projects. A regional meeting was held in June 2001 in Mérida, Yucatan, where each team presented its results. This meeting was judged very useful because it helped to develop a shared methodology as well as shared learning. After the next group of projects was selected, Phase II began. Another regional meeting was held in June 2002 in Costa Rica, which researchers from each project team attended. Participants reported that it greatly enhanced the quality of communication between the researchers, and that it gave rise to the establishment of a reference grid in which they had the opportunity to better define their opportunities for shared learning. One other change was that in this volume, all chapters of Phase II are based on a collective, comparative ethnographical approach rather than on single case studies. During Phase II, sub-regional meetings between groups of researchers were held in Mérida, Yucatan, in June 2003 and in Port of Spain, Trinidad, in

April 2004. A final regional meeting was held in the Dominican Republic in June 2004. Added to these efforts, the group from Laval University, Canada, made regular efforts to supply the projects with relevant documentation. They constantly communicated with the project staff and the regional partners to enable the creation and consolidation of this volume.

We need to emphasise another positive learning experience. This was researchers' efforts to interact with their communities in order to establish research protocols, discussion groups, and workshops for the dissemination of information. Unfortunately, resources were not available for a systematic evaluation of the various initiatives that took place among the projects. However, in many of them we know this has been a well-received strategy that built stronger, mutually trusting relationships with local stakeholders. The CINVESTAV team's experience described in chapter 2 illustrates the investment required for the promotion of a stronger participatory approach. It demonstrates the value of well-structured sessions of information sharing, both on continuing work and on outcomes of the project, with the local population. However, without a detailed knowledge of the social dynamics that prevail in a given context, this exercise might be useless or even misleading in terms of real understanding and participatory project planning (Fauroux 2002). During Phase II, more significant exchanges were implemented among all the programme's participants. But there is no doubt that with fewer projects, financial restrictions in this regard would have been less onerous. Once again, our pan-Caribbean orientation forced us to engage in some compromises.

Collective writing and result dissemination

A basic orientation of this publication, stemming from Phase II of the programme, has been the promotion of collective writing efforts, which reinforce its initial interdisciplinary and pan-Caribbean objectives. In addition to encouraging more structured face-to face exchanges between the projects, we thought greater emphasis on collective writing efforts would be an important capacity-building component of the programme. This volume represents but one part of the overall dissemination effort. Many of the projects engaged in other forms of dissemination including videos, Web sites, atlas production, scientific articles, participation in conferences, posters, and so on.

Long before the completion of the field research within the projects, the scientific committee started to work on a general draft plan of the publication, in close consultation with the project leaders. There were delays in getting project leaders involved immediately, as most were preoccupied with their research projects. As time passed, however, and especially as related to the consolidation of Part 2 of the publication, the project's leaders had to intervene more directly, since this step was concerned with the use of their own data. An interaction then began. This process first addressed the issue of who should assume leadership in the writing. This was particularly important since each chapter included two or three main writers and various colleagues. Agreement was reached rapidly, greatly facilitated by the researchers' previous acquaintance and exchanges. Thereafter, the most difficult part of the operation began, that of developing a common demonstrative framework in which, without losing sight of their particular case, writers could validate the use of a comparative approach around the central theme of the publication: the communities' heterogeneity. For many of the researchers, undertaking a joint writing effort with colleagues from a different country and of another discipline was a new experience. Factoring in the geographic and language barriers, this writing phase has probably been one of the most intensive, but at the same time most enriching, aspects for the researchers. Related challenges in the comparative chapters represented particular challenges posed by the difficulties of cross-community analysis. For instance, population sizes ranged from 300 to 12,000 people. This provided interesting systems to study, particularly when combined with important differences in management mechanisms that were also in place.

The part-time involvement of the researchers within the SGA led to delays and postponements in the submission of a first draft manuscript. The schedule previously agreed upon before the Dominican Republic regional meeting in June 2004 was not fully respected, and the same prevailed for the accepted revised date after the meeting. This sort of delay is probably understandable and forms part of a collaborative learning process involving a highly diversified group of researchers. Nevertheless, it should be the object of additional reflections in the future when similar programmes are being designed. The major problem was that increased time constraints forced the scientific committee to postpone its final judgement on the quality of the publication. This was because the committee did not have all the necessary information, which led to a reduction in its consultation efforts with the researchers during the final editing phase. It is hoped that this overall experience will bear several lessons for the programme's participants who wish to promote collective research and writing efforts in the future.

We present these issues so the reader can have a critical look at the CBCRM 2000–2005 programme in the Caribbean. In accordance with the general orientation of this publication, in which the concept of heterogeneity has an important analytical weight, this programme took place in a particular context and has its own specificity. But by extracting some variables within the iterative framework of the programme, readers can transpose several lessons to other programmes or regions in which gaps also exist between theories and practice. Reflections on management issues, whether at the administrative, research, and monitoring levels or at the writing and results-dissemination level, ought to focus on the reduction of these gaps between theory and practice, and the promotion of interdisciplinary and 'integrated' research.

Recommendations for Researchers and Decision Makers

This concluding section aims to formulate some recommendations that will be useful to people interested in coastal management issues, in which CBCRM is considered as a valuable approach. At the beginning of this volume, we argued that the first logical step to take in dealing with the Caribbean context was to take into account its great heterogeneity. Afterwards we documented this general feature by focusing on the malleability and diversity of the region's coastal communities; in the core chapters we showed how similar management problems could be approached differently, according to local contexts. A clear need for more and better interdisciplinary research emerged through this demonstration. The results of this could reduce the gaps between the official discourses, the ready-to-use models, and the understanding of people's behaviour and perceptions.

Our plea for greater local autonomy in order to solve coastal management problems is not intended to isolate communities. Instead, we hope that their social capital will be better recognised by the scientific milieu and the state agencies, which, we hope, will include the communities in a more significant and visible partnership. This general orientation should be taken as a guide for the comments that follow.

Policy and research at national and international levels: Fragmentation and persistence challenges

In the Caribbean there are various organisations that seek to reinforce collaboration between national agencies and regional bodies involved in examining environmental issues, such as CRFM, the Association of Eastern Caribbean States (AECS), and the Caribbean Sub-commission of the United Nations Intergovernmental Oceanographic Commission of UNESCO (IOCARIBE). Also present are various international organisations with their sub-regional offices and representatives. These include the World Bank, IADB, CIDA, CIRAD, the Economic European Community (EEC), FAO, the French Research Institute on the Sea Resources (IFREMER), IOI, the Research Institute on Development (IRD), and the US Agency for International Development (USAID). All are pursuing more or less similar goals designed to solve management problems. Their collaboration is probably influenced by the geographical, political, and linguistic fragmentation of the region; thus it incorporates several shortcomings that considerably reduce the effectiveness and efficiency of their exchanges. The result is that there is a tendency to establish individual programmes that are the object of sporadic exchanges. These do not generate the real, controlled comparison that is so essential for regional development.

Periodic conferences gather various participants together, but they are generally characterised by weak follow-up activities; attempts to create regional networks do not last long once additional funds are unavailable. Without a real and comprehensive information-sharing mechanism, several initiatives have a repetitive and localised content that does not favour a cumulative know-how process. In addition, many of these initiatives are conceived through natural-sciences frameworks that do not sufficiently take into account the sociocultural elements of the particular sub-regions.

The result is that local collaboration and participation, which are often described as key elements in any CBCRM programme, are diluted in the face of state agencies' needs for justifying their existence and plans of action. During the five-year existence of the CBCRM Caribbean programme, little success has been achieved in this regard, despite efforts to inform other institutions of IDRC involvement in the region. This negative institutional resilience should be the object of serious questioning in the near future.

Challenges in adaptive learning teams: Lack of institutional support for researchers

Most of the research teams involved in the CBCRM Caribbean programme included three or four individuals, although some teams comprised up to twice this number. The rationale for the larger size was partly explained by the programme's interdisciplinary requirements. The complexity of the management issues studied, and the necessity to deepen a series of variables linking the dynamics of given ecosystems with particular communities, also required some collective research. The limited time that the researchers could devote to their project within their overall responsibilities also probably led to larger team sizes. But whatever the number of individuals involved in the projects, several were faced with the same problem of lack of higher-level organisational support.

Several institutions, especially universities and research centres, welcomed the arrival of research funds that could increase their visibility and their potential image on the development scene. But at the same time, many of these organisations did not really encourage the researchers to invest time in an interdisciplinary CBCRM programme. This type of research presupposes significant stays in the community, including being available to interact with the local population to build trust and related relationships, organise workshops, and produce popularised documentation. All such efforts were far more complex if the community was not located close by.

These necessary inputs, which are central to the notion of participation, are in contradiction to academic requirements surrounding the usual performance-review standards for the evaluation of researchers. This is because the latter, in general, focus strictly on high-level scientific publications. In many institutions, there is a clear lack of recognition of what some call 'non-academic' work, which represents an essential input in implementation and development of a CBCRM project. In any future promotion of similar programmes, greater efforts must be undertaken to convince the administrators to rectify such situations, if they actually want their professors and researchers to contribute to solving local and national development problems.

Better recognition of the contribution of social sciences in management programmes

In various sections of this publication, the ongoing asymmetry characterising the relationship between natural and social sciences in management initiatives has been pointed out. The imbalance is accentuated when dealing with coastal management issues because, in most institutions, marine sciences long preceded social sciences at the research and decision-making levels. Without repeating here all the arguments previously discussed, the fact is that maintaining this asymmetry has led to negative consequences from a CBCRM perspective because the social dimensions of the community's components are generally thought of as independent variables.

This is a clear illustration of the existing gaps between theory and practice. In spite of their scientific assets, academic institutions can barely escape from the logic of capitalism in which there exists a constant need for creating new products in an expanding market characterised by a strong competition for attracting new clientele. The field of coastal management has been exemplary in this regard. Almost completely absent from university programmes a few decades ago, its consolidation progressively gave rise to an increased number of courses, books, readers, and conferences. That process was greatly enhanced by the discourses of international agencies rendering these 'academic products' more fashionable. In various institutions, new graduate programmes are emerging that are oriented not only towards coastal management but even towards such topics as 'integrated coastal management', in which 'interdisciplinarity' supposedly becomes a key word. But a close look at the content of these programmes reveals that some of them are guided exclusively by natural scientists, and also that there is still a long way to go before attaining a better representation by the social sciences. In other words, it is not easy to achieve a CBCRM perspective, in which the notions of community and ecosystem receive equal attention.

Taking into account the overall projects of this Caribbean programme, in which the situation described above is easily verifiable, we are convinced that one way to reduce this disciplinary asymmetry is to put more emphasis on training young social-science students in coastal-communities research. These efforts should take place at key institutions on both the English and Spanish sides, with adequate financial and other support incentives. Another potential initiative consists of concrete support by the CBCRM-IDRC for a bilingual or trilingual social-science network, oriented towards coastal management in the Caribbean. In both cases, a few individuals' efforts will not be sufficient; some form of institutional visibility is needed that will ensure a better equilibrium between the disciplines.

Greater insistence upon women's productive role

Gender analysis formed an integral part of the majority of development programmes in many of the projects. Several studies and specialised journals exist that emphasise women's contributions to the livelihoods and development of local communities. But the gaps between theory and practice are probably more obvious in coastal and fishing communities than in agrarian mainland communities, in which women's productive role seems to be more visible. Several factors explain this situation. The limited interest of social scientists in the study of coastal communities has led to a gap in the development of information on their economic organisation. To date, the limited studies that are available suggest that before the consolidation of capitalism in fishing, women were deeply involved in some labour processes related to the activity (Thompson 1985; Cole 1991; Nadal-Klein and Davis 1988). On the other hand, the consolidation of the bio-economic sciences in many fishery administrations in the 1950s and 1960s increased the 'masculinised' view of the activity, mainly by conferring a productive role on men, while women were often excluded from work at sea. Finally, as is often the case in ministries linked to the management of natural resources, there are generally more male than female researchers and administrators in fisheries. They implicitly define the producer as a male actor extracting value from the environment.[1]

The foregoing aims at making the reader aware that in CBCRM programmes, the visibility of women's productive roles is embedded in some specific constraints and stereotypes that must be overcome if we are to obtain a better understanding of women's contribution. If we add the fact that usually the key actors on the local political scene are male, it is clear that it is not always easy to emphasise women's overall importance in coastal communities. However, in the present Caribbean programme, some projects have strongly insisted on this orientation, thus showing that additional research efforts can be undertaken to obtain a richer view of the real situation.

In Trinidad, women actively participate in capital investments in fishing and are in the process of forming a regional association. In Jamaica, they significantly engaged in a mangrove reforestation plan. In Mexico, a group of San Felipe women works directly at sea and recently formed their own fishing cooperative to sell their products. In Sarteneja, Belize, several women are involved in community groups aimed at local and regional economic diversification. These clear examples prove that additional research is needed at the local level to counteract the dominant images that prevail in coastal communities. Such images deny women's potential to innovate and to enter into domains that are still generally reserved to men.

Renewed images of indigenous communities

A good part of the literature dealing with CBCRM gives a lot of importance to some indigenous communities that present, before and after the presence of capitalism, a certain degree of social cohesion and low social stratification with a reduction in the size of the productive zone. These features represent positive elements in the use of community-based devices for management problems because they facilitate decision-making processes and conflict resolution. But a brief look at indigenous cultures in the Caribbean indicates that the frequent references to indigenous communities as relatively isolated and integrated social units does not correspond to either past or present reality.

Long before their conquest, the Maya developed a state form of political organisation. In spite of the absence of urban centres, there existed a clear division of labour and various social classes. Although the colonisation period negatively affected groups such as the Taino and the Caribs, 'they did not all become extinct within the first fifty years, as has been wrongly repeated in primary school text books', and 'unlike the case in the insular Caribbean, there is no place for the extinction ideology on the continental rimland' (Palacio, Coral, and Hidalgo 2004, 10). The Kuna and Garifuna ethnographies discussed in chapter 3 indicate that, as in any other human groups, indigenous communities have undergone significant internal changes through time. They have been able to revitalise their culture and group status, and they evolved in connection with transformations taking place in the larger society. Contrary to the prevalent image in many present-day governing institutions, indigenous groups form differentiated social units living in communities with a wide variation of contexts. Future CBCRM research in these communities should be more rooted in their diversity and development patterns.

These brief remarks are aimed at making researchers and administrators more aware of some existing 'biases' in the implementation of CBCRM programmes in the Caribbean and elsewhere, and at pinpointing the relevance of interdisciplinary research at the local level. While representing only one analytical approach in the overall research efforts in coastal management, these programmes sought to promote flexible management frameworks in which science and participation can be effectively merged to meet livelihood challenges of coastal communities.

Overall, we intend to examine various means to pursue many of these recommendations ourselves, and we will be looking for partners to work with us in attempting to move ahead on these challenges.

Note

1. Women in fisheries is the subject of *Yemaya*, the biannual newsletter of the International Collective in Support of Fishworkers, Brussels.

References

Begossi, A., and Brown, D. 2003. Experiences with fisheries co-management in Latin America and the Caribbean. In *The Fisheries co-management experience: Accomplishments, challenges and prospects*, ed. Nielsen Wilson and Degnbol Kluwer, 136–52. London: Academic Publishers.

Berkes, F., and Folke, C. 2002. Back to the future: Ecosystem dynamics and local knowledge. In *Panarchy: Understanding transformations in systems of humans and nature*, ed. L.H. Gundersen and C. S. Holling, 121–46. Washington DC: Island Press.

Brosius, J.P., A. Tsing, and A. Lowenhaupt. 1998. Representing communities: Histories and politics of community-based resources management. *Society and Natural Resources* 11: 157–68.

Brosius, J.P., and R. Russel. 2003. Conservation from above: An anthropological perspective of transboundary protected areas and ecoregional planning. *Journal of Sustainable Forestry* 17(1–2): 35–60.

Cole, S. 1991. *Women of the Praia: Work and lives in a Portuguese coastal community*. New Jersey: Princeton University Press.

Den Heyer, M., and K. Savard, 2000. Proposed monitoring and evaluation guide for community-based resources management in the Caribbean: A small grant approach. Ottawa: IDRC.

Doyon, S. 2003. L'environnement « révolutionnaire »: Pratiques, discours et dynamique socio-environnementale de la gestion des ressources côtières à Cuba. PhD diss., McGill University.

Fauroux, E. 2002. *Comprendre une société rurale: Une méthode d'enquête anthropologique appliquée à l'Ouest malgache.* Paris: Editions du GRET.

Haughton, M., R. Mahon, P. McConney, A. Kong, and A. Mills. 2004. Establishment of the Caribbean Regional Fisheries Mechanism. *Marine Policy* 28: 351–59.

IOI-CFU-LAVAL-IDRC. 2002. *Balancing people and resources: Interdisciplinary research and coastal areas management in the Wider Caribbean.* Heredia, Costa Rica: Editorial Fundación, UNA.

Jentoft, S., and B.J. McCay. 2003. The place of civil society in fisheries management: A research agenda for fisheries co-management. In *The fisheries co-management experience: Accomplishments, challenges and prospects,* ed. D.C. Wilson, J.R. Nielsen, and P. Degnbol, 293–307. London: Kluwer Academic Publishers.

Jones, R.W. 2004. The heterogeneity of Caribbean communities: Resilience and adaptive responses in coastal management. Ottawa: IDRC.

Kearney, J. 2004. The impending global fisheries crisis and the problem of governance. Paper presented at the IDRC-IASCP panel of fisheries, Oaxaca, Mexico, August.

Marshall, R.J., and J.M. Lowther. 1997. CSIRO. Paper submitted to the International Conference on Work Teams, Dallas-Fort Worth, Texas.

Nadal-Klein, J., and L. Davis, eds. 1988. *To work and to weep: Women in fishing economies.* St Johns, NL: Memorial University, Institute of Social and Economic Studies.

Nichols, K. 1999. Coming to terms with 'integrated coastal management'. Problems of meaning and method in a new arena of resource regulation. *Professional Geographer* 51(3): 388–99.

Olsen, S. 2001. Future directions in coastal governance. The consensus from Block Island, Rhode Island University.

Palacio., J., C. Coral, and H. Hildalgo. 2004. Territoriality, technical revitalization, and symbolism in Caribbean indigenous communities. Manuscript. Belize: University of the West Indies.

Pomeroy, R.S., R. Pollnac, B.M. Katon, and C.D. Predo. 1997. Evaluating factors contributing to the success of community-based coastal resources management: The Central Visayas Regional Proect-1, Philippines. *Ocean and Coastal Management* 36(1–3): 97–120.

Thompson, P. 1985. Women in fishing: The roots of power between the sexes. *Comparative Studies in Society and History* 27(1): 3–32.

Wilson D.C., J.R. Nielsen, and P. Degnbol, eds. 2003. *The fisheries co-management experience: Accomplishments, challenges and prospects.* London: Kluwer Academic Publishers.

Contributors

Jorge Ángulo
Centro de Estudios Marinos, Havana, Cuba

Yvonne Arias
Grupo Jaragua, Dominican Republic

Yvan Breton
Université Laval, Québec, Canada

David N. Brown
CARICOM Regional Fisheries Mechanism, Belize

Maria Elena Castellanos Gonzalez
Centro de Estudios Ambientales de Cienfuegos (CITMA), Cuba

Ratana Chuenpagdee
St Francis Xavier University, Antigonish, Nova Scotia, Canada

Marisa Clarke-Marshall
Institute of Marine Affairs, Port of Spain, Trinidad

Camilo Coral, Sociologist
OXFAM, Bolivia

Brian Davy
International Development Research Centre, Ottawa, Canada

Gregory de Souza
Institute of Marine Affairs, Port of Spain, Trinidad

Jorge I. Euán-Ávila
CINVESTAV, Mérida, Mexico

James Finlay
Spring, St Georges, Grenada

Julia Fraga Berdugo
CINVESTAV, Mérida, Mexico

Liliana M. Gomez Luna
Universidad de Oriente, Santiago, Cuba

Milton Haughton, Biologist
CARICOM Regional Fisheries Mechanism, Belize

Herbert Haylock
Programme for Belize, Belize

Hugo Hidalgo, Biologist
Fundaeco, Guatemala

Rosemarie Kishore
Institute of Marine Affairs, Port of Spain, Trinidad

L. Ciro Marcano
Fundacion Claudio Perna, Caracas, Venezuela
Clark University, Worcester, Massachusetts, USA

Clara E. Miranda Vera
Universidad de Cienfuegos, Cienfuegos, Cuba

Luis Ovares, Sociologist
Universidad Nacional Autónoma, Heredia, Costa Rica

Joseph Palacio, Anthropologist
University of the West Indies, Belize

Zulay Poggy
Asociacíon Punto Verde, Caracas, Venezuela
Universidad Gran Mariscal de Ayacucho, Venezuela

Hema Ramsundar
Institute of Marine Affairs, Port of Spain, Trinidad

Daniel Robledo Ramirez
CINVESTAV, Mérida, Mexico

Silvia Salas Márquez
CINVESTAV, Mérida, Mexico

Winsome Townsend
National Environment and Planning Agency, Kingston, Jamaica

Index